Knights Errant
and True Englishmen

'We ought to be tired of our Knight Errantry which has made us hitherto act so, that a drum is not to be beat in Europe but we straight sound to arms.'

John Freind, Tory MP, 1726.

'The people, as far as I can observe . . . fancy they have got an English King again or at least one that has an aversion for foreigners, which is about half the character of a true Englishman.'

Edward Cooke, 1727.

Knights Errant and True Englishmen:

British Foreign Policy, 1660-1800

Edited by
JEREMY BLACK
Lecturer in History
University of Durham

JOHN DONALD PUBLISHERS LTD
EDINBURGH

To

Eveline Cruickshanks and Philip Woodfine

ISBN 0 85976 226 2

Typeset by Beecee Typesetting Services
Printed in Great Britain by Bell & Bain Ltd., Glasgow

Preface

The history of British foreign policy has been a marginal subject for several decades. During these decades much good work has been produced, especially for the period 1660-1800, on the diplomacy of the 1670s, the 1710s and 1720s, but, on the whole, this work has not been integrated into the general scholarship of the period. Many textbooks, commonly written by experts in high politics, offer a hurried account of foreign policy that is a jumble of names and dates often unrelated to the problems discussed in the rest of the work. The extent to which foreign policy posed crucial problems of political management and debate is insufficiently appreciated. The strong diplomatic bias of foreign policy studies has led to the production of many works that have few points of access for the general scholar. The domestic context of foreign policy and, in particular, the extent to which policy was debated are subjects that have received relatively little attention.

Much of the research on diplomatic history consists of studies of bilateral relations. This reflects the nature of doctoral research on the subject. Doctoral students, understandably, are encouraged to study a well-defined, readily comprehensible topic following clearly established methods in considering a small range of well-known sources. These studies are very valuable in that they clearly establish the course of negotiations, but they often fail to provide an explanatory account, largely because they tend to search for the causes of action in the very diplomatic sources that do not always contain them. Furthermore, these scholars have often betrayed a lack of interest in the domestic background of diplomatic activity; their sensitivity to the nuances of diplomatic behaviour has not necessarily been matched by an appreciation of the domestic context of foreign policy.

The essays in this book do not offer accounts of bilateral relations. Instead, they concentrate on a number of forces that influenced the formulation and execution of foreign policy: the intervention of foreign powers in British politics, the role of British diplomats, the influence of the monarch, especially in light of the Hanoverian connection, and the dynamics of ministerial relationships. Dwyeyd Jones provides a valuable reminder of the economic and financial costs of an active interventionist policy and H.M. Scott indicates the importance of contemporary views on Britain's role. Collectively these essays illustrate the complexity of the relationship between British diplomacy and the domestic context, a complexity that is not always clarified by phrases such as 'a parliamentary foreign policy'.

Thanks are due to the British Academy and the Wolfson Foundation. Janet Forster and Wendy Duery typed successive drafts of much of the book. John Tuckwell has again proved the most helpful of publishers.

Jeremy Black

Notes on the Contributors

Jeremy Black	Lecturer in History, University of Durham. Publications include *British Foreign Policy in the Age of Walpole* (1985); *The British and the Grand Tour* (1985); *Natural and Necessary Enemies: Anglo-French Relations in the Eighteenth Century* (1986); *The English Press in the Eighteenth Century* (1987); *The Collapse of the Anglo-French Alliance 1727-1731* (1987); ed., *Britain in the Age of Walpole* (1984), *The Origins of War in Early Modern Europe* (1987); co-ed., *Essays in European History in honour of Ragnhild Hatton* (1985), *The Jacobite Challenge* (1988), *The British Navy and the Use of Naval Power in the Eighteenth century* (1988).
T.C.W. Blanning	Reader in Modern European History at the University of Cambridge and a Fellow of Sidney Sussex College. He has published numerous books and articles on the history of Germany, France and the Habsburg Monarchy in the eighteenth century and the revolutionary-Napoleonic period, his most recent books being *The French Revolution in Germany* (1983), *The Origins of the French Revolutionary Wars* (1986) and *The French Revolution* (1987).
Michael Duffy	Lecturer in History, University of Exeter. Publications include *The Englishman and the Foreigner* (1986) and *Soldiers, Sugar and Seapower. The British Expeditions to the West Indies and the War against Revolutionary France* (1987).
Carl Haase	Until his retirement in 1978, Director of the State Archives of Lower Saxony at Hanover. He has published extensively on the history of Germany, and especially of Hanover, in the eighteenth century. His publications include *Leibniz* (1966) and *Ernst Brandes* (2 vols., 1973-4).
D.W. Jones	Dr. D.W. Jones was an undergraduate at the University College of Wales, Aberystwyth, and a post-graduate at Merton College, Oxford, where he completed his D. Phil. thesis in 1971. Since 1965 he has been on the staff of the history department at York University. After embarking on a study of the East India Company and the city of London in the 1690s for his D. Phil thesis, he has since broadened the study to consider what the wars of the Grand Alliance involved for the English economy. His *War and Economy in the Age of William III and Marlborough* (Blackwell) appeared in 1987.
James R. Jones	Professor of History at the University of East Anglia since 1966. His main publications include *The First Whigs* (1961); *The Revolution of 1688 in England* (1972); *Country and Court,*

England 1658-1714 (1978); *Charles II: Royal Politician* (1987); 'English Attitudes to Europe in the Seventeenth Century', in *Britain and the Netherlands in Europe and Asia,* edited by J.S. Bromley and E.H. Kossmann (1968); 'Dutch Sea Power and National Survival', *International History Review,* February 1988. His main current research work is concerned with a multi-author volume setting the Revolution of 1688 in its widest context, which he is editing for the Center for the History of Freedom at Washington University, St. Louis.

Geoffrey Rice Senior Lecturer, University of Canterbury, New Zealand. Has published on both eighteenth-century international relations and modern New Zealand history, including a book on the 1918 influenza epidemic.

H.M. Scott Lecturer in Modern History at the University of St. Andrews. A specialist in eighteenth-century diplomatic history, he is the author of *The Rise of the Great Powers 1648-1815* (1983, with Derek McKay) and of *British Foreign Policy in the Age of the American Revolution* (forthcoming) and editor of *Enlightened Absolutism: Reform and Reformers in Later Eighteenth-Century Europe* (1989). He is presently completing a study of the emergence of Russia, Prussia and Austria as major powers in the middle decades of the eighteenth century, to be published by John Donald.

Abbreviations

Add. MS	Additional Manuscripts in the British Library.
AE	Paris, Quai d'Orsay, Archives du Ministère des Affaires Etrangères.
Ang	Angleterre.
BL	London, British Library, Department of Manuscripts.
Bodl	Oxford, Bodleian Library.
CP	Correspondance Politique.
CTB	*Calendar of Treasury Books, IX-XXVIII*, 1689-1714, ed. W.A. Shaw (HMSO, 1931-1955).
D'Avaux	*Négociations de Monsieur le Comte d'Avaux en Hollande depuis 1679* (6 vols., Paris, 1752-53), edited by E. Mallet.
EcHR	*Economic History Review.*
Hanover	Hanover, Niedersachsisches Hauptstaatsarchiv.
HHStA	Vienna, Haus-, Hof-, und Staatsarchiv.
HLMSS	*The Manuscripts of the House of Lords*, 1678-1714 (15 vols., HMSO, 1887-1962).
KAO	Kent Archives Office, Maidstone.
NUL	Nottingham University Library.
PRO	London, Public Record Office, State Papers.
SRO	Shrewsbury, Salop Record Office.

Contents

CHAPTER 1

French Intervention in English and Dutch Politics, 1677-88

James Jones

If his master James I had not been so short of money, Sir Henry Wotton could have added the words 'bribe and form parties' to his celebrated and over-candid definition of the role of an ambassador, that he was an honest man sent to lie on behalf of his master. In England the diplomatic representatives of rival or hostile powers — Habsburg and Valois in Tudor times, Gondomar and his Dutch opponent Caron during James's reign — worked and intrigued at the royal Court, spending a great deal of money in building an interest or party. They purchased the support or sympathy of ministers, favourites, servants and Court ladies with the ultimate objective of gaining an ascendant influence over the sovereign. After his assumption of the direction of policy in 1661 Louis XIV continued to use these traditional techniques in most of the Courts of Europe. For example his diplomats consistently favoured the clerical party in the Viennese Court, so as to mobilise their influence against alliances with protestant German princes which might impede French foreign policies, while at Berlin they played on suspicions and fears created by the increase in Habsburg power. In 1697-1700 French diplomats prepared the way for the accession of Philip V to the Spanish throne by the success with which they fostered and exploited jealousies of the House of Austria.[1]

Two crucial differences marked off England and the United Provinces from all other European states, necessitating the use by Louis (and Mazarin before him) of significantly different techniques of intervention. First, since neither country possessed stable political systems, Louis had constantly to include in his calculations the possibility that the existing forms of government might be completely altered in the near future. Traditionally France regarded the stadholders of the House of Orange, and especially Frederick Henry and William II, as reliable allies. After their republican opponents forced through a separate peace with Spain in 1648, at Münster, the French gave William encouragement in his campaign to increase his authority, expand the strength of the army and then re-enter the war against Spain as the ally of France. The failure of William's attempted coup against Amsterdam, followed by his sudden death in September 1650 which inaugurated the stadholderless period of True Freedom, resulted in a sharp and prolonged reduction in French influence.[2] By 1662, when Louis re-established an alliance with the Dutch, close and friendly relations with the republicans suited his foreign policy purposes, and France entered the war against England in 1666.

In 1667-8 Johan de Witt, pensionary of Holland but in practice the chief

1

executive officer of the Dutch Republic during the stadholderless period, formed the Triple Alliance to prevent France annexing the Spanish Netherlands. Louis turned against the republicans, and planned to revive the former connections with the Orange party. He calculated that he could reduce the United Provinces to a state of permanent dependence by installing the young Prince William as their hereditary ruler, freed from constitutional restrictions, but dependent on external support from France and England.[3] William had been educated as 'child of state' but barred by the Perpetual Edict from becoming stadholder of Holland. By 1670 he and his partisans were beginning to assert his claims, and were seen by both Louis and Charles as future protégés: a clause in the secret treaty of Dover envisaged the dissolution of the republican forms of government, on the assumption that William would collaborate with the victorious enemies of his country.[4] By 1683 Louis reversed his position, assuring the republican party that he would intervene to protect them and the True Freedom in the event of William attempting to establish himself as absolute prince.

Mazarin and Louis had similarly to take into account the instability of each successive regime in England. A state of undeclared war between France and the Rump followed the execution of Charles I, but Mazarin subsequently won the race with Spain to establish an alliance with the Protectorate of Oliver Cromwell. But subsequently Mazarin and Louis were seriously misled by the information which they received from their representative in London, Antoine Bordeaux, and failed to anticipate the collapse of the Commonwealth and the restoration of Charles II.[5] As a result Louis never subsequently lost sight of the possibility of further changes of regime. During the Exclusion Crisis of 1679-81 he required frequent and full analyses of the situation from his ambassador, Paul Barrillon. Eventually Louis decided to renew offers of subsidies to Charles, and concluded a personal treaty in March 1681 which enabled the latter to dissolve the Oxford parliament, and so defeat the Whig bill to exclude James from the succession.[6]

Louis's primary objective in intervening to support Charles was to pre-empt William intervening. Similarly in 1685, when Monmouth provoked a rebellion in the west of England there was more danger to French interests from William rallying to support James (for reasons of his own), than from Monmouth himself, who had little chance of success. In 1688 Louis had detailed advance information about William's naval and military preparations for the invasion of England, and his ambassador at the Hague, d'Avaux, fed some of this material to the obtuse and generally inactive English representative there, d'Albeville, in the hope that such intelligence would alert James to the danger. However, Louis neither promised nor gave James any significant assistance.[7] It suited his overall purposes to let

William involve himself and a sizeable proportion of the Dutch army in what Louis expected would be a prolonged civil war in the British Isles. The absence of William on an expedition which could be represented as an attempt to dethrone James and seize sovereignty for himself, or alternatively as a protestant war of religion, would help Louis advance French territories and influence in the Rhineland without provoking a general war. All Louis's calculations were upset by the rapid collapse of James's authority and strength, and as in 1659-60, unsound information and misjudgements by his representative in London, the ambassador Barrillon, contributed largely to the ensuing débâcle. Although d'Avaux provided information about the activities of William's agents in England, his warnings were not verified by the complacent Barrillon, who for some time had largely confined his contracts to the inner circle of James's confidants, and saw everything through their eyes.[8] Like Bordeaux in 1659-60, Barrillon failed to anticipate a total alteration in English affairs. But whereas Louis had been able to recover his influence in England in the first years of Charles II's reign, the Revolution of 1688 made it certain that hostilities in the Rhineland would escalate into a general, and as it proved totally exhausting, European conflict, with England under William as one of France's enemies.

The second major difference between England and the United Provinces, and all other major European states, was to be found in the constitutional position occupied in these two countries by representative institutions, and in the influence which they could exert over the decisions of executive government. The importance of the States General and Parliament demanded the use of different techniques of intervention, open or clandestine, from those employed in other countries. In the United Provinces d'Avaux exploited all the opportunities presented to him by the complexities of the Dutch system of government, so as to block William's attempts to expand the army, raise new taxes and form new alliances. He openly canvassed delegates from the provincial States, who came to meetings of the States General mandated to follow their instructions, against responding to speeches by William or Gaspar Fagel, de Witt's successor as Pensionary of Holland but William's loyal lieutenant.[9] By persuading delegates to stand obstinately by their instructions, and by persuading provincial States to adhere to their policy decisions, d'Avaux could at the very least obstruct William's initiatives. In 1683-4 he blocked William's attempt to raise new levies of men for the army, and prevented him moving army units into the Spanish Netherlands, which were about to be invaded by a French army.

D'Avaux established close working relationships with William's most consistent and influential opponents, the Regents in the city governments and the provincial States of the leading province of Holland. His most important contacts were those whom he called Messieurs d'Amsterdam, the tight-knit oligarchy of burgomasters and other magistrates who not only controlled the city government but also provided the Dutch government and its allies with loans and banking services. D'Avaux also canvassed support from members of the Frisian and Utrecht delegations to the States General, and tried with indifferent success to exploit the jealousy which Jan Casimir, stadholder of Friesland and head of the cadet branch of the House of Orange, felt for William.[10] D'Avaux himself resided at the Hague, and frequented the small Court maintained by William and Mary, where he behaved with extraordinary boorishness, losing no opportunity of insulting the prince and princess, and on one occasion nearly involving himself in a physical scuffle for a chair with the latter. His unpleasant behaviour reflected his frustration. William's Court consisted entirely of trusted friends, officers and long-term associates. As compensation for his failure to build anything resembling a French party at Court, d'Avaux constructed a network of valets and menial servants, whom he paid to report conversations and (very effectively in 1688) the names of those who visited William, and especially English and Scots.[11] Salaried officials of the States General and of the Amsterdam Arsenal proved to be equally susceptible to French money: in 1688 they supplied d'Avaux with valuable information about William's preparations, including the crucial intelligence that horse transports were being fitted out, which indicated conclusively that William would use the army for an invasion of England, and not for a move into the Rhineland to counter the imminent French attack.[12]

Money provided the inducement for humble servants and officials to keep d'Avaux supplied with secret information, although some as Catholics could be persuaded that they were serving the interests of their religion. But how did the Regents rationalise their behaviour in sabotaging William's attempts to check French advances in the Spanish Netherlands and Luxemburg? And how did Louis bring himself to further the interests of a republican party, and to protect a republican constitution, established originally as a result of a successful rebellion against the legitimate monarchical authority of the king of Spain?[13]

Common interests of two kinds connected the Regents and Louis. First, d'Avaux repeatedly and explicitly promised his Regent associates protection for the True Freedom against encroachments by William. For them the True Freedom meant in principle the rights of the Dutch cities and provinces, recognised in the Union of Utrecht.[14] In practical governmental and political terms it meant the preservation of a clumsy and slow-moving system (if, indeed, that word can be used). Each province sent delegates to meetings of the States General, furnished with instructions from which they could not deviate. If new issues arose, then the delegates had to seek fresh instructions from their principals, the States of their province, and members of the States would have to receive new mandates from their principals, mostly the city governments. In theory the agreement of all seven provinces in the States General was required, but this could be circumvented in practice: only the province of Holland could actually enforce a veto. To add to the difficulties of getting decisions from the States General, the composition of the provincial delegations constantly changed, and the office of president rotated weekly among the provinces, so that there was little continuity of membership, and only limited opportunities for individuals to gain experience, or for either the States General or the provincial States to develop the corporate character and cohesion developed by the House of Commons in the 1620s and again in the Cavalier Parliament of 1661-79.

This extraordinarily clumsy system of representative government, one made in Sir William Temple's words for rest, but not for motion, by which he meant that it was static, not dynamic, represented no threat or challenge to monarchical government. It was defensive, concerned to preserve the liberties and rights of certain territorial entities — provinces and cities — which had been established in medieval times, and which Philip II and his minister Granvelle had tried to subordinate. The Dutch Revolution had been aimed against royal attempts at centralisation, and the local rights which it preserved did not differ significantly from those which the French kings allowed certain provinces — for instance Languedoc — to retain.[15]

By supporting those whose principal concern was to defend the True Freedom by restricting the authority and powers of the stadholder, Louis reduced William's ability to form and maintain alliances designed to check further French advances. Louis also relied on commercial concessions to win over Regent interests. These played a crucial part in persuading the States General to conclude the peace treaty of Nijmegen, against William's opposition, and unilaterally, ignoring the protests of the allies.[16] This proved to be a major diplomatic coup, in that the separate peace concluded by the Dutch destroyed the alliance which William had formed and left him humiliated and isolated. Only such a significant advantage could justify Louis making concessions in an area which fell within his prerogative powers; for reasons of interest of state he abandoned the protectionist policies which Colbert had introduced to foster French commercial and industrial development. But once these commercial concessions had served their purpose Louis withdrew them, unilaterally breaking the treaty. This was not so much because of the economic damage which might be suffered, but because Louis regarded the making of any concessions in matters of domestic affairs as derogatory to his honour and authority. For him the re-imposition of tariffs was a vindication of his sovereign authority, and he ignored the representations which d'Avaux made about the resulting alienation of mercantile interests, hitherto favourable to France on both economic and ideological grounds.[17]

Louis did not think of d'Avaux's Dutch associates as friends whose views and interests had to be treated with consideration. For him their status was that of dependents whose interests coincided with his own for the time being, and up to a point (which Louis would determine). Moreover he seems to have believed that they had no alternative means of withstanding William's policies, other than French support and encouragement. His attitude became even clearer after the Revocation of the Edict of Nantes, when he obstinately refused to allow the relatives and friends of leading Regent families in Amsterdam to leave France. Although Dutch by origin, they had become naturalised French subjects, in order to gain commercial advantages for themselves; Louis insisted that as his subjects they must obey his laws. D'Avaux urged Louis to let the most prominent and well connected leave France, rather than conform to Catholicism, and forecast that this would create a favourable impression and counteract furious anti-French propaganda, but the fact that publicity would be given to any concession made it impossible for Louis to make exceptions. As a result many of d'Avaux's most influential connections severed their links with him.[18]

In his dealings with England, as with the United Provinces, Louis was concerned entirely with furthering his own interests. He did not intervene to protect the monarchy as a form of government, nor would he prejudice his policies by openly intervening to protect the Catholic religion. Generally he preferred to work with Charles and James personally, but if a situation demanded a change of tactics — as it did in 1678 — he had no hesitation in encouraging and subsidising the parliamentary opposition, in order to check royal moves that he calculated would affect France. Louis intervened to destroy ministers, and even in order to determine the selection of the English ambassador to his own Court.[19]

In concluding the celebrated, or infamous, secret treaty of Dover in 1670, Louis enlisted Charles as his subsidised ally for a pre-arranged and aggressive war against the Dutch, which was declared in the spring of 1672. In the most historically controversial clause of the treaty, Charles undertook to announce his conversion to Catholicism, at a date to be decided by him, and Louis promised to give him subsidies in return. If the announcement provoked disorders, he would provide armed assistance.[20] One may be entirely cynical about Charles's intentions, since he was never publicly to declare his conversion, but for Louis a Catholic king in England was one who would be permanently dependent on French support, or the promise of support when needed, against his own subjects. It would fix the position of the king and restrict his freedom of action. In the correspondence between Louis and his ambassadors in London and The Hague it is assumed that Charles and James had ultimately to decide whether to rely on French support, or fall increasingly into a state of dependence upon their own subjects. They saw as advantageous to French interests the determination expressed by James to free the monarchy from its institutional and practical dependence on Parliament, and to abandon the practice of his brother Charles in allowing his ministers to make, as well as execute, major policy decisions. The tactics used by Louis were determined by this view of Charles as impressionable. Not only was he personally indolent and excessively tolerant, but his financial and legislative dependence on Parliament made him susceptible to pressure.

This dependence of the English monarchy on Parliament greatly reduced the value of England as an ally for France, and Louis made only half-hearted efforts to persuade Charles not to make peace with the Dutch in February 1674. For the rest of the period down to (and including) 1688, French purposes were best served by neutralising England, and that meant intervening in its affairs to prevent William, Spain and the Emperor drawing the country into the anti-French alliance that was fighting the war of 1672-8, and which William tried to reassemble after the peace of Nijmegen. Neutralisation at a modest price was the objective of the subsidy treaty concluded in February 1676: in return for £100,000 Charles undertook to dissolve Parliament, which would make it impossible for him even to contemplate intervening in the war. In the event Charles did not fulfil his undertaking, substituting an eighteen-month prorogation, which meant that he could not intervene in either 1676 or 1677, and Louis accepted this as value for money.[21] But the fact that Charles had to sign and seal the treaty himself, because neither of his principal ministers, the earls of Danby and Lauderdale, dared to do so, revealed to Louis the potentially dangerous isolation of the king and his brother James in wanting friendly relations with him.

Spectacular French advances in the Spanish Netherlands early in 1677 provoked furious debates in the spring session of Parliament, with demands for the recall of all English forces in the service of France, and an Address calling on Charles to conclude alliances in order to prevent further French advances.[22] Country or opposition MPs received encouragement and were supplied with information for use in these debates from the Spanish, Imperial and Dutch ambassadors. To counter this the French ambassador provided Charles with £11,000, for distribution to MPs, that is as a supplement to the patronage and money being dispensed by Lord Treasurer Danby.[23] This money had little effect. In an Address on 29 March

1677 the Commons described the recent French conquests as a danger to England, and not only called on Charles to conclude new alliances (which was an encroachment on the prerogative), but explicitly advocated a war in order to stop the great and 'over-balancing' power of Louis. Promising to vote supply once war was declared, MPs claimed that this was 'the unanimous sense and desire of the whole Nation'. But they voted only £200,000 for preliminary naval and military preparations, whereas Charles claimed that he needed at least three times as much. In the debates and the exchanges between the Commons and the king each side, the Court and the MPs of the Country opposition, tried to saddle the other with the blame for the weaknesses of the English position, rather than try to rectify the defects.[24]

In the autumn of 1677 Charles offered his services to Louis as a mediator with the allies, in return for fresh subsidies.[25] He greatly over-estimated his own diplomatic skill and the amount of influence he could bring to bear on William and the allies. He had no chance of obtaining from the latter concessions of a magnitude sufficient to satisfy Louis. He bungled the attempt to induce William to abandon his determination to continue the war. Charles claimed to Louis that he could persuade William to conclude an early peace, by holding out to him the prize of a marriage to Mary, James's daughter, but a marriage that would be solemnised only after peace had been made. What Charles overlooked was the availability to Louis of a much more certain method of forcing William to end the war. French agents were already in contact with the war-weary Dutch republicans. By playing on their fears that William would, like his father, make an attempt to increase his authority at the expense of their constitutional rights and liberties, and by offering commercial concessions, Louis was to persuade them to exert extreme pressure on William. The States General was to refuse him additional tax revenues.[26]

Charles also bungled relations with William on the visit which he made to England in October. By giving permission for him to come over, Charles raised universal expectations that an immediate marriage would take place, but the king had made no such decision, and James was strongly opposed. By keeping William waiting Charles tried to postpone making a decision that was bound to affect not only English policies towards Europe and the war, but the future course of the war itself. All Europe was watching William's visit; during it the negotiations at Nijmegen came virtually to a halt. William felt humiliated by the delay; a refusal to allow an immediate marriage would have been a shattering blow to his prestige, and it would also have provoked furious recriminations in England. But once Charles authorised the marriage he found that William began to intensify his attempts to draw England into the war, and indeed this constituted his short-term objective.[27]

From the French perspective the most disturbing feature of William's visit was the part played by Lord Treasurer Danby, who had earlier if reluctantly participated in Charles's attempts to obtain subsidies from Louis. His pressure on Charles had produced the authorisation for the marriage, and he began immediately to identify himself with William's interests, instigating the despatch of an emissary to Louis with proposed terms for peace which were unrealistically and unacceptably favourable to William and the allies.[28] Danby's policies provoked a sustained French reaction that was characteristically deft in probing a number of alternative options. Barrillon, the new French ambassador in London, received orders to stop payments due under the earlier subsidy treaty. He told Charles that a resumption of payments, and an agreement to pay additional subsidies, depended on his making a public commitment not to enter the war against France. Such a statement, presumably through the medium of a royal speech to Parliament, would provoke furious reactions and ensure the rejection of all requests for supply. However, Barrillon was to offer the calculatedly inadequate sum of £200,000. This would make it impossible for Charles to reverse his policies again, by going to William's aid. As a cynical but customary additional gambit Louis offered Danby a massive bribe, but although the lord treasurer was notoriously avaricious and greedy he wisely declined it. The third and most fruitful option was for Louis to enter into a working relationship with the parliamentary opposition. Some of its leaders had already made an approach in the autumn of 1677, but at first received a non-committal response. In December Louis established contact.[29] The men with whom he was now prepared to work had consistently denounced him and his policies, international, domestic and religious. They had condemned the failure of Charles and Danby to check French advances, and vociferously championed the protestant religion.

Sir John Dalrymple's revelation that many of the stalwarts of the constitutional opposition to Charles had volunteered their services as the mercenary agents of France, including the future Whig martyrs lord William Russell and Algernon Sydney, created a storm of controversy and incredulity.[30] What were the reasons for such apparently deceitful and dishonourable behaviour? How can one account for their readiness to continue to denounce French policies in violent terms, while simultaneously working to sabotage any possibility of England assisting the allies against France? First, most of the prominent opposition spokesmen, for example lord Hollis among the older generation, lord William Russell of the younger leaders, genuinely and profoundly distrusted Charles in general, and suspected (rightly) that he had no real intention of going to war against France. They feared that the army which Danby raised, with ominous speed, in the first months of 1678 was really intended (as they believed the army raised in 1672-3 had been intended) for use at home, to deter the nation from resisting the king when he deprived it of its liberties, and established royal absolutism.

All the activists in the parliamentary opposition had become totally frustrated by Danby's success in building up a patronage system within the 'standing' Cavalier Parliament, elected seventeen years before.[31] There were no indications that this Parliament would be dissolved, and indeed by his success in arranging William's marriage to Mary Danby had strengthened his position and was even thinking in terms of a 'reversionary interest', that is, looking ahead to Mary succeeding either Charles or James. Desperately frustrated Country MPs like Henry Powle, William Sacheverel and William Garroway could see no other way of getting the Cavalier Parliament dissolved, and so making it possible to dislodge Danby, than by working underhand with France.[32] Some of their colleagues were actuated entirely by mercenary greed, or by the desire to oust a minster who refused to give them office.[33] Other MPs who collaborated with the French ambassador had connections with members of the Dutch republican groups who had similar contacts with the French diplomats at the Nijmegen negotiations. They had imbibed from the latter the fear that William's motive in marrying Mary, and establishing a friendly relationship with Charles and Danby, was to obtain their backing for an attempt to increase his authority at the expense of the liberties of the Dutch provinces and cities.[34]

By offering all their contacts money Louis and his diplomatic agents calculated (like the KGB today) that the acceptance of money, even in small amounts, would compromise their dependents and render them vulnerable to blackmail if they ceased to be co-operative. French promises were seldom honoured in full, it would appear, so that a man like Ralph Montagu had to return repeatedly in the hope of further instalments, and so was kept available for service.[35] Lord Hollis had compromised himself long before, when ambassador in Paris, by accepting presents from Louis, and the duke of Buckingham had often received substantial payments.[36] In his egocentric and imaginative way Buckingham still fancied himself to be Louis's first choice as his friend in high places in England. In October and November 1677 Buckingham was making what proved to be his last serious bid to become a leading (or even chief) minister. Danby's success in persuading Charles to authorise Mary's marriage spelled the end of this bid.[37] Consequently in December Buckingham took the initiative in sending an emissary to Louis, the excessively untrustworthy Sir Ellis Leighton, and seems to have claimed that this mission had Shaftesbury's approval. The first earl of Shaftesbury was not yet acknowledged as leader of the Country opposition, although Danby recognised him as his most dangerous enemy, and had him committed to the Tower in February 1677 for arguing that

Parliament had been automatically dissolved by the fifteen-month prorogation, and kept him there until 27 February 1678. It is now impossible to know whether Shaftesbury did have anything to do with Leighton's mission, and nothing seems to have come of it, but after his release he became the politician whom Barrillon thought would be the most valuable of all in the service of France. There is no evidence to indicate that Shaftesbury ever had any direct dealings with Louis or Barrillon, and although several of the latter's contacts claimed that they could influence him, this also seems unlikely.[38]

Buckingham's initiative ran counter to all French operating practices. Louis and Barrillon preferred to keep all initiatives in their own hands, rather than respond to approaches. Moreover, with the exception of the negotiations that led to the secret treaty of Dover in 1670, which were conducted through the medium of the personal correspondence between Charles and his sister, the duchess of Orléans, Louis invariably restricted all clandestine dealings — with Charles, James, ministers and opposition peers and MPs alike — to the English end, to the royal Court and Westminster.

In the earliest phase of his contacts with the opposition in December 1677 Louis astutely employed as his principal emissary the Huguenot soldier and diplomat Henri de Ruvigny, who was related to the Russell family, and had more insight into the workings of Parliament, and the mentality of its members, than had Barrillon.[39] Ruvigny, Barrillon and their contacts worked out an effective and simple strategy which was applied during the fragmented sessions of the spring and summer of 1678. While continuing to press their previous line of argument calling for immediate war against France, and condemning the Court for failing to do anything to check the increasingly dangerous French advances, those MPs who were co-operating with Barrillon raised and insisted on conditions which they knew Charles and Danby would not concede. The king must reveal details of his newly concluded treaties with the Dutch, which after all had been published in newspapers in Holland, and give the Commons information about current negotiations with foreign states. As everyone knew, not only were foreign policy matters exclusively part of the royal prerogative, but Charles had already refused to communicate such information. Secondly they demanded the dismissal of all ministers and councillors who had advised Charles to disregard the Commons resolution of February 1677, which had called for action against France.[40]

Opposition MPs demanded an immediate declaration of war against France, and a commitment to continue it until entirely unrealistic objectives had been achieved: the reduction of France to the frontiers of 1659, of the treaty of the Pyrenees, which would involve Louis surrendering all the territories he had gained by the 1666-8 war of Devolution, as well as his conquests in the current war. Considering the military situation in the spring of 1678, when the French took Ghent and Spanish resources and morale were near to collapse, such proposals were absurdly unacceptable. In addition, so as to create more difficulties, MPs insisted that all the allies must agree to cease all trade with France, something that the Dutch (and particularly the commercial interests represented by the republicans) would never accept, given their traditional practice of permitting trade with enemy countries in southern Europe, first Spain but now France. MPs also made furious attacks on alleged misbehaviour by soldiers in the new army units, and alleged that many of the officers were papists.[41]

Most damaging of all, opposition MPs successfully propagated the notion that Charles had no intention of making war on France, and that talk of a war was merely a cover for sinister absolutist designs. Secretary Coventry referred almost despairingly to the general 'incredulity of a war (and) aversion to land forces'.[42] There really was reason for these suspicions, and it is now virtually impossible to say precisely what Charles and Danby actually intended, that is, which of the various options they preferred. While continuing to talk publicly of entering the war, Charles negotiated a secret treaty with Louis on 17/27 May: in return for subsidies he undertook to disband all newly raised forces by July.[43] At first Charles had tried to obtain a three-year agreement, but at this time Louis was concerned entirely with short-term objectives, with maximising the advantages which he could extract from the peace negotiations at Nijmegen. Charles made the mistake of assuming, when he concluded the 17/27 May treaty, that a general peace was imminent. But after coming to a preliminary agreement with the States General, Louis then declared that he would not sign or ratify the peace unless his ally Sweden received full restitution of its lost territories. By this move Louis not only expected to retain Swedish friendship, but to drive a wedge between the Dutch and the elector of Brandenburg-Prussia, who would blame the States General for his having to give up his conquests. As a result the war continued unexpectedly, and Charles's warlike rhetoric made it impossible for him to disband his new forces while hostilities continued in Flanders. But because he did not disband by the stipulated time he did not get the subsidies promised.[44]

By preventing armed English intervention, and showing that Charles could not be relied on to turn his declaration into actions, Louis induced the States General to sign a separate peace. This left other allied powers to reach a settlement with Louis individually. William was powerless to prevent this catastrophe, which detonated the Confederation which he had formed. However, Louis was determined to increase William's isolation by destroying his new associate, lord treasurer Danby. Louis's chief instrument in this destructive intervention was the former English ambassador in Paris, Ralph Montagu. An extremely able, ruthless and ambitious politician, whom Danby feared as a potential rival, Montagu ironically had penetrated Louis's intentions the previous December (1677), and warned Charles and Danby about the real purpose of Ruvigny's mission. A year later Montagu became the chief agent for Louis in Parliament; the explanation for this change is that he had lost his embassy and been denied the secretary-ship of state to which he thought himself entitled.[45]

In a coup pre-arranged with Barrillon, and with the promise of political asylum in France if things went wrong, Montagu revealed evidence on the floor of the Commons about the part played by Danby in earlier negotiations with France. Danby was shown to have been asking for subsidies from Louis at a time when his publicly proclaimed policy was for a war. This demonstration of his duplicity apparently confirmed all the strong suspicions about his real intentions in raising new army units. An enraged Commons voted for his impeachment.[46] Charles had to dissolve a Parliament that his minister could no longer control, and Danby had later to resign. The French-instigated attack took him out of politics for a decade. More significantly it also helped to plunge England into the turmoil of the Exclusion Crisis.

Barrillon never paid Montagu the full amounts he had been promised. The latter was kept on a string by being made occasional payments, so that when he became potentially valuable again, as a leader of the small group of Whigs who challenged Shaftesbury's domination of the party at the end of 1680, he provided the French with a new means of preventing William exploiting the situation in England. Montagu and his associates tried to negotiate a secret deal with Charles, who was to grant them high offices and concede Exclusion. From the French angle, accepting that it was indeed possible that Charles would eventually give way on Exclusion, it was preferable for this to be done in co-operation with Whigs who possessed French connections than with the Court group of Sunderland, Godolphin and Henry Sidney, who worked in William's interests.[47] But Louis did not avail himself of Montagu's offer to work with Barrillon, preferring to subsidise Charles, on condition that he did not call another Parliament, for the duration of the agreement, and that he would not fulfill the obligations stipulated in a treaty signed with Spain in 1680. Effectively Louis purchased Charles as a dependent, neutralising England.[48]

Between 1678 and 1684 the subversive and diplomatic interventions of the French ambassador at The Hague confirmed the pessimistic prophecy made in the Commons by Sir William Coventry that in major matters the comte d'Avaux would have greater influence there than the Prince of

Orange.[49] D'Avaux entered with great skill and total ruthlessness into the interplay of Dutch domestic politics, encouraging William's opponents and augmenting their fears and suspicions to the point where the city of Amsterdam and the provinces of Groningen and Friesland did not think themselves safe, and seriously considered the possibility of seceding from the United Provinces, and placing themselves under the protection of Louis.[50] D'Avaux developed a bitter personal animosity towards William, but also in time a large measure of contempt for the republicans whom he used against William. Experience of their irresolution and willingness to compromise led d'Avaux to see himself as the only person who really possessed the necessary determination to defy William and Fagel. At times d'Avaux seems almost to have lost sight of the actual objectives that Louis was trying to achieve — the acquisition of specific territories, Strasbourg in 1681, Luxemburg in 1682-4, without provoking a general war.

D'Avaux shared the advantage which Barrillon exploited in England in 1678, profound suspicion of their rulers by significant political groups, in the Dutch case the oligarchical Regent government of Amsterdam, together with its allies and dependents in the States of the province of Holland. In addition he had an advantage stemming from the commercial concessions which Louis gave the States General in 1678, as an inducement to make a separate peace at Nijmegen, and which he continued until 1684. During the war of 1672 Dutch merchants had suffered severely from the burden of exceptionally high war taxation, combined with heavy losses of ships and cargoes at the hands of French privateers. The return of peace and the French concessions restored some measure of prosperity, which now seemed at risk from William's apparent eagerness to renew the struggle against France.

Like John de Witt in the years after 1666, when Louis went to war to enforce his 'devolutionary' claims to parts of the Spanish Netherlands and annexed parts of them, William had as his first objective the preservation of Flanders as a barrier to French expansionism. But after he failed to prevent the States General making a separate peace he had to warn the Spanish governors in Brussels, and the remote government in Madrid, that the Dutch had little inclination to go to war again to preserve Flanders.[51] He also knew a great deal about the connections which d'Avaux was establishing with the burgomasters and sheriffs of Amsterdam and of the fears of the republicans that the only way in which he could mobilise the resources of the United Provinces for a new war was by overriding their rights and breaking the constitution. William's predicament was that any attempt to expand the army, to send forces into the Spanish Netherlands as a precautionary defensive move, or to send out a fleet to support allied Sweden against Denmark, the client of France, would be interpreted by the republicans as aggressive warmongering, and as a prelude to an attempt to increase his authority arbitrarily and illegally. As d'Avaux put it, with characteristic malice, Amsterdam would seek French protection, preferring a great king who would protect their liberties to a little prince who would oppress them.[52]

In September 1683 William proposed measures to the States General which, hopefully, would deter Louis from making an attack on Luxemburg, or, alternatively, would bolster Spanish resistance to an attack there, and on other key fortresses. William already possessed authority, from the period of an earlier threat to Luxemburg in 1682, to move 8000 men into defensive positions in the Spanish Netherlands but he needed to augment the army by 16000 soldiers overall in order to create a credible deterrent.[53] From Louis's point of view an augmentation of this size would strengthen William's chances of bringing about a general European war over Luxemburg, by encouraging Spanish intransigence. The proposal also confirmed the official French view of William as an inveterate enemy, with whom no settlement could be negotiated. Louis therefore initiated a policy which combined the application of pressure on Spain, which began with an attack on the fortress of Kortrijk in November 1683, with intensified intervention by d'Avaux. He was to use the Amsterdam republicans, and their allies in Friesland and Groningen, to sabotage all William's attempts to come to the assistance of Spain.[54]

As later in 1688, Louis calculated that he could seize what he wanted, Luxemburg in 1683, Phillipsburg in 1688, without provoking a general war. On both occasions he used the same technique, the selective use of intimidatory force, against Spain in 1683, the Palatinate and the German princes in 1688, while relying on diplomatic intervention and manoeuvres to prevent other states and rulers coming to the assistance of the one which he chose as his target. While Kortrijk was under attack French bands ravaged the rural areas of Flanders, and preparations were made to besiege Luxemburg. Meanwhile d'Avaux's Amsterdam connections remained unmoved by appeals from Gaspar Fagel, the Pensionary of Holland and William's lieutenant. One of the city's deputies commented that war would ruin trade, and that it was not worth risking the prosperity of the fishing trade (important for North Holland) for the sake of frontier towns in the Spanish Netherlands. William's answer to this was that if d'Avaux had been present, and allowed to speak, he would have used the same words.[55]

The tactics used by the Amsterdam deputies in the States of Holland, and by the Holland deputies in the States General, closely resembled those used by the opposition MPs working in Parliament in co-operation with Barrillon, in the sessions of 1678. In the States they rejected the levy of 16000 men, and attached impossible conditions to the voting of extra money: they demanded that the other and poorer provinces must pay all their arrears, within a month, knowing that it would take them years to raise the money. They made allegations of embezzlement of revenues voted during the war, and the diversion of money to uses other than those intended.[56] Blatantly the counter-proposal was made that d'Avaux should be sounded about ways in which the Spanish authorities could be compelled to accept French demands. Most significantly of all, the Amsterdam deputies showed that they would not authorise military action even if Louis continued or even extended his offensive actions. All these points had been rehearsed with d'Avaux, who kept in constant touch with the burgomasters, on one occasion melodramatically meeting their representative at night at a country rendezvous. Even a personal appearance by William in the States, and his use of both entertainment and intimidation, failed to persuade the Amsterdam deputies to agree to extra men and money, and this humiliating failure gave them greater confidence.[57]

William's difficulties grew when, despite his earlier warning and his lack of success in increasing his armed forces, Spain unilaterally declared war on France on 1 December 1683, hoping to draw in the Dutch, the Emperor (now that Vienna had been saved from the Turks) and the German princes. The intensification of pressure on Amsterdam by William only resulted in their appealing to d'Avaux for increased support. However, Louis mercilessly used the republican party. He ignored their requests that he improve their position in relation to William, by lowering his demands on Spain and extending the time limits in which the latter had to come to terms. Revealingly in his despatches to d'Avaux Louis insisted on tight time limits if Amsterdam was able to block William, but gave authority to extend them if William got his way.[58] Louis and d'Avaux both despised the Regent class, merchants and magistrates, as men who would always succumb to pressure in order to safeguard their material interests. Consequently the best way of using them to further French policies was to maintain pressure upon them, to make them fear Louis more than they feared William. Having embarked on appeasement policies, the Dutch republicans found that they lost all leverage on France, and it suited the French for relations between them and William to deteriorate further.

D'Avaux in his despatch of 9 January 1684 gave Louis a full account of the fears and anxieties of his republican contacts, whom he described and detailed. Grana, governor of the Spanish Netherlands, intercepted and deciphered this despatch, which William read to the States of Holland on 16 February.[59] His denunciation of leading Amsterdam republicans, Hooft and Hop, by name and his charges of treasonable behaviour in maintaining connections with d'Avaux had a sensational effect, but only in the short term. The Amsterdam house in the Hague was sealed up after the city's deputies to the States General fled by night. The gates of Amsterdam were closed early each night, as a precaution against a coup.[60] But in the longer term William's charges produced little effect. Those whom he accused acknowledged that they had kept in contact with d'Avaux, but claimed that they had done so for the purpose of protecting the city's trading interests. D'Avaux not only protested that the interception of his despatch constituted a breach of international law, but that Grana had deliberately distorted his words for propaganda purposes. William did not go to the extremity of trying to seize the men whom he denounced. Encouraged by this sign of weakness, Amsterdam continued obstinately to obstruct the levy of additional soliders, and in the States General the deputies of Groningen and Friesland, with whom d'Avaux also maintained close relations, joined in opposition.

From William's angle the final result was as damaging a reverse as the separate peace of 1678. He found himself unable to give the governor of the Spanish Netherlands sufficient assistance to withstand French incursions. The Dutch troops already there had to be kept on passive garrison duty in towns which the French chose not to attack, while they burnt the suburbs of Brussels and ravaged the countryside. Finally Luxemburg fell. William had no success in trying to form a new anti-French alliance, and he could do nothing to stop the German princes concluding the twenty-year truce with Louis. This represented a French triumph comparable to that of Nijmegen, and it was a similar triumph that he planned and expected to achieve in the winter of 1688-9. Once again in 1684 he succeeded in negotiating a settlement with other states separately, one by one. In his negotiations with the States General Louis refused to include any discussion of the affairs of the German princes and the Empire, or of Northern European affairs, the Holstein question and other disputes between Denmark and Sweden.[61] The Swedish envoy at the Hague naturally complained about the selfish behaviour of the States General, and its complete disregard of existing treaty obligations. The Spanish government, humiliated again by having to accept French terms, heaped reproaches on the Dutch.[62]

Encouraged by his success in checkmating William, d'Avaux tried to obtain the dismissal of Fagel as pensionary, and talked with his contacts about Louis taking Amsterdam, Groningen and Friesland under his protection (by means of a French army invited by them), and their secession from the United Provinces.[63] However, d'Avaux's influence had peaked. His contacts had been subjected to ruthless pressure in 1683-4 and treated like pawns, not as allies or associates whose views and interests deserved some form of consideration. Moreover d'Avaux failed to convince Louis that in one crucial area he had to tailor his policies to Dutch views and interests. In his despatches he referred, rather diffidently to an absolute master, to the central importance attached by Amsterdam and the republicans to trade, and the value they placed on the concessions which Louis had granted in 1678.[64] In reply Louis prohibited his entering into any discussion on specific commercial matters; he was to confine himself to giving vague general assurances. These were in fact entirely insincere, since Louis was about to withdraw the concessions. In retrospect d'Avaux admitted that his master's action amounted to a breach of the Nijmegen treaty, and deplored its effects.[65] These were little short of disastrous. Former connections who had been ready to work with d'Avaux against William expressed real resentment, and rejected the casuistical and unconvincing explanations which the ambassador offered. Many supported economic reprisals against French commodities, which in turn were seen by Louis as an unfriendly act. Merchants who had formerly opposed any policy likely to lead to war now changed their attitude towards France, thinking (wrongly, as it proved) that involvement in a new war could not be more damaging to their interests than existing French policies.

Religious persecution in France completed the destruction of the network of contacts which d'Avaux had manipulated with such success. When pressure on the Huguenots began, in the early 1680s, he reported that his contacts, being mostly arminians (or known as remonstrants) would not be antagonised by measures taken against dogmatic French calvinists. But even before the Edict of Nantes was formally revoked in October 1685, he found that in reality his influence was annihilated. Former connections shunned him. In the years 1687-8 he was reduced to controlling and operating no more than an efficient espionage network, and wielded very little political influence.[66]

Paradoxically by 1688 French influence in England had increased, and seemed to be securely established, but within a strictly limited social and political circle. The period of active French collaboration with MPs and members of opposition groups and parties proved to be a relatively short interlude between long periods in which the primary duties of the French ambassador were to maintain close and continuous contact with the sovereign himself. At the end of 1683 Louis ordered Barrillon to sever contact with Montagu, in case it became known and upset the relationship with Charles, and because there was now no likelihood of another Parliament meeting during his reign.[67] Both before and after Charles's death, it is clear that Louis saw James as his most useful and reliable friend. Consequently Barrillon virtually confined himself during James's reign to maintaining close contact with the king and his inner circle of ministers, together with a group of prominent catholic courtiers. For Louis and Barrillon these were men whose positions and policies necessarily inclined them to seek French friendship. None of them, after Lawrence Hyde's dismissal at the end of 1686, were suspected of having links with, or expectations from, William and Mary. As a result Barrillon saw and reported events and possible developments in the British Isles very much through James's own eyes, and shared his blind confidence in the strength of the royal position.

Almost all the intelligence information which Louis received in the course of 1688 about the formidable character of William's preparations to intervene in England, and the chances of their succeeding, came from d'Avaux at the Hague. Barrillon's despatches, like those of Bordeaux in 1659-60, gave a misleading impression of the strength of the regime. On the other hand the advice which d'Avaux offered to Louis had little relevance to the faulty strategy which the latter adopted. As his influence on the republicans declined, and as he came to despise them for their weakness in not standing up to William, d'Avaux began to advocate the use of direct intimidation against the Dutch, as the only sure means of checking William.[68] In the late summer of 1688, as he reported William's military preparations, d'Avaux urged Louis to make an attack on Bergen-op-Zoom or, more realistically, the southern and exposed fortress of Maastricht. As he realised that Dutch preparations were in fact aimed against England, he claimed that a military attack would prevent William sailing for England with a substantial part of the Dutch army, including most of its élite units.[69]

D'Avaux failed to understand the way in which William's invasion of England fitted into, or even hopefully facilitated, Louis's strictly selective and restricted offensive plans. By attacking the fortress of Phillipsburg on the Rhine, invading the Palatinate and installing his protégé Furstenberg as archbishop-elector of Cologne, Louis expected to break up the League of Augsburg without having to fight a general war. William, by crossing to England with an army and becoming involved in what Louis expected on the basis of Barrillon's reports to become a long civil war, would be leaving the German princes to look after their own defences. This would expose William to French allegations that he was behaving as selfishly, in pursuing his ambitions to usurp the English throne, as the States General had done in 1678 to further their trading interests. The French would add, for the benefit of the Emperor and the Catholic princes, that William was fighting a protestant war of religion in the British Isles, and that they should dissociate themselves from him.

Louis still hoped, in addition, to exploit the timidity of the Dutch republicans and get them to hamper William, as they had done in 1683-4. At that time Louis relied on a combination of persuasion with pressure. In 1688 Louis applied naked intimidation, knowing that d'Avaux no longer had the confidence of the republican party. On 9 September d'Avaux presented a memorial to the States General, threatening them with war if they tried either to keep Furstenberg out of Cologne or to support an attack on James.[70] The States General ignored both parts of this ultimatum. Significantly Louis only acted to substantiate his threat, and declared war on the Dutch, much later on 26 November 1688, when he knew that William had established himself in the west of England and that James's army was concentrating against him, and not earlier when allied Brandenburg and Dutch forces took up defensive positions in, and to cover, the territories of Cologne. Louis's eyes were fixed on the Rhineland and reactions in Germany, where he relied on intimidation. He gave the Emperor and the princes until 1 January 1689 to make a settlement on French terms, and the first systematic, terrorist burnings of towns began in November. If these tactics had worked and the German states had agreed to peace, the States General would have found themselves in a precarious state, without allies, with William and the best part of the army engaged in England and without a clear lead — Fagel was dying.

Of course developments quickly brought down this card castle of French expectations. The devastation of towns, palaces and villages in the Rhineland made the Emperor and the German princes more determined not to accept French terms. They recognised William and Mary's title as king and queen surprisingly soon after they accepted the offer from the Convention Parliament.[71] Since the French could not mount an immediate threat to the United Provinces, even d'Avaux's former associates initially supported the war. Revealingly one of William's first executive actions, in January 1689, although technically it was outside the temporary powers given to him by the Assembly in December, was to give Barrillon peremptory orders to leave the kingdom. As king of England, William declared war on France in May, and in the same month an alliance was concluded between the States General and the Emperor, which Spain, Denmark and Bavaria joined later.[72] D'Avaux had had to leave the Hague in November, but his abilities and experience ensured him immediate and important new employment. He accompanied James to Ireland as ambassador, but his real mission was to ensure that the interests of France would be served by James and his adherents.[73] In other words Louis and his agent d'Avaux applied themselves to control and manipulate a new set of puppets, the Jacobites, in a new situation and for a new set of purposes.

NOTES

1. G. Pagès, *Contributions à l'Histoire de la Politique Francaise en Allemagne sous Louis XIV* (Paris, 1905), pp. 45, 61, 66, 72-3, 82-3.

2. P. Geyl, *Orange and Stuart* (1969), pp. 60-6.

3. *Ibid.*, pp. 316-17. The treaty of Heeswijk (16 July 1672) bound both Louis and Charles to give William sovereignty over what was left of the United Provinces.

4. A. Browning, *English Historical Documents*, viii (1966), 864.

5. F.J. Routledge, *England and the Treaty of the Pyrenees* (Liverpool, 1973).

6. PRO, Baschet transcripts: Barrillon, 24, 27 March 1681.

7. Geoffrey Symcox, 'Louis XIV and the Outbreak of the Nine Years War', *Louis XIV and Europe*, edited by Ragnhild Hatton (1976), p. 202.

8. J.R. Jones, *The Revolution of 1688 in England* (1972), pp. 258-60.

9. He began canvassing from the very start of his mission, with the full approval of Louis: *D'Avaux*, i, 28-30, 32, 135, 138, 173, 179-81.

10. *D'Avaux*, i, 100-2; ii, 263-4, 267; iv, 99-103, 163-4, 169-70, 330.

11. *D'Avaux*, i. 7-8, 9-11, 260-1. J.J. Jusserand (ed.), *Recueil des Instructions données aux Ambassadeurs ou Ministres de France* (Paris, 1929), xxv, 423.

12. *D'Avaux*, vi, 155-6, 187-8, 191-2, 202-3, 204-5, 218, 225, 231, 248-9.

13. Louis assumed that it was the republican constitution of the United Provinces that worked to the advantage of France, because it made for external weakness. English conservatives, and later Jacobites, saw the United Provinces as a source of ideological infection: Bevill Higgons, *A Short View of the English History* (1723), pp. 379-80, 420.

14. *D'Avaux*, i. 271-3, 289-90; ii, 43-5.

15. Sir William Temple, *Works* (1740), i. 89.

16. J.A.H. Bots and A.G. Weiler, *The Peace of Nijmegen* (Amsterdam, 1980).

17. *D'Avaux*, iv, 6-7, 58, 346; vi, iii, 138, 153, 195-6, 210, 224-5, 299-300, 322, 326.

18. *D'Avaux*, v. 140, 144-7, 200-1, 222-3, 232, 266-7; vi, 12-14, 94-5, 105-6, 108.

19. Marquise Campana de Cavelli, *Les Derniers Stuarts à Saint-Germain en Laye* (Paris, 1871), ii, 115, Louis XIV to Barrillon, 2 August 1686.

20. Browning, *English Historical Documents*, viii, 864.

21. Sir John Dalrymple, *Memoirs of Great Britain and Ireland* (1773), ii, appendix, 102-5. Jusserand, *Recueil des Instructions*, xxv, 97-9.

22. F.A. M. Mignet, *Négociations relatives à la succession d'Espagne sous Louis XIV* (Paris, 1835-42), iv, 532, 535-6.

23. Dalrymple, *Memoirs*, ii, appendix, 110.

24. Anchitell Grey, *Debates of the House of Commons* (1769), iv, 331-4.

25. Mignet, *Négociations*, iv, 426-7, 445, 487-93, 514, 516-17, 518, 523, 572.

26. S.B. Baxter, *William III* (1966), pp. 150-1.

27. Ragnhild Hatton, 'Nijmegen and the European Powers', *The Peace of Nijmegen*, edited by J.A.H. Botts and A.G. Weiler (1980), p. 11.

28. A. Browning, *Thomas Osborne, Earl of Danby* (Glasgow, 1951), i, 250-5. Sir William Temple, *Works*, i. 454-5. S.B. Baxter, *William III*, pp. 148-50.

29. Baschet transcripts, Barrillon, 13 November 1677. Dalrymple, *Memoirs*, ii, appendix, 128, 129-30.

30. Jusserand, *Recueil des Instructions*, xxv, 258-9. Dalrymple, *Memoirs*, ii, appendix, 131.

31. Browning, *Danby*, i. 167-73, 205-7; iii, 96-111.

32. Baschet transcripts, Barrillon, 22 July 1680, 'memoire de ceux à qui on peut faire des gratifications'. Also 14 December 1679.

33. Ibid., Barrillon depicted William Harbord, Sir John Baber and Algernon Sydney as the contacts most concerned with money.

34. Among Barrillon's contacts Sydney, with Thomas Papillon and the elder Hampden, was linked with the republican or Louvestein party. Baschet transcripts, Barrillon, 7 September 1679. D'Avaux i, 15.

35. Baschet transcripts, Barrillon, 28 July, 22 September and 24 November 1681; Louis to Barrillon, 5 August 1681.

36. Baschet transcripts, Barrillon, 11 April 1681.

37. Browning, *Danby,* i, 240-2, 263-5.

38. Baschet transcripts, Barrillon, 24 January, 9 February, 14 March 1678. On claims of indirect management of the earl of Shaftesbury, 22 July 1680. *Historical Manuscripts Commission, Finch,* ii, 36.

39. Baschet transcripts, Barrillon, 14 March 1678. Jusserand, *Receuil des Instructions,* pp. 263-5.

40. Baschet transcripts, Barrillon, 24 March 1678. Dalrymple, *Memoirs,* ii, appendix, 146-7, James to William, 2 February 1677/8, O.S.

41. Grey, *Debates,* vi, 29, 69-70, 79-86, 216-25, 278-85, 307-14.

42. *Historical Manuscripts Commission, Ormonde, new series,* iv, 403.

43. Dalrymple, *Memoirs,* ii, appendix, 159-62, 165-8. Jusserand, *Recueil des Instructions,* pp. 260-1.

44. Dalrymple, *Memoirs,* ii, appendix, 174, James to William, 21 May 1678 O.S., 180.

45. *HMC, Finch,* ii, 12. Baschet transcripts, Barrillon to Pomponne, 10, 24 October 1678.

46. Dalrymple, *Memoirs,* ii, appendix, 205, James to William 20 December 1678, O.S. Grey, *Debates,* vi, 337-59 (19 December); 359-64 (20 December); 366-87 (21 December).

47. Baschet transcripts, Barrillon, 18, 22 July, 29 August, 12 September, 31 October, 11 November 1680. Jusserand, *Recueil des Instructions,* pp. 267-9. J.R. Jones, *The First Whigs* (1970), pp. 131-3, 149-54.

48. Baschet transcripts, Barrillon, 13 January, 13 February, 3, 24, 27 March 1681.

49. Grey, *Debates,* v, 291.

50. *D'Avaux,* iii, 50-1, 92-3, 190-1; iv, 20-1, 200.

51. *Ibid.,* i, 238-9. Baxter, *William III,* pp. 188-90.

52. *D'Avaux,* i, 142.

53. *Ibid.,* i, 204, 206-7, 208, 321, 324-6, 328-30, 344, 347-8, 359-60, 378.

54. *Ibid.,* i, 372-4.

55. *Ibid.,* i, 378-9.

56. *Ibid.,* i, 384-5.

57. *Ibid.,* ii, 8-14, 51-2.

58. *Ibid.,* i, 389-90; ii, 23-8, 29, 83-8, 113-14, 164-7, 184-6.

59. *Ibid.,* ii, 116-20, 121-4, 195-8, 211-13.

60. The delay between the interception and William's revelation of the content of the despatch had the effect of diminishing its impact: *D'Avaux,* ii, 136-7, 195-201, 203, 216-17, 222-3.

61. *Ibid.,* iii, 167-8, 229-30, 244-7.

62. *Ibid.,* iii, 183.

63. *Ibid.,* iii, 120, 161, 162-3, 190-1; iv, 20, 41, 48, 64, 99-100.

64. *Ibid.,* iv, 19, 40-1, 64, 152-3, 310-11, 327; vi, 190, 198, 229, 271, 299.

65. *Ibid.,* vi, 319.

66. *Ibid.,* v, 140, 144-7, 185, 209, 222-3, 231-2.

67. Dalrymple, *Memoirs,* ii, appendix, 79-80.

68. *D'Avaux*, v, 70, 86-7; vi, 274. Jusserand, *Recueil des Instructions*, pp. 403-4.
69. *D'Avaux*, vi, 213, 252-3, 257, 271.
70. *Ibid.*, vi, 215.
71. Baxter, *William III*, pp. 251-2.
72. J.R. Jones, *The Revolution of 1688 in England* (1972), p. 310.
73. J. Hogan, *Négociations de M. le Comte d'Avaux en Irlande, 1689-90* (Dublin, 1934).

CHAPTER 2

The Economic Consequences of William III

D. W. Jones

It has long been recognised that the great European war William III committed England to fight against France once he had gained the throne in 1688/9, brought unprecedented burdens for the country. But these burdens were also very dangerous so that by 1696-7 England suffered one of the most critical crises of her history, certainly in pre-twentieth century terms. For early in 1696, after confidence had been lost late in 1694 in what, by then, was a heavily clipped silver coin, a decision had to be taken to recoin even though England was still at war. Already, during 1695, the initial loss of confidence had precipitated a currency hurricane. Throughout the year, massive quantities of gold were speculatively imported and England's exchange depreciated alarmingly. Already, also, transactions had become ever more perplexed by the state of the silver coin.

But once recoining had been decided upon, these difficulties were considerably compounded. Recoining was bound to take time; between taking in the old coin and reissuing it as newly minted (and as a much smaller face-value amount of) new coin, there was bound to be a severe shortage of cash. Accordingly over the second half of 1696 and the first half of 1697 economic activity at home fell severely thanks to what indeed turned out to be a chronic shortage of cash. Early in 1697, the wagons which normally left Trowbridge full of Exeter serge for London were said to have gone almost empty;[1] while a little later in the year, cloth was claimed to be virtually unobtainable in London, once clothiers had been forced to lay off their weavers.[2] Most seriously of all, for a time during the previous year when the exchange remained at a heavy discount, the government, through the Bank of England, failed to pay bills drawn for the army in Flanders. Consequently, for nearly four months between late June and early October 1696 the army received virtually no funds from England.[3]

The explanation for this desperate situation is to be found in the highly ambitious, yet dangerously contradictory, strategy adopted by William III. Quite apart from the scale of the war effort, from virtually the beginning of the war England was undertaking a Double Forward Commitment of both the military and naval arms. No other European military power, whether of the immediate past or the present, had attempted, or was attempting, such a thing (the Dutch alone excepted perhaps). On the one hand, an English army was committed forward in Flanders (and with allies, notably Savoy, being subsidised as well), while on the other, the English navy was also committed forward most of the time, whether covering the Irish operations of the years 1689-91, covering and participating in two massive 'Descents' on the French coast in 1692 and 1693, attacking French corn ships over the winter of 1693-4, and then operating in the Mediterranean over the years 1694-5.

A naval commitment of this scale and character was of itself dangerous. Naval manning requirements were bound to starve trade of the seamen it required and to impose upon it a dangerously unseasonal pattern of sailings. At the same time, the forward commitment was unlikely to leave many ships of the line free to defend trade against the privateering attacks that the French were only too likely to launch against English commerce. But what made the forward naval commitment particularly dangerous was the second aspect of William's strategy — namely, the forward commitment of an army

Table 1. Weight of supplies and shipping required to supply the Flanders army in the mid-1690s for the year

Supplies	Consumption	Weight [d] (tons)	Shipping [h] (tons)
Bread	60,000 x 1.5 lb Brabant per day[a]	15,155	40,312
Beer	60,000 x 5 pints per day[b]	61,105	72,715
Fodder	2,000,000 rations of 15 lb Brabant hay, 6 lb straw and 3 pecks (14 lb per peck) oats for 200 days winter quarters[c]	25,305 hay 10,118 straw 68,437 oats 103,860 total fodder	140,569 hay 56,205 straw 66,384 oats 263,158 total fodder
Other Food		9,778 [e]	9,778
Wine		1,376 [f]	1,376
Fuel (coal)		54,000 [g]	54,000
		245,274	441,339

Notes and Sources:

[a]   BL Add. MS 10,123 fo. 106 (Brabant 1 lb = 470 grams).

[b]   PRO SP 8/12, no. 14; T 64/173.

[c]   BL Blenheim Papers, F2-22, 27.

[d]   To arrive at the weight of supplies annually required, the consumption shown for bread, beer and fodder has been scaled up to 365 days (one gallon of beer = 10 lbs). Had we estimated on the basis of feeding green forage to the horse in summer, then following G. Perjés, 'Army Provisioning, Logistics and Strategy in the Second Half of the 17th century', *Act Historica Scientarium Hungarica*, XVI (1970), 16-7, the estimate for fodder would have stood at 150,841 tons.

[e]   Estimate based on M. van Creveld, *Supplying War* (Cambridge, 1977), p. 24.

[f]   Estimate of wine consumption, see Jones, *War and Economy*, p. 31.

[g]   Estimated on the basis that London, with a population of some 500,000, imported 450,000 tons of coal annually.

[h]   The ton burden has been taken to be a ton of 2240 lb weight and of a capacity of 53.2 cubic feet (see M. Oppenheim, *A History of the Administration of the Royal Navy* (1896), pp. 30, 132, 266-8). PRO SP 8/14, no. 101 provides the ratio for converting weights of hay and straw into the ship tonnage required to carry them. For the remainder, the ratios have come from R. W. Stevens, *On the Tonnage of Ships and their Cargoes* (Plymouth, 1858), pp. 15-7, supplemented by P. Garoche, *Stowage Handling and Transport of Ship Cargoes* (New York, 1941).

and allies fighting abroad and for whom, because their needs could not be directly supplied from England's shores, remittances had to be sent across the foreign exchanges for spending by them as they saw fit.

The sheer impossibility of direct supply from England becomes immediately apparent from Table 1.

This shows that supplying the Flanders army would have required a 'lift' of some 245,000 tons annually, for which, allowing for the bulk of the hay and straw, a ship-tonnage of some 441,000 tons would have been needed. We can compare this with the 475,000 tons that annually sufficed to carry the whole of England's foreign trade in the later 1680s.[4] True, ships can be made to work harder and sailings to Flanders involved only short-haul voyages. Yet even if we suppose that ships in a supply shuttle could have been worked to make fully twice the voyages trading ships ordinarily made in trade with the Low Countries, the requirement still works out at at least 40,000 tons, or over 10% of England's total shipping tonnage at this time.[5] Moreover, the manning of this tonnage would have placed further pressure on scarce seafaring manpower at the same time as the supply shuttle, by presenting the French with the best possible target to attack, would also have required much of that naval protection which trade would only too likely be short of as well.

Even had these problems not applied, direct supply from English shores would still not have been practical. Unless horse regiments were to be bogged down when summer campaigning in a morass of wagon trains bringing fodder from the rear (which was impractical anyway), the horse had to be able to buy locally the green fodder needed, wherever it was to be obtained. It was also better for the officers and men to be free to buy locally freshly baked bread (instead of biscuit), and fresh meat (instead of salted meat). Moreover, since the Low Countries were one of Europe's long-standing cockpits, a whole host of local (and especially Jewish) entrepreneurs existed there long versed in the business of supplying armies; their military supplies were also exempted from local excises. The operations of two of these, Fonseca and Pereira, who contracted for the army's bread in the 1690s, are graphically described by Richard Hill, Deputy Paymaster to the army in Flanders, when he wrote in 1694 that:

> Pereyra . . . has allready his provision of corn, of ovens & of bakers at Gand as providor to ye Danes whom he has fed these 2 years & Ffonesca has ye same at Bruxelles, Louvain, as providor to all ye Spanish troops. Ffonseca has ye use of a 100 waggons as providor & a great many boats to transport his provision. They have comis and serv[t] in every town allready as they furnish ye troops every[where] with bread and for ye same reason have credit everywhere, they have provision of corn excise free in all towns, they have waggons to bring 'em in straw and wood as forrage . . . Ffonseca has his own grounds and farms

near Bruxelles where he designed to keep a stock of cattle and bring his provision as he had occasion, he has his own magazines and graneryes at Bruxelles & every town to lay up his provisions . . .[6]

All things considered, it was reckoned that supplies could be bought in the Low Countries some 10-20% cheaper than they could in England, and this without reckoning the freight and transshipping charges that would have applied had direct supply been attempted.[7] In the meantime, recipients of English subsidies also needed to be able to spend these as they saw fit.

Thanks to the impracticality of direct supply, there had to be remittances instead, and it was the fact of these remittances that exposed England to a whole host of economic dangers only direct supply could have avoided. That direct supply would have been free of economic dangers is obvious enough. For then all taxes and net loans raised in England for the war abroad would have been spent at home, thus taking up the savings extracted by the taxes and loans out of home consumption. Home-employment would remain undisturbed. Correspondingly, with no remittances being sent across the foreign exchanges, the stability of England's balance of payments would not have been imperilled either. But these dangers were bound to apply when there were remittances. Their transfer across the exchanges would obviously imperil balance of payments' stability and so risk monetary outflow and a contractionary monetary squeeze at home. While as transfers of taxes and net loans raised in England to be spent not at home (where the tax and loan savings had been extracted), but abroad, the remittances would likely reduce home spending and so additionally risk a fall in English output and unemployment. Nor as Table 2 makes plain were the sums involved trivial. Rising to over a million annually by the middle years of the 1690s, at these levels the military remittances were roughly double England's pre-war European trade surplus of some £600,000 annually,[8] and roughly equal to

Table 2. England's remittances to Troops and Allies Abroad, 1689-1697 (in £s).

	Total Spent Abroad	Net Borrowings Abroad	Remitted from Home	To the North	To the South
1688-9	169,335		169,335	169,335	
1689-90	795,547		795,547	795,547	
1690-91	557,866		557,866	426,200	131,666
1692	788,420		788,420	732,430	56,000
1693	876,114		876,114	781,032	95,082
1694	1,508,137	150,000	1,358,137	1,254,137	104,000
1695	1,255,621	17,000	1,238,621	1,099,821	138,800
1696	1,174,717	133,000	1,041,717	966,717	75,000
1697	806,922	100,000	706,922	706,922	

Figures for 1688-91 inclusive are for Michaelmas years, the rest for calendar years. For sources, see D.W. Jones, *War and Economy*, p. 319.

the total resources England was annually committing to her Atlantic trades at this time. In money terms, at least, they are also greater than anything Spain in an earlier age had remitted to her Flanders army.[9]

On the face of it, then, the remittances alone would appear to have threatened England's economic stability. Of course economists might suppose that at least some of the spending abroad might come back for English goods, or that part of it might intercept some of the imports England previously consumed: either would help restore employment and balance of payment stability. Equally, economic historians might argue that because England had achieved something of a commercial revolution over the second half of the seventeenth century, perhaps the remittances could be handled with ease. More specifically, both economists and economic historians would agree that were there sufficiently large surpluses, then there should have been no danger. For saving serving to keep England's import purchases below what otherwise her foreign earnings could have afforded her, has to be the counterpart of such surpluses. Surpluses, therefore, would not only furnish a government wishing to remit with the required foreign exchange without imperilling balance of payment stability, but they would also mean that any taxes and loans remitted across them would, in effect, have appropriated this saving and not spending. Current spending, and hence current output and employment, would thus be left undisturbed.

No doubt all this is fine in principle. But the remittance outstripped England's pre-war trade surpluses as just noted, while the likely grave consequences of the naval side of William's war for trade must also be considered. Moreover, with so much local purchase a necessity as we have seen, it is unlikely that very much of the spending abroad even could, and let alone would, come back as purchases of supplies from England. Estimates[10] of how England's foreign spending was composed are not easy to construct. However, it is clear that much the greater part went on providing feed for the horse, and fresh bread, beer (very bulky), and meat for the men, all of which had to be provided locally. Only some 38%, at most, went on items that at least could have either boosted English exports (e.g., butter and cheese, possibly, and grain to make bread and beer), and/or diverted erstwhile English import consumption (e.g., wines and linens purchased by the officers and men). And in practice, of course, far less than this was likely to be achieved. The only provision laid down by the government was to require the army's bread contractors in Flanders to export annually out of England a quantity of grain *equivalent* to the amount they used in making the army's bread (this, in the 1690s, being stipulated to be made out of Prussian rye).[11] But the value of the grain involved could not have amounted to much more than some £90,000's worth each year.[12] For all other supplies the Dutch were far better placed to provide what was required by shipping supplies down the rivers into Flanders; while throughout the 1690s French luxury goods, including wines, were also readily available there to entice, possibly, much of the officers' spending.[13]

Where any hope that England's foreign spending would solve the remittance problem by coming back to England's shore thus turns out to be almost wholly illusory, prospects that English trade might solve the problems turn out to be equally unpromising. Indeed, considerable though England's commercial achievements had been, it would be difficult to think of any commercial pattern more at risk in the likely circumstances of a French war and when a navy was so committed to forward operations. Two things in particular made for the vulnerability of English trade. The first was that by the mid-1680s England's trade balance, to the tune of some £250,000 annually,[14] had become dependent on the surplus Ireland had in her trade with Europe, and especially so with France. Thanks to an Irish deficit on trade with England, and the remittance of rents to English absentee landlords, Ireland was in deficit with England; and this she cleared, in effect, by making over her European surpluses for England's use (i.e., to help England pay for her European imports). Once there was war between England and France, however, trade prohibitions were bound to be imposed bringing Irish trade with France to an end no less than English, and so costing an important part of sterling's earnings. In the event, also, there was to be an Irish rebellion and a campaign to put it down which had severe effects on Irish trade throughout most of the 1690s.[15]

The second reason for the extreme vulnerability of English trade was that some £800,000's worth annually in net earnings accruing to sterling were generated by England's Atlantic trades.[16] For each year, the earnings of these trades for England's balance thanks to the sugars, the tobaccos, and the dyestuffs and so forth sold as re-exports in Europe, and thanks to the Newfoundland and New England cod sold directly in the Iberian peninsula, were greater by some £800,000 annually than the European import purchases that had to be incurred, whether as naval stores (for building and equipping the ships), or as linens and metalwares (for sending out to the colonists), to run these trades each year. But, of course, it was precisely the Atlantic trades that would be most at risk in William's war. Naval manning requirements were bound to reduce their level very considerably by taking away the seamen who manned the shipping upon which they were so dependent. Moreover, it was these trades which were likely to suffer most from storm losses when, to give priority to naval manning requirements, most voyages would likely have to be winter ones; whilst in the Western approaches and the length of the Channel there would be the attentions of the French privateers to contend with.

Between these Irish and Atlantic 'balances', therefore, England could only too easily lose the equivalent of what could well be rather more than the £600,000, or so, overall total of her surpluses with Europe in the later 1680s. In the meantime, however, the one thing that could *not* be hoped for would be some compensatory expansion in the inherently more secure domestic exports, and notably English woollen exports. For in Europe English woollens faced stern competition coming from such great centres and regions of production established at Leiden, or in and around Tilburg, Helmond and Eindhoven in the southern extremities of the Dutch Republic and in and around Vervier in the vicinity of Liège; while a little further afield there were even greater centres of production established in Saxony, Lusatia and Silesia. It was only the East India trade which, in principle, offered more promising possibilities. For each year the European dimensions of this trade normally involved both massive re-export sales to Europe and massive purchases of bullion from Europe for sending out to India.[17] Cutting back on these latter purchases, therefore, would produce a substantial gain for the balance of payments. For imports from India (the fruits of past investment) could still come in for some considerable time and, as re-exports, would thus continue to earn credits in Europe but in the absence now of the usual, offsetting, bullion purchases. Unfortunately, however, no such effect could work for William III (and as it was to do so spectacularly, in fact, for Marlborough). The East India Company, which controlled the trade, had been seriously weakened by a major interloping attack in the early 1680s so that by the later 1680s the trade was at a very low ebb.

The dangerously contradictory character of William's strategy must now be clear. On the one hand, supporting the army without endangering economic stability at home required a rather better trade performance as far as the balance of payments was concerned than was being achieved immediately prior to the war. On the other hand, the massive commitment to the navy and its deployment on forward operations threatened to destroy the very trade performance upon which support of the army would depend.

Table 3. *English Trade 1686-1701* (in £000's at 1699-1701 average customs valuations)

	Near Europe				The North				The South			
	(1)	(2)	(3)	(4)	(1)	(2)	(3)	(4)	(1)	(2)	(3)	(4)
	Export	Re-export	Sum 1+2	Imports	Export	Re-export	Sum 1+2	Imports	Export	Re-export	Sum 1+2	Imports
1686	1,445	989	2,436	2,310	296	78	375	613	976	219	1,195	1,260
	(1,666)	(865)	(2,031)	(1,595)					(1,255)	(343)	(1,598)	(1,975)
1693	1,512	324	1,837	1,276	255	42	297	548	906	58	964	921
1694	1,511	366	1,877	1,601	431	49	480	468	978	117	1,099	836
1695	2,015	499	2,513	1,087	289	63	353	499	976	57	1,034	1,347
1699-01	1,859	1,163	3,022	1,328	255	80	335	583	1,484	224	1,708	1,555

In the UK port books (PRO E 190) which are our source for the figures for 1686, too often only 'France' is given as the destination of exports and re-exports. Ideally, however, English trade with the French Biscayan ports should belong to the 'South' and not to 'Near Europe' where we have included it in the first line of the figures. Accordingly, the figures in parentheses provide an estimated re-allocation of the French Biscayan trade from 'Near Europe' to the 'South' in 1686. Comparisons with the 1690s within these two categories should be conducted with the adjusted, and not the unadjusted figures. Sources for the other figures are: 1693-5, compiled from House of Lords Records Office, Parchment Books 32-42; 1699-1701, compiled from PRO Cust 3/3-5.

These dangers are fully borne out by what actually happened in the 1690s. From Table 3 we see that the longer-distance trades had been thoroughly disrupted; that the re-export trade with Europe had been gravely reduced; and that export performance over the years 1693-4 was indifferent (some £150,000's worth of the apparent export 'expansion' to Near Europe (i.e. the Low Countries and Germany) simply reflecting how more export to Southern Europe went overland now to avoid the privateers).[18]

Table 4. Trade performance in the 1690s (in £000s)

THE WIDER WORLD BALANCES IN 1686 AND 1693-5

	(1) East India Re-export	(2) Atlantic Re-export & cod	(3) Total Sales in Europe	(4) Bullion for India	(5) European Import for India	(6) European Import for Atlantic	(7) Total Import Bill	(8) Net India Balance	(9) Net Atlantic Balance	(10) Net Wider World Balance
1686	300	1,136	1,436	368	16	344	728	−84	792	708
1693	42	543	585	95	5	137	237	−58	406	348
	−258	−593	= −851	+273	+11	+207	= +491	+26	−386	−360
1694	98	557	655	147	5	175	327	−54	382	328
	−202	−579	= −781	+221	+11	+169	= +401	+30	−410	−380
1695	153	566	719	0	5	144	149	148	422	570
	−147	−570	= −717	+368	+11	+200	= +579	+232	−370	−138

THE EUROPEAN BALANCES IN 1686 AND 1693-5

| | | | | | | | | WARTIME GAINS AND LOSSES BY: | | | | | | | | | |
| | | | | | | | | DOMESTIC EXPORTS TO | | | | IMPORTS FROM | | | | | |
	(1) Net Wider World	(2) Net Profit and Freight	(3) Ireland	(4) Net Total (1)-(3)	(5) Home Import/Domestic Export Balance	(6) French Home Import Domestic Export	(7) French Post Prohibition Gain	(8) Baltic	(9) Near Europe	(10) The South	(11) Net	(12) Baltic	(13) Near Europe	(14) The South	(15) Net	(16) Sum of Gains and Losses (7)+(11)+(15)	(17) Overall Balance 1686+(4) +16
1686	708	534	250	=1,492	−305	−767											420
1693	348	123	0		−305	0											
	−360	−411		−250 =−1,021			+557	−41	+546	−9	+496	+64	−128	+45	−19	+1,034	420+13=433
1694	328	139	0		−305	0											
	−380	−395		−250 =−1,025			+557	+130	+527	+124	+781	+145	−495	+114	−236	+1,102	420+77=497
1695	570	145	0		−305	0											
	−138	−389		−250 =−777			+557	−7	+1,008	+65	+1,107	+114	−1	+179	+292	+1,915	420+1,138 =1,558

For the structure and sources of this table, see Jones, *War and Economy,* pp. 52-5, 212-7, 224-8, 325-9. The valuations used differ somewhat from those used in Table 3, while here 'Near Europe' excludes France, which is dealt with separately. The surplus of £420,000 shown for 1686 differs from the £600,000 mentioned in the text simply because of the inevitable discrepancy between the trade surplus estimate and that provided by net monetary movements.

Moreover when we look at Table 4, we see that in addition to the loss of the Irish balance, it was indeed the Atlantic balance which had been severely hit. This is not to say that there were no favourable features. Quite substantial gains on the balance of payments were in fact made through the ending of French trade (in which there had been a substantial deficit against England) and thanks to sundry export gains and import savings made in the Southern European and Baltic trades. (The import savings of the latter trades, though, reflect the crippling of English trading activities, and hence a lower import of Baltic naval stores overall notwithstanding the navy's extra purchases.)

These gains, however, were virtually outweighed by the destruction of the Irish balance, by the halving of the Atlantic balance and by the severe losses on freight and profit earnings incurred when much of England's European trading was taken over by foreign shipping (profiting from the crippling of her own shipping);[19] and when much of the export trade with Near Europe became conducted increasingly for the accounts of principals abroad (instead of on English account as previously).[20] Little wonder, therefore, that as the remittances mounted, more and more silver bullion, culminating with the massive export of some £700,000's worth in 1694 (see Table 5), had to be exported to pay the army's debts.

Table 5. Bullion Movements and the Exchange Rate, 1680-1701 (in £s).

	Mint Output	Bullion Outflow To Europe		Net Inflow/ Outflow		Guilder Exchange Rate
1680	671,624	(nd)		+671,624		+ 3.89%
1681	338,801	(36,480)		+338,801		+ 3.56%
1682	180,989	(137,684)		+180,989		+ 2.45%
1683	507,927	(114,351)		+507,927		+ 4.76%
1684	312,287	(81,277)		+312,287		+ 3.92%
1685	551,893	(30,828)		+551,893		+ 3.66%
1686	593,030	(13,977)		+593,030		+ 3.58%
1687	562,800	(67,847)		+562,800		+ 3.37%
1688	557,445	248,359		+309,086		+ 0.63%
1689	193,828	385,270		−191,442		(nd)
1690	44,516	—	734,433	—	c. −534,433	(nd)
1691	51,048	—		—		− 1.44%
1692	104,171	—		—		+ 0.20%
1693	46,975	219,214		−172,239		− 3.29%
1694	62,023	698,896		−636,873		− 6.11%
1695	630,838	226,132		+404,706		−14.42%
1696	Recoinage	(nd)				− 9.27%
1697	Recoinage	(nd)				+ 2.57%
1699-1701	571,903	10,158		+571,903		+ 3.20%

For sources, see Jones, *War and Economy,* pp. 322-3. Figures of bullion outflow shown in brackets are for exports to Holland only, but such exports always comprised by far the greater amounts. Exchange quotations for 1690 are very scarce.

Matters at least appear to have dramatically improved in 1695; but once we allow for the severe exchange depreciation plus the gold inflow coming in to buy English goods cheap, it can be shown quite easily that the net trade performance was still insufficient, by some margin, to meet the remittances without an export of silver. In the meantime, throughout these years it was Dutch supplies shipped down the rivers into Flanders that the army was buying, very little of the spending coming back as a demand for English exports; also, the officers did indeed consume French wines and brandies for which it was very difficult, given the prohibition of French trade, for English exports to pay. On these points, Richard Hill was again particularly graphic when he wrote towards the end of 1695:

> There has been little help from Trade since the war, and none at present, for Hollande supplys allmoste everything which is wanting for ye use and consumption of the Army . . . they send butter and cheese and Bread, Rhenish wines and fish and foreage, spices and rice and Everything for the subsistence of their own and our Troops, and of all Brabant and Flanders . . . and this year last past [i.e., 1695] has been so plentifull in corn and other provisions that allmost nothing of that kind can come from England; and ye Trade to France being opened with those provinces their goes more of our money in France at present for wines, brandies and baubles than there goeth to England or Ireland for any kind of provisions.[21]

Reasons for this parlous state of affairs are just as predictable as the pattern we have just seen. Since nothing untoward seems to have happened to competing European centres of woollen textile production (and as was so strikingly to happen to Marlborough's benefit in the 1700s), there was little scope for English exports to expand very much. Gains there certainly were in sales of kersey, bays and some other cloths used for making uniforms (and of which England produced the most and the best);[22] but these gains were almost wholly offset by losses incurred by English exports through the generally disturbed trading conditions of the 1690s. It is with these latter conditions, indeed, and the way they hit the Atlantic trades particularly hard, that we find the major reason for the near-disaster of the 1690s. Thus to safeguard naval manning requirements, but inevitably crippling for the Atlantic trades which were so dependent on shipping and seamen, a system of draconian controls was introduced from the very beginning of the war to limit these trades to under half the shipping and men they had employed in the later 1680s.[23] Also, since it was laid down that no ships could sail out before naval manning had been completed by the end of May, and that all ships had to be back before the manning season commenced in February,[24] a

totally unseasonal pattern was imposed on trade, and one which was bound
again to hit the Atlantic trades very hard. Arriving in tropical waters
towards the middle of the year meant that ships employed in these trades
would be departing during the hurricane season and reaching home waters
during the stormy winter months. Then returning home through the
Western approaches and running the length of the Channel made these
ships, along with those coming from Southern Europe and India, very
vulnerable to French privateering attack and particularly so when far too
few ships-of-the-line were committed to the protection of commerce.

No comprehensive account of losses in the Atlantic trades is available but
some impression of their scale can be gained from how, over the years
1694-5, the value of cargo lost by the Royal Africa Company was put at
£57,219; that by the Jamaica, New England, and Leeward Island merchants
at £68,500, £114,000 and £138,000 respectively; and that by the Barbados
merchants at a massive £387,100.[25] Of this, £187,000 had been incurred by
storm and the rest at the hands of a French naval squadron commanded by
Nesmond in the Channel Soundings. The Barbados merchants explained
how the departure of their ships from London had been delayed for five
months; how this had obliged their ships to be leaving Barbados at the
height of the hurricane season; how eleven of their ships were duly lost in a
hurricane even before they had weighed anchor for home; how another
hurricane cost a further eight ships shortly after departure; and how once in
the Channel Soundings a further sixteen were taken by Nesmond thanks to
the utter inadequacy of naval cover. Nor were the Barbados merchants in
any doubt about the significance of the losses they had suffered when they
wrote that:

> The losses from the plantations are double for the nation being all goods that would have
> been exported to have supplied the army with the proceeds, and kept up the exchange . . .
> for if we have not effects to pay our army, the foreigners will have our silver to be sure, for
> the exchange is governed by the balance of trade. . . .[26]

On the face of it, therefore, England in the 1690s should have been
suffering mounting unemployment. The bullion outflow should have been
producing a severe contraction of the home money supply when, with so
little of the foreign spending coming back for the savings extracted out of
English consumption by the taxes and loans remitted abroad, home
spending should also have been seriously deficient. Thanks, however, to the
clipping of the coin — the major economic consequence of William III —
both these dangers were warded off, at least until 1696-7.

What made clipping possible was that the old hammered silver coin
minted until 1663 (and this coin still comprised the largest single
component of England's money stock) lacked the raised, protective, milled

edge of the milled silver coin minted from 1663 onwards.[27] It became the practice, therefore, to remove small slivers of metal from the hammered silver coin, and to melt down these clippings into bullion for sale while passing on the coin at face value. Hence the profitability of the business. Yet, by as late as 1686, when there was some official concern about clipping, even the most clipped coin, judging from excise receipts which were sampled, had lost no more than 12% of its metal content.[28]

Table 6. The Exchange, Molten Silver Export, Silver Coin and Silver Plate Making.

Calendar Years	Gilder Exchange (+/−% of Par)	Molten Silver Export (a) To Europe oz's	(b) To East oz's	at June 21st	% Deficiency in Metal Content of Silver Coin	June–June	% Annual Deterioration of Metal Contents	Silver Hallmarked at Goldsmith's Hall, oz's
						1683		
1684	+ 3.92%			1684		1684		c.719,091
1685	+ 3.66%			1685	13.13%	1685	+1.71%	
1686	+ 3.58%			1686	11.42%	1686		c. 684,509
1687	+ 3.37%			1687	12.48%	1687	−1.06%	
1688	+ 0.63%	670,900	234,000	1688	15.32%	1688	−2.84%	
1689	nd	1,360,000	32,000	1689	15.98%	1689	−0.66%	c. 533,688
1690	nd	2,400,000		1690	18.82%	1690	−2.84%	537,742
1691	− 1.44%			1691	21.20%	1691	−2.38%	529,704
1692	+ 0.20%		216,938	1692	27.50%	1692	−6.30%	634,402
1693	− 3.29%	832,554	336,571	1693	33.27%	1693	−5.77%	526,300
1694	− 6.11%	2,444,149	57,490	1694	39.85%	1694	−6.58%	544,944
1695	−14.42%	407,046	770,430	1695	49.38%	1695	−9.54%	c. 514,218
1696	− 9.27%	6,754,649	1,647,938	1696	54.97%	1696	−5.58%	c. 390,307

8,402,078   TOTAL

(Total Lost from Silver Coin 1688-1695 = 9,174,200 oz's)

Details of plate making come from the Renter Warden's accounts at the Goldsmiths' Hall, London. BL. Lansdowne Ms 801, fo. 39 provided details of the deterioration of the silver coin. This information has been combined with J. Craig, *The Mint*, p. 193 to produce the estimate of how much silver was lost from the coin between 1658 and 1695.

Thereafter, however, as Table 6 shows, the rate of deterioration increased rapidly once, first, silver was exported from England to profit from the higher silver prices paid in the Dutch Republic over the years 1688-91 to mint the debased *schellingen* then being minted there;[29] and once, second, England's military remittances increasingly outstripped the performance of her trade, thus requiring even larger amounts of silver to pay her debts.

How the clipping business was organised emerges clearly from the depositions of York assizes.[30] The business was organised on a three-sided basis involving the clippers with their skills and instruments; the goldsmiths of such centres as Manchester, Pontefract, Leeds, Wakefield, Halifax and York who, with a float of cash (including clipped coin) always on hand, were prepared to buy molten clippings as *bone fide* bullion, but at rates of between 4s.0d and 4s.6d per ounce as compared with market rates of above 5s.2d per ounce; and finally, all manner of dealers such as clothiers, dyers, drovers, graziers and even clergymen who, as receivers of large amounts of cash, could cull their receipts for the heavier coin most suitable for clipping.

The latter dealers would thus put out coin to be clipped and at rates, to start with, of only some 21s.6d clipped coin to be returned for each pound's worth of heavy money put out to be clipped; the rate soon rose, however, to reach some 24s.0d clipped coin to be returned. Once the clippers had finished their work, they took the clippings to the goldsmiths who melted them down, paying the clippers clipped money for it. So adding this clipped money to the money they themselves had clipped, the clippers were then able to return clipped money to the dealers at the rate agreed with them. (Though, obviously, to have something left over for themselves, the clippers would have removed rather more metal from the coin than the rates agreed with the dealers implied.)

Of course, there could be many variants of these relationships. On occasion, it was the dealers who took the molten clippings round to the goldsmiths and then settled up with the clippers; quite frequently, too, goldsmiths put out coin to be clipped for they themselves then to receive back the newly clipped coin as well as the clippings. But whichever way, clipping had clearly become a major business, organised by men of substance. Indeed, it was precisely these that the clerk of the York Assizes wanted to get his hands on when he wrote in 1697 that if a certain Parvin were convicted, a very large 'discovery' would be made of some very 'considerable figures' who otherwise would 'escape condigne punishment for having impoverished the Kingdome more than the war'.[31] Thanks to the dealers, cash receipts were being systematically culled for the heavier coin that was then put out to be clipped; whilst thanks to the goldsmiths, molten silver clippings were entering the bullion market. The goldsmiths thus played *the* key role, for the profitability of clipping depended as much on finding buyers for the clippings as it did on being able to pass on clipped coin at face value.

What is equally clear, finally, is that it was indeed the demand for silver to settle foreign debts that was driving the clipping business. Partly, this is just a matter of how well the rate at which the coin was being clipped correlates with the chronology of bullion export out of the country (see Table 6) even if, to compare with the calendar year details of the latter export, details of the former are available only on a midsummer year basis; also we lack a figure for bullion export in 1692. None the less, where the acceleration of the later 1680s coincides well with what was being exported to profit from the high prices paid for silver to be minted into *schellingen* in the Dutch Republic, that of the (midsummer) years 1693-4 and 1694-5 neatly straddles that record year of (calendar) year export, 1694. Moreover, there is a marked acceleration of clipping over 1691-2 which also correlates well with the marked stepping-up of remittances to Europe from 1692 onwards. It is also the case that the total recorded export of molten silver of 8,402,078 ounces between 1689 and the end of 1695 (East India export of molten bullion included in this since clipping was by far its likeliest source) compares well with the total of 9,174,200 ounces known to have been lost from the silver coin between these dates. To be sure, some of the export might have been of full-bodied coin melted down, except that most of this must have been hoarded in the hope of a sterling devaluation, and not exported abroad. In any case, some of the clippings must surely have gone into plate making which remained surprisingly high at a time when little silver could have been coming in from abroad.[32]

Above all, each link in the chain whereby the despatching of bullion abroad from London created the demand for molten bullion, and whereby this demand was then met by the supply of coin and molten silver from the provinces, can be documented. Thus, tellingly, we read in a deposition at the York Assizes of a York goldsmith recasting some molten clippings brought to him at his shop in Leeds: 'the reason of casting the said bullion in the shape he did' being 'in order to the sending it to London as plate melted down'.[33] Equally significantly, two London goldsmiths and two money men were prosecuted in 1695 for having used the internal remittance network to drain coin from the provinces to be clipped in London;[34] and some remittances of coin from Swansea and Carmarthen were suspected of having been made for the same purpose.[35] Early in 1695, in fact, Bristol carriers were said to be no longer accepting bills but 'bring-up' instead £1,000 weekly, taking only broad and unclipped money.[36] Nor can there be any doubt that it was the despatching of bullion abroad to pay the army's debts that was the source of the demand fuelling the clipping of the coin. In October 1693 the customs authorities attempted to discourage the export of bullion by ordering two London goldsmiths, Floyer and Johnson, to remove and bring to the mint a number of silver consignments which, with but one technical infringement (i.e., a switching of ships), they had duly entered out to go on two men-o'-war for the settlement of the army's debts.[37] Now when this was done, silver prices, it was said, fell for a time and so the incentive to clip the coin.[38]

It may not be immediately apparent how clipping, an illegal activity debauching England's silver coin, should have saved the country under William III. A moment's reflection, however, shows that it certainly did. For it was only through clipping that the bullion needed to pay the debts that England had no other way of paying for, was provided. Normally, of course, such bullion export would have enforced an intense money squeeze, but as long as the clipped coin passed at face value, as was the case down to late 1694, through the clipping of the coin England was spared such a squeeze. In the meantime, the fact that the business of clipping had become a major industry in the land gave those who participated in it new incomes (and thus spending) which served to counterbalance the deficiency of spending produced at home when increasingly England's trade was not matching the external remission of funds. Moreover we can be certain that since what was clipped from the coin closely matched the bullion exported abroad as we have noted, the income generated by clipping closely matched (and thus offset) the income deficiency created by England's deficits. Clipping, in other words, not only spared England from a money squeeze but also staved off that collapse of spending, and thus that collapse of output and employment, which the remittances and the failure of trade would otherwise have produced.

True, sooner rather than later confidence would be lost in the silver coin once it became so clipped that it could no longer be regarded as any sort of store of intrinsic worth. And this did of course happen late in 1694. Yet even then the game was not quite up for England since the combined effect of the resulting collapse of the exchange, and of the gold coming in to profit from rocketing English gold prices, was to produce a boom of activity in England and thus keep things going for another year. And it was during this year, of course, that William recaptured Namur, and so gained an essential negotiating card in his dealings with Louis XIV.

Thanks therefore to the dangerous contradictions at the very heart of William's chosen war strategy — the navy's forward deployment compromising the very trade performance upon which the successful forward deployment of the army depended — for England William's war became a finely balanced race between the inexorable deterioration of the coin and his military achievements. Certainly Richard Hill's correspondence, whether of 1695 after the exchange had collapsed, or of the summer of 1696 after payments to the army had failed, leaves us in no doubt that survival to the peace, signed at Ryswick in September 1697, was a very close-run thing indeed.

NOTES

1. J. de L. Mann, 'A Wiltshire Family of Clothiers: George and Hester Wansey 1683-1714', *EcHR*, 2nd Ser., 9 (1956), 251.

2. KAO, Papillon MSS C44, pp. 6-8 (Philip Papillon to William Rawston and John Mawdsley, 23 Mar. 1697).

3. For a reconstruction of this episode, see D.W. Jones, *War and Economy in the Age of William III and Marlborough* (1988), pp. 23-6.

4. R. Davis, *The Rise of the English Shipping Industry in the Seventeenth and Eighteenth Centuries* (1962), p. 200.

5. Davis, *Shipping Industry*, p. 398.

6. Bodl MS Eng. Hist. d 146 (1), fo. 7.

7. NUL PwV 59, fos.9-10; BL Add. MS 18,759, fo. 129.

8. For sources and techniques this estimate is based on, see Jones, *War and Economy*, pp. 212-7.

9. Jones, *War and Economy*, pp. 47-8; G. Parker, *The Army of Flanders and the Spanish Road 1567-1759* (Cambridge, 1972), pp. 232-65; I. A. A. Thompson, *War and Government in Hapsburg Spain 1560-1620* (1976), p. 288.

10. Jones, *War and Economy*, pp. 112-14.

11. Bread contracts for the 1690s are in SRO 112/75, 186; PRO T 48/12. And see *CTB* IX. 1647-8, X. 1065, 1251, 1361, 1421 and BL Add. MS 9735 fo. 48 for bread contractors exporting grain.

12. BL. Add. MS 10,123 fo. 106.

13. For French imports in the Spanish Netherlands, see J. de Smet, 'Commerce et Navigation de Bruges et Ostend', *Bulletin de la Commission Royale d'Histoire*, 94 (1930), 180-97; F. van Kalken, *La Fin du régime Éspagnole aux Pays-Bas* (Brussels, 1907), pp. 107-8; R. de Schryver, *Graaf van Bergeyck 1644-1725* (Brussels, 1965), pp. 84-6; I. Bog, *Der Reichmerkantilismus* (Stuttgart, 1959), pp. 114, 116, 117.

14. For sources of this estimate, see Jones, *War and Economy*, pp. 55-7.

15. L. M. Cullen, *Anglo-Irish Trade 1660-1800* (Manchester, 1968), pp. 40-1; *idem, An Economic History of Ireland* (1972), pp. 27-34; and see Jones, *War and Economy*, pp. 140-1.

16. Jones, *War and Economy*, pp. 54-5.

17. *Ibid.*, pp. 55, 58-9.

18. For references to this trade, see *The Parliamentary Diary of Narcissus Luttrell 1691-1693*, ed. H. Horwitz (Oxford, 1972), pp. 428-30. Our estimate of the exports involved is based on the value of southern European imports coming overland.

19. Davis, *Shipping Industry*, p. 26; PRO CO 388/6, A 1, 4, 7, 11, 13, 15, B 49.

20. Jones, *War and Economy*, pp. 253-60.

21. BL Add. MS 10,123, 'Considerations about the Payments of his Majesties Armyes in Flanders from Mr Hill 1695', fos.124ʳ-124ᵛ, 126.

22. For the 'military' textiles, see Jones, *War and Economy*, pp. 182, 185-6, 188-90, 191, 201-3, 205-6. The value of the 'military' textile sales to the Low Countries and Germany was as follows: 1686, £317,815; 1693, £486,405; 1694, £547,904; 1699-1701, £428,130.

23. PRO CO 389/12, fos.108, 151, 222, 249, 279; 13, fos.1-2, 143; Davis, *Shipping Industry*, pp. 59, 398.

24. *CTB* IX and X: index s.v. 'Embargo'; PRO CO 389/12, fos 28ᵛ-30ᵛ.

25. *HLMSS 1695-7*, pp. 64, 65, 66, 76-82, 87-8.

26. *Ibid.,* p. 77.

27. Hopton Haynes, 'Brief Memoires Relating to the Silver Coins of England . . .', BL Lansdowne MS 801, fos. 34-6, 38.

28. Ibid., fo. 39.

29. H. Enno van Gelder, *Munthervorming tijdens de Republiek* (Amsterdam, 1949), p. 133; J. G. van Dillen, *Van Rijkdom en Regenten* (The Hague, 1970), pp. 442-3.

30. The most revealing depositions are PRO Assi 45/13/2/72; 14/2/137; 15/2/59; 15/4/60B; 16/1/1, 2, 3, 5; 16/3/4, 49; 16/4/1, 4, 5; 17/2/5.

31. Ibid., 17/2/89.

32. For sources and details of plate making, see Table 1.6.

33. PRO Assi 45/16/1/5.

34. PRO T1/33/22.

35. PRO T1/34/43.

36. All Souls College Library (Oxford), MS 152/5, paper from Dutton Colt, February 1695.

37. PRO T1/24/53; *CTB* X. 382-3.

38. BL Add. MS 18,759, fo. 131.

CHAPTER 3

Parliament and Foreign Policy in the Age of Walpole: the case of the Hessians

Jeremy Black

'they [the Hessians] were kept up with a view to save the Publick Money, and to preserve the Peace of Europe, by being ready to march on any service our Treaties might oblige us to provide Troops for; and that they actually hindered any Rupture, while they were retained in the Pay of Great Britain, is certain.'

Daily Courant, 27 April 1734.

In the early eighteenth century two types of political organisation can be distinguished in the states of Europe. On the one hand were those states that possessed representative assemblies able to debate policy. The most prominent such state was Great Britain which possessed two parliaments, one at Dublin representing Ireland, the other, at Westminster, representing Scotland, Wales and England. Other prominent states with powerful representative assemblies were Sweden, the United Provinces (or Netherlands) and Poland. The second type of state was that which either lacked a representative element completely or only possessed one with limited powers. Most European states, including the vast majority of Catholic states, fell into the latter category. The absence of powerful representative institutions did not mean that these states saw no discussion of governmental policies. In France, for example, there is evidence of a sustained public interest in, and discussion of, governmental policies: the ministry was sufficiently anxious about metropolitan opinion to commission a regular series of police reports upon opinions being expressed in public places.[1] These reports testify to the often highly sophisticated nature of public opinion in a supposedly autocratic state.

However, the public discussion of ministerial policies was easiest in those states that possessed representative assemblies able to contest governmental policies. It is no accident that the two states that possessed the freest newspaper presses in Europe, Britain and the United Provinces,[2] were the states with the most important representative assemblies. Though the Swedish and Polish Diets possessed vast powers, they did not meet every year as the British Parliament and the Dutch Estates General did. One of the most spectacular manifestations of the political power of the British and Dutch representative assemblies was their ability to discuss foreign policy. In most European states this was the most jealously preserved prerogative of sovereignty. In Britain, however, though the legal right of Parliament to discuss foreign affairs was heavily circumscribed, the governmental need to secure parliamentary fiscal support for the costlier manifestations of foreign policy, such as subsidy treaties and naval armaments, ensured that Parliament was able to discuss foreign policy.[3] Furthermore, the habit of discoursing at length upon unrelated subjects ensured that even when MPs were asked to discuss only very limited subjects they tended to consider the whole range of foreign policy. In particular discussion of foreign policy played a major role in the debates over the addresses from the two Houses of Parliament in response to the royal speech that opened each parliamentary session. To a great extent the government encouraged such debate as they hoped that success in it would lead foreign powers to conclude that British foreign policy enjoyed wide support. Conversely the opposition sought to use discontent over foreign policy to discredit the ministry. Due to the importance of parliamentary support there is evidence of foreign envoys opposed to Britain, such as the Prussian envoy Reichenbach in 1730 and the French envoy Chavigny in 1733-5, encouraging the parliamentary opposition.

In the first half of the eighteenth century some of the bitterest parliamentary debates over foreign policy centred on the issue of the payment of subsidies to the Landgraves of Hesse-Cassel. It is the intention of this chapter to consider why this issue aroused so much fervour, and to show how free Parliament was in discussing it, and how an examination of the debates can illustrate the more general point of the need, in Britain, for a ministry to face the fact that its foreign policy could be fully debated.

It was the failure to secure a long-lasting Anglo-Prussian alliance that made the British ministry negotiate treaties with Hesse-Cassel by which, in return for annual subsidies, a designated number of troops were set aside to be ready to serve, if required by the British government. Though Hessian troops were sent to Britian to aid in the suppression of the Jacobite rising of 1745, and to guard against a threatened French invasion at the beginning of the Seven Years' War, and though Hessian troops were sent to America in the War of American Independence,[4] on the whole the anticipated use of the Hessian troops was for operations in the Empire. Indeed, their major function was to aid in the defence of the Electorate of Hanover.[5] During the early eighteenth century Hanover was threatened by five powers, Russia, Sweden, Denmark, Prussia and France. The Swedish threat stemmed from Hanover's acquisition, during the Great Northern War, of the former Swedish possessions of Bremen and Verden. However, Swedish weakness after the death of Charles XII and the intimidation of Sweden by Russia ensured that the Hanoverians did not have to fear Sweden. Indeed the good relations of George I and George II with King Frederick I of Sweden, the eldest son of Landgrave Karl of Hesse-Cassel, were an important factor in preventing Swedish opposition to Hanoverian interests. By supporting Frederick I in his struggles with his domestic opponents, George I and II helped to create better relations with Hesse-Cassel, and by subsidising Hesse-Cassel better relations with Frederick were produced. For the Georges relations with Hesse-Cassel and with Sweden were two sides of the same coin. The diplomatic offensives of 1726-7 to win Swedish and Hessian assistance complemented each other. Equally, it is noticeable that in the early 1740s British relations with both powers deteriorated in step. As George II shifted from a Swedish to a Russian alliance tension with Hesse-Cassel increased, whilst Franco-Swedish relations were complemented by closer links between France and Hesse-Cassel.

The Danish threat to Hanoverian interests was a minor one. It was due to the Danish interest in southward expansion, an interest that had led to the Danish absorption of the Duchy of Schleswig, to Danish interest in the Mecklenburg disputes, to the dispatch of Danish troops to East Friesland in the 1720s and to continual Danish pressure upon the independence of Hamburg. This infringed Hanoverian interests in the Lower Saxon Circle and led to military action at Steinhorst in early 1739. However, Denmark was a minor military power that tended to prefer British subsidies to clashes with Hanover, and the assistance of Hessian troops against Denmark was not required.

The deployment of Russian troops in Jutland and Mecklenburg in 1716-17, and the dynastic links between Peter the Great and the anti-Hanoverian Dukes of Mecklenburg to Holstein-Gottorp, represented a powerful Russian threat to Hanover during the reign of Peter the Great. However, after his death, Anglo-Russian relations slowly improved. This improvement was slow at first. Hopes that Peter's death would lead to an Anglo-Russian reconciliation proved abortive. In 1726 Russia, under Peter's widow Catherine I, allied with Austria against Britain and in the following year a British fleet was sent to the Sound to protect Sweden from possible Russian attack. Relations continued poor until the Anglo-Austrian reconciliation of 1731 opened the way for better relations. Thereafter Britain increasingly saw Russia as a power that could be used to intimidate Prussia and to prevent Prussian moves against Hanover. In 1733-4 Britain used Russia to pressurise Prussia during a Prusso-Hanoverian dispute over Mecklenburg. From 1741 Britain sought to use Russia in order to threaten Frederick the Great. Russian strength was a far better protection for Hanover than Hessian forces, but it was more difficult to secure. The commercial treaty of 1734 was an important landmark in Anglo-Russian relations, and in 1735 Britain supported the march of Russian troops to the Rhine, and in 1748 subsidised a similar march.

The major threats to Hanover came from France and Prussia. From 1716 until 1731 Anglo-French relations were good, but thereafter they markedly deteriorated, and at the beginning both of the War of the Austrian Succession and of the Seven Years' War French invasions of Westphalia forced Hanover into humiliating neutralities. In both cases Hessian support was sought but the disproportionate strength of the French, and the ambivalence of Prince William of Hesse-Cassel's position in 1741, meant that the Hessians could do little to help Hanover.

The Prussian royal family was the family to whom the Hanoverians were most closely related. George I was the uncle and father-in-law of Frederick William I; George II the cousin and brother-in-law of Frederick William, and the uncle of Frederick II. However, relations were bad, particularly after the accession of George II, and attempts supported by various British ministers, such as Horatio Walpole, Robert Walpole's diplomat brother, to create a Protestant League of Hanover, Hesse-Cassel, Britain, Prussia, Sweden, Denmark and the United Provinces, were defeated by the bad relations of George II and Frederick William I. Tension between Hanover and Prussia was caused in general by their wish to dominate north Germany and the Protestant interest, and in specific terms by their conflicting claims to the contested inheritance of East Friesland and the administration of Mecklenburg.[6] The eventual resolution of both issues in Prussia's favour during the reign of Frederick the Great marked the Prussian victory over Hanover for the domination of north Germany.[7] Bad family relations were also a major problem. Frederick William I and George II clashed over George I's will as Frederick William claimed that George II had suppressed clauses in favour of Sophia Dorothea, Frederick William's wife. Attempts to arrange marriages between the children of George II and Frederick William failed, and proved to be a major source of dispute and tension.

The struggle between the two powers began in earnest in 1726 when Prussia left the Anglo-French Alliance of Hanover, and joined the Austro-Russo-Spanish Alliance of Vienna. It was a struggle in which the Hanoverians attempted to enlist the support of Hesse-Cassel, the third most powerful Protestant state in the Empire. Hesse-Cassel was the leading German state not to possess the status of an Electorate, and it was considered for this status at several times during the century. The army of Hesse-Cassel impressed contemporaries, and, although it was rather deficient in the experience of battle, it could be classed as the second best army in northern Germany, after the Prussians. George II was most impressed by the Hessians when he reviewed them, and his high opinions were shared by Major-General Richard Sutton sent to Cassel as British Envoy Extraordinary in 1727-9, 1730 and 1731. In 1729 the Undersecretary of State in the Southern Department, Charles Delafaye, wrote to his counterpart in the Northern Department, 'Your Hessian troops cut a figure; our Flanders officers say they were always better than any other troops in the army; auxiliary to be sure they mean'. In March 1729 Sutton compared the Hessians favourably with the troops of Brunswick-Wolfenbüttel which 'for air, exercise, dress and discipline, fall so far short of my Hessians, that they are in no manner within the compass of comparison'. Two years earlier Sutton had been told by the French envoy in Berlin that the Hessians were better soldiers than the Prussians.[8]

The most important services rendered by the Hessians to Hanover occurred in 1729-30, the period that marked the high-point of tension between Frederick William I and George II.[9] The breakdown of Anglo-Prussian marriage discussions in the spring of 1729 and the visit of George II to Hanover that summer provided the background for a series of minor clashes. Prussian enlisters in the Electorate of Hanover were arrested, reprisals ordered, atempts to negotiate failed and an irate Frederick William prepared for a major invasion of the Electorate. On 12 July (ns) Sühm, the Saxon envoy in Berlin noted, 'on affecte plus de tranquillité, qu'on ne se répand pas en menaces, et qu'il paroit qu'on a le coeur ulceré et rempli d'un désir de vengeance, dont l'exécution dépendroit de peu de chose, et ne manque de la moindre incitation'. He reported that Frederick William had ordered the encampment on the Elbe near the frontier of Hanover of fifty-two battalions by mid-August. Sühm commented that Prussia had made warlike preparations before, but that hitherto they had been done openly. He believed that Frederick William intended to attack. The Prince of Anhalt, one of the leading Prussian generals, was sent to reconnoitre the valley of the Elbe down which the Prussians hoped to advance cutting off Mecklenburg from Hanover. On 19 July (ns) Guy Dickens, secretary to Brigadier Du Bourgay, the British envoy in Berlin, reported that Frederick William was eager for action: 'the King of Prussia waits with impatience for an opportunity to do some action, which, to use his own expressions, may make some affronting stroke on the side of Hanover'. On 21 and 22 August (ns) Du Bourgay reported that Prussia had decided to attack.[10] Faced with an imminent invasion, George II requested Hessian assistance on August 23rd (ns).[11] The swift Hessian response[12] delighted George and pleased the British Secretary of State accompanying him, Viscount Townshend, who wrote, 'H.M. thinks himself in a very particular manner obliged to the Landgrave of Hesse Cassel . . . who by his great fidelity and readiness in executing his engagements, has extreamly contributed to the happy turn which this affair seems now to have taken'.[13] George attributed Frederick William's decision not to invade to the assistance he received from his allies, particularly Hesse-Cassel.

In the beginning of 1730 fears of an invasion revived. Townshend informed Edward Finch, envoy in Stockholm, that he had been instructed by George II to tell him 'that he has received secret advices concerning the warlike preparations of the peace in that part of Germany. These advices have been confirmed from several quarters . . . His scheme seems to be . . . to begin hostilitys by attacking the King's German Dominions'. Again George turned to his allies, and again the Hessians hastened to demonstrate their readiness to help.[14] Hostilities did not however materialise, and the signature the following spring of the Anglo-Austrian Second Treaty of Vienna served to defuse the dangerous situation in north Germany, as the Austrians attempted, with some success, to restrain their Prussian ally. Although difficulties persisted for the rest of the 1730s and became temporarily very serious, as in the summer of 1735, and in 1738, they never became as serious again during the reign of Frederick William as they had been in 1729-30. Indeed, the failure of the British to renew the subsidy treaty with Hesse-Cassel testified to a feeling that the situation was less serious. The decision was taken despite great pressure from the Hessian envoy Diemar.

It was therefore in the late 1720s and early 1730s that the alliance with Hesse-Cassel was of the greatest political and military significance, and it is in that period that parliamentary interest in the Hessians was strongest. The need to secure parliamentary consent for the voting of funds with which to pay the annual subsidy to Hesse-Cassel ensured that the issue was fully discussed. The subsidy treaty, signed on 1 March 1726, had provided for the Hessians holding 12,000 troops ready for use. The annual debates on the subject are a source of great interest. Records of parliamentary debates in this period are scanty and sometimes unreliable.[15] Fortunately the diaries of two MPs survive for this period. Sir Edward Knatchbull, MP for Lostwithiel, and Viscount Percival, MP for Harwich, both tended to support the minstry, but both preserved considerable independence, and their diaries are a valuable source for the period.[16] Both attended debates on the Hessian subsidies. This was hardly surprising as the Hessian subsidies were one of the major parliamentary issues of the period. The ministry came under increasing strain on the point. In 1727 the subsidy was carried by 191-98, a majority of 93, in 1728 by 280-86, a majority of 194, in 1729 by 298-91, a majority of 207 and in 1730 by 248-169, a majority of 79.[17] Majorities of 93 and 79 might not appear serious, but it was widely held that if the majority was not large or if the opposition vote exceeded 150, then the government would fall.[18] The majority of 79 in 1730 was the lowest governmental majority in a major debate for ten years, a testimony to the seriousness of the Hessian issue.[19]

Parliamentary anxiety over the Hessians did not reflect any animosity to the ruler, people or country of Hesse-Cassel. In the debates over the use of

Hessians during the War of American Independence opposition was to be voiced in Britain to a ruler who could hire out his subjects for money. This was not the case earlier in the century. Indeed Protestant Hesse-Cassel was highly regarded, and its system of government was not attacked in Parliament, in contrast to autocratic Denmark. The hiring of Hessians was attacked not out of any disgust with Hesse-Cassel, but because it was felt to symbolise the manner in which British policy was being distorted for Hanoverian goals. A major plank in the opposition critique was that the interests of the Electorate of Hanover were dominating British foreign policy to the financial detriment of the British taxpayer and the political detriment of British national interests. The annual retainer of £125,000 paid to ensure the first call on the Hessians' services was attacked as an expense that led to the outflow of bullion, and could be ill-met during a period of economic recession. The opposition alleged that the cost of Hessians was equivalent to 6d in the £ on the land tax, a figure that represented one eighth of the tax load in the late 1720's. This claim was frequently repeated in the press: *The Craftsman* of 20 April 1734 is a good example. Another leading London opposition paper, *Mist's Weekly Journal*, in its issue of 20 August 1726, asked, 'what Dependence can be laid upon the succour of that state, which only goes into an Alliance with another for the Money it can draw from it? . . . giving money for Alliances is no more than a new term for paying tribute to your neighbours . . . the paying money for an Alliance must be a mark of high Disgrace, for the state which submits to it, makes a discovery of its own weakness, and seems to own, that it cannot subsist without foreign assistance'. Knatchbull recorded that in the debate on 7 February 1729 the opposition argued that the Hessian subsidy 'was giving foreign princes access to our treasury here, and exporting too much money and impoverishing the nation'.[20] A year later the opposition returned to the same theme. Walter Titley, envoy in Copenhagen, responded to the news that the Hessian subsidy had been carried by noting, 'That is such a camel for a country squire to swallow, that I am extremely glad to find it went down so easily'.[21]

These criticisms were justified, given the heavy cost of the Hessians. In 1731, when the last grant in the early 1730s was voted, Walpole managed to persuade Parliament 'that £241,259 1s 3d be granted to his Majesty, for defraying the expence of 12,000 Hessians taken into his Majesty's pay, for the service of the year 1731'.[22] However, though these sums were significant, particularly given the fact that Anglo-Hessian trade was minimal and that therefore little of the bullion that Britain paid returned through trade, it was the political consequences of the subsidies that aroused most disquiet.

The ministerial MPs argued that the Hessians were not simply hired to protect Hanover, but that they were part of a wider strategic plan. 'Secretary Pelham . . . showed that the true design of the Hessian troops was never to defend Hanover, but to guard one part of Europe from the ambitious views of another.'[23] In particular, it was claimed that the Hessians were designed to preserve the United Provinces from Prussian or Austrian attack. The United Provinces were militarily the weakest section of the Alliance of Hanover. They were vulnerable to attack from the Austrian Netherlands to the south or from the Prussian Rhenish and Westphalian possessions, Cleves, Mark, Lingen, Teckebenburg, Upper Gelderland and Minden. Prince William of Hesse-Cassel was a powerful figure in Dutch politics, the commander of the largest Dutch garrison, Maastricht, and a candidate for the vacant Dutch stadtholderships. On the evening of 2 February 1730 the Prime Minster's brother, the diplomat Horatio Walpole, paid a visit on the wavering Viscount Percival to urge him to stand fast to the ministerial side. He told Percival that the Hessians 'are not kept as the malcontents pretend to defend the Hanover dominions, but really to fulfil our engagements with the Dutch, who having nobody to fear but the Emperor, would not in reason accede to the Treaty of Seville, till they were sure they should be defended from the Emperor's attacks by land; that unless a Formidable army covered them on the side of Germany, they would in case of an attack be obliged to accommodate themselves with the Emperor, and so be obliged against their wills to quit our alliance, a thing to be prevented by all means'.[24]

This argument was specious. In the correspondence of Diemar there are no signs that the British ministers, with whom he enjoyed close personal relations, intended that the Hessians should be used to aid the Dutch. Rather it is clear that they were intended for the defence of Hanover. This point was reiterated with vigour by the opposition in all the major debates of the period. As the Jacobite MP, William Shippen, baldly put it in 1730, 'To me plain that these are only for the defence of the foreign dominions'.

The opposition Whig MP, Walter Plumer, advanced another line, held in private by some ministers, when he claimed during the 1736 Commons debate on the Navy Estimates for that year, 'I have always observed, that no foreign Prince would lend us any of his troops, without our engaging, not only to pay them, but to grant him a subsidy, perhaps greater than the pay of those troops, upon their own footing, would have amounted to; and that even in cases where the Prince stood obliged, perhaps by former treaties, to assist us with troops at his own expence, and often in cases where his own preservation was more immediately concerned in the event of the war than ours'.[25] The opposition also argued that the distortion of British policy for Hanoverian ends represented by the Hessian subsidies, was illegal and unconstitutional. The Hessian debate of 4 February 1730 was the occasion on which George Heathcote, a wealthy West India Merchant, and the hitherto ministerial MP for Hindon, went into opposition. He made a speech described by another MP, Lord Hervey, as 'a flaming speech against the Court, which he had collected from a common-place book on tyranny and arbitrary power and extracts of treatises on a free government'. Heathcote claimed that George II's right to the throne was based upon his observance of a contract with the population, a contract stipulated in the Act of Succession. He stated 'that the not defending Hanover at the expense of England' was included in the contract, and that therefore by subsidising the Hessians, George was in breach of his right to the crown.[26] Robert Vyner, MP for Lincolnshire, claimed that voting for the Hessian subsidies was committing treason 'against the people'.[27]

Thus, the debates over the Hessians provided an opportunity for discussing, or rather declaiming upon, the constitutional position of the monarch. By encapsulating the issue of relations between Britain and Hanover, the Hessian subsidies provoked consideration of the relationship between George II, in his ambivalent position of King and Elector, and the elected representatives of the people of Britain. The high cost of foreign policy, the Hanoverian interests of the King, and the relatively limited interest of eighteenth-century governments in internal affairs ensured that the major issues over which the position of the monarch vis-à-vis the representative institutions could be tested were those of foreign policy. George II's strong personal interest in, and determination to control, foreign policy increased the importance of the issue.[28]

The debates did not reveal much knowledge of the intricacies of German politics. Throughout the period the British government provided support for the claim by Hesse-Cassel to place a garrison in the strategic fortress of Rheinfels. This fortress controlled one of the major crossings on the middle Rhine, an obvious route for the French to enter northern Germany. In the late 1720s when Britain was in alliance with France, George I and George II were concerned to facilitate Hessian control of the fortress, in order to provide a secure bridging-point through which French forces could move into northern Germany to protect Hanover against a potential Prussian or Austrian attack. By the War of the Polish Succession of 1733-5 policy had changed. Britain was neutral in the war but George II was a keen partisan of the Austrians in their war against the French and 10,000 Hanoverian troops served in the Imperial army on the Rhine. George pressed Diemar to persuade William of Hesse-Cassel to send troops to Rheinfels, to block a possible French seizure of the fortress, and George used the British minister Plenipotentiary in Vienna, Thomas Robinson, to exert influence upon the Austrians to condone a Hessian seizure of Rheinfels. It was the threat, in the spring of 1734, that Marshal Belle-Isle's French Army would seize

Rheinfels and invade Hesse, thus threatening Hanover, that led George II
to send his Hanoverian troops to the Rhine. He had delayed doing so in
early 1734 when Austria had pressed for assistance after the French
declaration of war the previous October but moved as soon as Hanoverian
interests were threatened.[29]

Thus, in the case of Rheinfels, the British diplomatic system was used to
further a Hanoverian goal, despite (in 1733-5) the neutrality of the British
government. Fortunately for George II, these transactions were kept a
secret and there was therefore no parliamentary storm over the matter.

Parliamentary opposition to the Hessian subsidies was no secret, and it
was used by the Prussians in an attempt to dissuade Hesse-Cassel from
supporting George II. On 4 September (ns) 1729 the Prussian Resident in
Cassel, Sasstroff, informed the Hessians 'that the Parliament will never
support H.M. in any war he may undertake in defense of his German
Dominions', and argued very strongly that the Hessian troops being voted
for by Parliament, were not to act in any cause 'that did not regard Great
Britain in particular'.

The role of Parliament in the granting of subsidies was frequently
referred to by British ministers and diplomats. In 1726 when St. Saphorin,
British envoy in Vienna, was sent to Munich to attempt to arrange an
alliance with Bavaria, Townshend told him that he could not offer
peacetime subsidies as Parliament would never consent, and without
Parliament they could not be afforded. Four years later Finch informed the
Swedish government that peacetime subsidies were impossible as
Parliament would never accept them. It is possible to argue that sometimes
the British ministry used Parliament as an excuse for not doing what they
did not wish to do. An example would be the return of Gibraltar, promised
in 1721, and urged in the 1720s by Britain's principal allies, France and the
United Provinces. The British ministry claimed to be unable to do it
because it would 'put the whole nation in a flame' and fail to secure
parliamentary support.[30] In fact, as with the issue of subsidies, many
ministers did not wish to yield to foreign pressure. Sasstroff's claim is an
interesting instance of the diplomatic use of the argument that a state's
strength was related to its constitutional and political ability to mobilise
support. Assessments of the Balance of Power in the eighteenth century
tended to concentrate upon the size of a state, the number of its inhabitants
and the strength of its army.[31] However, in considering the strength of the
new dynastic conglomeration of Britain-Hanover it was clearly necessary to
assess the relationship between the monarch and the British Parliament.
Sasstroff was inaccurate in his assessment of what Parliament would do, but
correct in arguing that Parliament had to be considered. Had Parliament

refused to pay the Hessians, then George II would have been forced to yield to Prussia in the struggle for the domination of northern Germany.

A similar analysis was necessary in a consideration of the other contemporary dynastic conglomerations, Sweden and Hesse-Cassel, Poland and Saxony. Theoretically the vast accretions of strength represented by the acquisitions of Sweden, Poland and Britain by the rulers of Hesse-Cassel, Saxony and Hanover should have enabled them to dominate northern Germany, indeed northern Europe. Indeed other German rulers attempted to emulate them. Duke Leopold of Lorraine laid the basis for the eventual marriage of his eldest son, Francis Stephen, with the heiress of the Austrian dominions, Maria Theresa, because he hoped that this union would give Lorraine the strength necessary to break free from French tutelage. This goal was thwarted by the expulsion of the Lorraine dynasty from Lorraine after the War of the Polish Succession. Frederick William I considered a marriage between Crown Prince Frederick of Prussia and Anne of Mecklenburg, the niece of the childless Czarina Anna, a move that could have produced the dynastic union of Prussia and Russia.[32]

These schemes failed to produce lasting gains in power. Augustus II and Augustus III drew little benefit from Poland apart from the glory of a crown. Hesse-Cassel did not benefit greatly from the short-lived dynastic union with Sweden. The energies of Hanover's rulers were diverted into the internal politics of Britain. In each case the limitation of the constitutional and political powers of the crown, whether in Britain, Sweden or Poland, thwarted the schemes of their German princely rulers. Augustus II failed to increase monarchical power in Poland, failed to make the crown of Poland hereditary, and was forced to accept the exclusion of Saxon troops from Poland. George I and George II failed in their attempts to use British power to strengthen the Hanoverian position in the Empire. Though Parliament paid for the British fleets that served the Hanoverian diplomatic strategy in the Baltic in the late 1710s and 1720s, and for the Hessians who shielded Hanover from the Prussians in 1727-31, George II had to bow to pressure from his ministers. The Hessians were paid off in 1732, attempts to create an alliance with the Wittelsbachs in 1729-30 foundered on the unwillingness of the British government to provide the necessary subsidies, and in the War of the Austrian Succession (1740-8) George was forced to watch whilst his hated nephew, Frederick II, pushed Prussia into a dominant position. Hanoverian influence in Mecklenburg was eroded, Prussia acquired East Friesland in 1744 despite Hanoverian protests, and the British ministers insisted that British foreign policy should concentrate on producing a coalition aimed against France, that would include Prussia, rather than a coalition aimed against Prussia.

Thus the attempt to use the Anglo-Hanoverian dynastic union to foster

Hanoverian territorial interests failed, just as the more general attempt to create strength through strategic marriages failed. The later eighteenth century witnessed nothing to parallel the unions created by Hanoverian, Hessian and Saxon marital diplomacy. Instead it was those states that had witnessed internal consolidation and followed a policy of the acquisition of territory through conquest rather than marriage — Russia, Prussia and France — that came to dominate Europe. The most promising attempt to develop in the other pattern had been that of Hanover, but it had failed to overcome the independence of the British political structure. The opposition to the subsidy treaties with Hesse-Cassel is the best example of this. Though the treaties were never defeated in Parliament, the continued strength and vigour of the opposition on this point led Walpole to insist in 1732 that Parliament be asked to provide no more funds for this purpose. Despite George's wish to continue the subsidy he was forced to yield. Thus Parliament had forced a major alteration in British foreign policy. The attempt by George I and George II to use British money to weld together a Hanoverian and Hessian bloc capable of defying the Prussian attempt to dominate northern Germany had to be abandoned in the face of Parliamentary pressure.

NOTES

Unless otherwise indicated, all dates are given in old style. New style is indicated by (ns).

1. Bibliothèque de L'Arsenal, Archives de la Bastille, Gazetins secrets de la Police; E. G. Cruickshanks, 'Public Opinion in the 1740's: The Reports of the Chevalier de Mouchy' *Bulletin of the Institute of Historical Research,* 27 (1954), pp. 54-68.

2. G. C. Gibbs, 'Newspapers, Parliament and Foreign Policy in the Age of Stanhope and Walpole', *Mélange offerts à G. Jacquemyns* (Brussels, 1968) pp. 293-315, J. Black, 'The British Press and European News in the 1730s: The case of the Newcastle Courant', *Durham County Local History Society Bulletin,* 26 (1981), pp. 38-43; J. Black, 'Manchester's First Newspaper: The Manchester Weekly Journal', *Transactions of the Historical Society of Lancashire and Cheshire,* 130 (1981), pp. 61-72.

3. G. C. Gibbs, 'Laying Treaties before Parliament in the Eighteenth Century', *Studies in Diplomatic History,* edited by R. Hatton and M. S. Anderson (London, 1970), pp. 116-137; J. R. Jones, *Britain and the World 1649-1815* (London, 1980), pp. 184-5.

4. R. Atwood, *The Hessians* (Cambridge, 1980).

5. There was no doubt of the vulnerability of the Electorate. The Secretary of State for the Northern Department, Viscount Townshend, informed the British Envoy Extraordinary to Hesse-Cassel, Major-General Sutton, 'You are very well acquainted with the exposed situation, and extent of His Majesty's frontiers, and that, as he had no fortifications to defend it, if he be not supported by a considerable body of his allies, there will be great danger from the first impression . . .', Townshend to Sutton, 2 Sept. (ns) 1729, Public Record Office, State Papers (hereafter, PRO), 81/123.

6. M. Hughes, The Imperial Supreme Judicial Authority under the Emperor Charles VI and the crises in Mecklenburg and East Friesland (unpublished London Ph,D., 1969); M. Naumann, *Österreich, England und das Reich 1719-1732* (Berlin, 1932); Hesse-Cassel gave diplomatic support to George II at the Imperial Diet in Regensburg over the Mecklenburg issue, Sutton to the Duke of Newcastle, Secretary of State for the Southern Department, 10 June (ns) 1729, PRO. 81/123.

7. R. Lodge, *Great Britain and Prussia in the Eighteenth Century* (Oxford, 1923).

8. Sutton to Newcastle, 1 Aug. (ns) 1729, PRO. 81/123. Chavigny, French envoy in Hanover, to Chauvelin, French Secretary of State for Foreign Affairs, 12 August (ns) 1729, Paris, Archives du Ministère des Affaires Etrangères, Correspondance Politique (hereafter, A.E.CP.) Brunswick-Hanover, 47 f. 119; Delafaye to Tilson, 1 Aug. 1729, PRO. 43/80; Sutton to Tilson, 11 Mar., (ns) 1729, PRO. 81/123; Sutton to Townshend, 21 July (ns) 1727, 16 Aug. (ns), 2 Sept. (ns) 1728, Townshend to Sutton, 16 Aug. 1728, PRO. 81/122.

9. H. Schilling, *Der Zwist Preussens und Hannovers 1729-30* (Halle, 1912); J. Black, British Foreign Policy 1727-31 (unpublished Ph.D., Durham, 1982), pp. 278-89.

10. 'Je me prépare à la guerre', Frederick William I to Ferdinand Albrecht, Duke of Braunschweig-Bevern, 22 Aug. (ns) 1729, Staatsarchivs Wolfenbüttel, 1 Alt 22, Nr. 532 f.32. Sühm to Augustus II of Saxony-Poland, 12, 23 July (ns) 1729, Dresden, Sächsisches Hauptstaats-archiv, Geheimes Kabinett, Gesandschaften (hereafter Dresden), 3378, VI, f.146, 163; Dickens to Du Bourgay, 19 July (ns), Du Bourgay to Townshend, 21, 22 Aug. (ns) 1729, PRO. 90/24; Chavigny to Chauvelin, 23 Aug. (ns) 1728, AE. CP. Brunswick-Hanover, 47 f. 162-5.

11. Townshend to Sutton, 23 Aug. (ns) 1729, PRO. 81/123; Diemar, Hessian Envoy Extraordinary to the court of George II, to Prince William of Hesse-Cassel, 23 Aug. (ns) 1729, Staatsarchiv Marburg, Bestand. 4: Politische Akten nach Philipp d. Gr., England (hereafter Marburg, England), 195.

12. William of Hesse-Cassel to Diemar, 27 Aug. (ns) 1729, Marburg, England, 195; D'Aix, Sardinian Envoy Extraordinary to the court of George II, to Victor Amadeus II, King of Sardinia, 28 Aug. (ns) 1729, Archivio di stato di Torino, Lettere Ministri Inghilterra (hereafter AST. LM. Ing.), 35; Caillaud, secretary to Sutton, to George Tilson, Undersecretary of State in the Northern Department, 29 Aug. (ns) 1729, PRO. 81/123.

13. Townshend to Newcastle, 6 Sept. (ns) 1729, PRO. 43/80; Townshend to Sutton, 11 Sept. (ns) 1729, PRO. 81/123.

14. Townshend to Finch, 20 Jan. 1730, PRO. 95/54 F. 5. Townshend to Diemar, 27 Jan. 1730, Townshend to the Wolfenbüttel minister, Baron Stain, 27 Jan. 1730, Townshend to the Wolfenbüttel minister, Count Dehn, 20 Feb. 1730, PRO. 100/16; Black, British Foreign Policy pp. 313-14; Diemar to William of Hesse-Cassel 31 Jan. (ns) 1730, Marburg, England, 199.

15. M. Ransome, 'The Reliability of Contemporary Reporting of the Debates of the House of Commons, 1727-1741', *Bulletin of the Institute of Historical Research*, 19 (1942-3), pp. 67-79; P. Mantoux, *Comptes rendus des séances du Parlement anglais* (Paris, 1906); 'Parliamentary Debates in the Eighteenth Century', *American Historical Review*, 12, 2 (1906-7), pp. 244-269.

16. *The History of Parliament: The House of Commons, 1715-1754,* edited by R. R. Sedgwick (2 vols., London, 1970), II, 190-1, 336-8.

17. *The Parliamentary Diary of Sir Edward Knatchbull, 1722-30,* edited by A. N. Newman (London, 1963), pp. 63, 84-5, 151; Tilson to Lord Waldergrave, British Ambassador Extraordinary and Plenipotentiary in Vienna, 15 Feb. 1728, Chewton Hall, Somerset, Waldegrave Papers (I would like to thank Earl Waldegrave for permission to consult these

papers); Townshend to Sir Cyril Wych, British Resident in the Hansa Town, 20 Feb. 1728, PRO. 82/45 f. 59; Townshend to William Finch, British Envoy Extraordinary and Plenipotentiary in the United Provinces, 20 Feb. 1728, PRO. 84/299 f. 109; Vignola, Venetian Secretary in London to the Doge of Venice, 25 Feb. (ns) 1729, Archivio di Stato di Venezia, Lettere Ministri Inghilterra 98 f. 116; Diemar to William of Hesse-Cassel, 17 Feb. (ns) 1730, Marburg, England, 199.

18. Zamboni, Saxon Resident in London, to the Saxon minister, Manteuffel, 29 Mar. 1729, Oxford, Bodleian Library, Ms Rawlinson 120 f. 59.

19. J. H. Plumb, *Sir Robert Walpole. The King's Minister* (London, 1960), p. 207.

20. *Knatchbull*, p. 84; Ossorio, Sardinian envoy in London, to Victor Amadeus II, 30 Jan. (ns) 1730, AST. LM. Ing. 37.

21. *Knatchbull*, pp. 103, 151; Historical Manuscripts Commission, *Manuscripts of the Earl of Egmont, Diary of Viscount Percival* (3 vols., London, 1920-3), I, 24, 29; Titley to Tilson, 28 Feb. (ns) 1730, PRO. 75/54 f. 119.

22. W. Cobbett, *Parliamentary History of England,* Vol. VIII (London, 1811), p. 842.

23. *Egmont*, pp. 25-6, 4 Feb. 1730.

24. *Egmont*, p. 21, 2 Feb. 1730.

25. *Knatchbull*, p. 151, 4 Feb. 1730; Plumer, 26 Jan. 1736; Cobbett, *Parliamentary History*, Vol. IX, 1003.

26. Hervey to Henry Fox, 4 Feb. 1730, *Lord Hervey and his Friends 1726-38,* edited by the Earl of Ilchester (London, 1950), p. 47; *Egmont*, pp. 27-8, 4 Feb. 1730.

27. *Knatchbull*, p. 151, 4 Feb. 1730.

28. Black, *British Foreign Policy in the Age of Walpole* (Edinburgh, 1985), pp. 27-48; Black, *The Collapse of the Anglo-French Alliance 1727-1731* (Gloucester, 1987), pp. 210-11; Black, 'George II Reconsidered', *Mitteilungen des Österreichischen Staatsarchivs,* 35 (1982), pp. 35-56. Black, 'British Foreign Policy in the Eighteenth Century: A Survey', *Journal of British Studies,* 26 (1987), pp. 39-43.

29. Diary of Marshal Villars, 26 May (ns) 1727, Marquis de Vogüé (ed.), *Mémoires du Marechal de Villars* (6 vols., Paris, 1884-1904), 5, 67; Horatio Walpole to Tilson, 28 May (ns) 1727, BL Add. 48981 f.237; Diemar to the Austrian minister Prince Eugene, 20 Apr. (ns) 1734, Vienna, Haus- Hof-, und Staatsarchiv, Grosse Korrespondenz 85a; Diemar to Frederick I of Sweden, 23 Apr. (ns) 1734, Marburg, England 203; Edward Weston, Undersecretary in the Northern Department, to Robinson, 16 Apr. 1734, London, British Library, Department of Manuscripts, Additional Manuscripts 23790 f. 401; De Loss, Saxon envoy in London, to Augustus III, 21 May 1734, Dresden 638 IIa f. 458.

30. Caillaud to Tilson, 5 Sept. 1729; Black, *Foreign Policy in the Age of Walpole,* pp. 75-92.

31. M.S. Anderson, 'Eighteenth-Century Theories of the Balance of Power', in R. Hatton and M.S. Anderson (eds.), *Studies in Diplomatic History* (London, 1970), pp. 183-98; Black, 'Theory of the balance of power in the first half of the eighteenth-century: a note on sources', *Review of International Studies,* 9 (1983), pp. 55-61.

32. Hopes of dynastic benefit lay behind the Swedish and Russian marriages of the Dukes of Holstein-Gottorp, and the interest in Russian marriages displayed by the Houses of Braunschweig-Bevern and Braunschweig-Wolfenbüttel.

CHAPTER 4

'The True Principles of the Revolution': The Duke of Newcastle and the Idea of the Old System

H.M. Scott

Anyone who has turned the pages of eighteenth-century British diplomatic correspondence will be familiar with the recurring expressions which resonate through them: the 'balance of power', the 'liberties of (all) Europe', the 'ambitious House of Bourbon', the 'Maritime Powers', the 'common cause', the 'grand alliance'.[1] From the century's mid-point one phrase eclipses all others: the 'old system' or, less usually, the 'ancient system', and for the next generation it becomes the dominant refrain in British foreign policy. Not all contemporaries were persuaded of the validity of such expressions. France's leading minister in the 1760s, the duc de Choiseul, fulminated against 'the balance between nations, that empty phrase coined by William III after he became King of England in order to arouse all Europe against France'.[2] William Pitt was even more outspoken. Speaking to the House of Commons in 1755 he declared:

> We have suffered ourselves to be deceived by names and sounds, the balance of power, the liberty of Europe, a common cause, and many more such expressions, without any other meaning than to exhaust our wealth, consume the profits of our trade, and load our posterity with intolerable burdens.[3]

Pitt's diatribe itself testified to the potency of such phrases, though his purpose was to decry their influence. His stance was, on this occasion at least, that of the isolationist, the opponent of entangling alliances and military operations on the continent. Those who favoured such intervention and argued for 'continental' rather than 'American' warfare did so in terms of the 'balance of power', the 'liberties of Europe' or, increasingly, the 'old system'. This chapter is, therefore, an exploration of the interventionist strand in Britain's eighteenth-century diplomacy, rather than its isolationist wing. It investigates not the tactical considerations involved in any policy but the strategic assumptions which it embodied.

The problems posed, and the possibilities offered, by such expressions have not usually engaged historians, who all too often dismiss such language as unimportant or ignore it altogether: 'paltry rhetoric' was Richard Pares' decisive verdict.[4] This neglect has been encouraged by the tendency of most historians of eighteenth-century British foreign policy to study actual diplomatic negotiations, rather than investigate its underlying attitudes and assumptions. Yet to a generation more aware of the

C

significance of language, such neglect must seem questionable. The present concern with modes of discourse, with its appreciation of the importance of how ideas are expressed as well as what they mean, is particularly apposite for diplomatic history. The existence of voluminous official despatches and private correspondence enables the development of traditions to be studied with some precision over a period of years. This chapter examines the significance of the language in which Britain's eighteenth-century diplomacy was conducted. It investigates the origin of the phrase 'old system' in the later 1740s and its importance in the period up to the early 1780s. It demonstrates that, far from being 'paltry rhetoric' or 'names and sounds', expressions such as 'old system' are an invaluable guide to certain of the fundamental assumptions behind official policy.

The diplomatic strategy pursued at any point in the eighteenth century would evolve from a complex aggregate of factors: the prevailing European situation and the diplomatic options open; an assessment of the resources available and likely to be required by a particular line of policy; the domestic political scene; the attitudes of parliament and of powerful individuals, above all the king and leading ministers; perhaps a sense of the sentiments of the political nation at large and of the commercial classes — all these factors might influence the formulation and execution of policy. But that strategy would also reflect certain ingrained attitudes and beliefs, rooted in perceptions of the past. These unspoken assumptions, however elusive, form part of British foreign policy. The Old System seldom — if ever — can be said to have dictated Britain's diplomacy; mental rigidity was never so great as to allow this idea to dominate policy. But it provides an insight into the minds of the men who controlled Britain's diplomacy and a key to its fuller understanding. The Old System became the idiom in which they thought and acted. The thinking which it encapsulated influenced, sometimes decisively, British foreign policy throughout the age of Newcastle and North. Above all, it made the search for one or more continental ally the central theme in British foreign policy during the generation after the 1740s. This had not been the case during the preceding thirty years, whatever was subsequently believed, and it was principally due to the establishment of the idea of the Old System.

The most satisfactory definition of the Old System was that provided by George III at the beginning of the 1770s. 'I confess,' he wrote, 'my political Creed is formed on the system of King William, England in conjunction with the House of Austria and the (Dutch) Republic seems the most secure barrier against the Family Compact, and if Russia could be added to this, I think that the Court of Versailles would not be in a hurry to commence hostilities'.[5] The King correctly highlighted the four principal characteristics of the Old System: it was essentially a means of opposing

France, and of fighting her on the continent; it sought to do this by concluding alliances with major states, at first the Dutch Republic and Austria and subsequently Russia as well; it embodied the idea of a military barrier against French expansion; and it looked back to what were believed to be the precedents of the age of William III and Marlborough.

First and foremost, the Old System was a means of fighting and defeating France and, where this became necessary, her Bourbon ally, Spain. The fact that it was a system of alliances must not disguise its basic anti-French intent: co-operation with continental states was sought not for its own sake but in order to contain Louis XIV's successors on the French throne.[6] There was a second, essentially Whig, assumption: that this struggle must be fought predominantly in Europe rather than by the kind of 'blue-water' strategy advocated by many Tories. The desired alliances were secondary to the purpose of defeating France. The two principal opponents of French power in the decades around 1700 had been the Dutch and the Austrian Habsburgs, and therefore their co-operation had been secured, as had that of the powerful and strategically-vital north Italian state of Savoy-Piedmont.

England and the Republic had shared a common ruler between 1688 and 1702 as well as a common Protestantism, and this made their partnership particularly close. With Catholic Austria no such bond existed, save that of mutual need in the conflict with France, although this had been strong enough to override religious hostility between the two states. Anglo-Austrian co-operation was rooted only in their joint participation in the struggle against Louis XIV. There were no dynastic, cultural or even economical links to buttress a political partnership based uniquely on opposition to France, and Britain and Austria were and always remained 'Allies of Convenience'. This is an important point since, with the waning of Dutch power in the eighteenth century and British assumptions about the Republic's loyalty to England, the Old System became almost synonymous with revived co-operation with Vienna. The basis of opposition to France enabled such ideas to persist long after the Austrian alliance had been lost. The anti-French purpose, and the pragmatism on which it rested, also made it easier to incorporate other states, above all Russia, France's established rival in eastern Europe. The duke of Newcastle had a particularly clear grasp of this when he wrote in June 1762 that he 'ever was, and ever will be, for supporting as powerful an interest as I could procure, upon the Continent, to be composed of such powers, as would best, at the time, obstruct and defend us against the views and power of the house of Bourbon'.[7]

The Old System thus rested on Britain's self-interest. It became a banner under which ministers sought to enlist as many continental states as could be secured to fight France. Moreover, it increasingly became a search for armies rather than allies. Britain hoped to unite with as many states as could be persuaded to put their own soldiers into the field and so reduce her own military effort on the continent. This was the overriding purpose of co-operation with Austria and Savoy-Piedmont in the wars of 1688-1748, and it was the main attraction of adding Russia, with her abundant manpower, to the ranks of Britain's allies during the generation after 1740. Lacking a standing army of the kind possessed by the leading continental states, and their abundant demographic resources, British ministers sought instead to find foreign soldiers, while themselves concentrating on naval and military operations beyond Europe. One purpose of the search for alliances during the generation after 1748 was to limit Britain's own continental commitments in any war, thus freeing her for the overseas struggle with France.

The Dutch Republic was usually a less formidable military power than Austria, Russia, or even the Savoyard state. But its strategic position, abundant wealth and established dynastic links with Britain made it a founder member of the Old System and the guarantor of her Protestant succession. During the generation after 1688, the shared concern with French expansion was sufficient to override established naval and colonial rivalry between the two states. On the British side, the Dutch alliance was seen as linking England to the continent.[8] Strategically, its role was crucial. Both states were anxious to check France's growth as a military, naval and colonial power. Specifically, they sought to defend the Southern Netherlands against French military expansion: the Republic because of its weak southern frontier, England on account of a historic fear of invasion from across the 'narrow seas'. This was to be achieved by the Barrier, formally established by a treaty signed in 1715. It was the most obvious legacy of the wars against Louis XIV and in time became the living symbol of the Old System. The Southern Netherlands passed from Bourbon Spain to Habsburg Austria, which shouldered the major financial and military burden of defending the area, while the Dutch retained the right to garrison certain key fortresses in the newly Austrian territory. Ostensibly this provided defence for the vulnerable Republic, but the Barrier also protected a traditional and vital British interest: the security of the Low Countries.

The search for allies and armies against France was given a special flavour by the language in which it was conducted and by the historical precedents on which it was believed to rest. During the generation after 1688 the fledgling British state had fought two long wars — the Nine Years' War of 1689-97 and the War of the Spanish Succession of 1702-13 — avowedly to resist French hegemony on the continent and also to defend England's own Revolution Settlement. These conflicts had been undertaken in alliance with the Dutch Republic (the Stadtholder, William III, ruled Britain until 1702), Austria, Savoy-Piedmont and several minor powers, above all Brandenburg-Prussia. Their co-operation had been embodied in two Grand Alliances, those of 1689 and 1701, which were believed to have contained the Sun King's ambitions and so preserved the political and religious liberty of the other European states. The treaties concluded during and immediately after the wars of 1688-1713 remained the principal bonds between these states in the middle decades of the eighteenth century, and this provided one obvious link with that epoch.[9] It reinforced the retrospective element in British foreign policy. There is a sense in which all statesmen and diplomats think partly in historical terms and are guided by past precedent as well as by present opportunities. The potent traditions of William III and Marlborough ensured that this was certainly true of Britain's diplomacy in the 1740s and the 1750s.

The difference between the view of past events embodied in the Old System and what had actually happened was striking and significant. Co-operation against Louis XIV, particularly during the War of the Spanish Succession, had been less successful than was subsequently believed. Though the threatened union of France and Spain had been averted, a French Bourbon prince had ascended the throne in Madrid, while Louis XIV's substantial territorial gains during the first half of his reign were largely confirmed by the peace settlements of 1697 and 1713-14. Indeed, the Peace of Utrecht appeared to confirm France as the leading European power. Military and political co-operation had been less successful and certainly less smooth than later believed. Austria's participation had not been wholehearted: she had been diverted by the war with the Turks in the 1690s and by the Hungarian rebellion in the 1700s, while her armies, when they had met French forces in the field without Anglo-Dutch support, had suffered serious defeats which not even Prince Eugene's reputation as a commander could disguise. The mantle of 'soldier-king' sits uncomfortably on William III, whose military efforts were more obvious than his successes. The great duke of Marlborough, at times in partnership with Eugene, had certainly won a striking series of victories during the first half of the Spanish Succession conflict, and these long remained an inspiration to observers in Britain and in the Republic. These triumphs, and above all the victories at Blenheim and Ramillies, were the first serious check to French military power during Louis XIV's reign, but they had not produced the expected peace settlement. Their limited impact could be explained by the change of ministry in 1710, after which the Tories were believed to have abandoned Britain's allies and concluded an excessively lenient peace: such a view came easily to Whigs. Diplomatic co-operation between the members of the Grand Alliance had often been difficult, even between the founder members. With the important exception of the established Anglo-Dutch links, their partnership rested simply on a fear of French power, and their own rivalries were at times as apparent as their shared wish to resist French hegemony.

There was thus an important difference between the realities of the struggle against the Sun King and the later myth of the Grand Alliance. This was highlighted by the immediate fate of the partnership which had fought Louis XIV. This was later to form the heart of the Old System, but both the Anglo-Dutch alliance and its Anglo-Austrian counterpart had come close to disintegration in the very different circumstances which had prevailed during the generation after 1713, when neither the Barrier nor Britain's Protestant Succession had been threatened by France. In retrospect, however, the clear hiatus in the alignment of Britain, Austria and the Republic from the 1710s to the 1730s was obliterated by memories of the earlier wars. What had been, at the time, a temporary marriage of political convenience, an ephemeral period of military and diplomatic co-operation, became after 1740 a grand and glorious league, the basis of Britain's later greatness and Europe's freedom. One key to this transformation may be found in the struggle's impact on Britain herself. The wars after 1688 had — or could be portrayed as having — secured the Revolution Settlement, the Protestant and eventually Hanoverian Succession, the position of parliament in government and — ultimately — the Whig ascendancy itself. Foreign policy here overlapped with domestic political developments and, in time, the two were fused into a common view of the importance of that era for Britain and for Europe. It was assumed that England's own liberty and subsequent rise to greatness were the basis of Europe's freedom from French hegemony. This belief was exemplified in Sir Joseph Yorke's remarks to the duke of Newcastle in November 1761: 'you have recalled our wandering thoughts to the true principles of the Revolution, an epoch which has swelled our National Debt, but has made us the most flourishing nation in Europe'.[10] Herein lay the broader context of the Old System: a conviction that Britain's commercial prosperity, growing political importance and distinctive constitutional arrangements were linked, in some ill-defined way, to the decisive generation after 1688 — the age of William III and Heinsius, of Marlborough and Prince Eugene. When Britain was again directly threatened by France, as was clearly the case in the 1740s, the utility of a new Grand Alliance appeared obvious.

Yorke's comments also make clear Newcastle's central role in re-establishing the 'true principles of the Revolution' as the basis of British foreign policy and in ensuring that they were christened the 'old system'. There is an important distinction here between the ideas themselves and the language in which they were clothed. Newcastle first championed the principles behind the Old System and then, from the summer of 1748 onwards, described them in this distinctive way. Previous uses of the phrases 'old system' or 'ancient system' can be found.[11] In a similar way, the idea of an anti-French alliance including those states which had been in the forefront of the struggle against Louis XIV was an established theme both in European diplomacy as a whole and in the foreign policies of individual states, powers such as Austria and Hanover. It was particularly influential in the Dutch Republic, where the Orangists always upheld its doctrines, although they were not to be in a position to implement them between the ending of the Spanish Succession conflict and the Revolution of 1747. But in no country did the idea of the Old System have such enduring importance as it did in Britain. This was primarily due to Newcastle, who dominated and, at times, dictated foreign policy from the mid-1740s until his resignation in 1762. The duke not merely established the expression 'old system' but made the ideas behind it central to British foreign policy.

II

The concept took shape in the early years of the Pelham Administration, when Newcastle finally secured control over Britain's diplomacy. Though intimately involved in its day-to-day conduct for two decades, it was only with Carteret's fall and the formation of the 'Broad Bottom' ministry towards the end of 1744 that he was able to shape policy himself. The idea of the Old System acquired its mature form — and the phrase itself came into general use — during Newcastle's early years as 'acting' or 'responsible' secretary,[12] and it became the mainspring of his foreign policy after the Peace of Aix-la-Chapelle in 1748. The concept was a criticism of recent British policy and a prescription for the future, expressed in the idiom and asserting the ideas of a bygone age. It arose primarily from stategic considerations and was the corollary of Newcastle's invincible belief by the 1740s in the priority of opposing France.[13] Its emergence at this time was due both to Britain's serious predicament and to the duke's distinctive reaction to it. This was shaped by the influence which particular individuals had on his thinking and his policies. Newcastle's ideas were often derivative, for his was certainly not an original intellect, and this was true for the Old System as it was for his foreign policy as a whole. But the 'true principles of the Revolution' which it reasserted were an integral part of Britain's domestic politics as well as her diplomacy throughout the eighteenth century.

The general context of the Old System can be found in Whig ideas, particularly about foreign affairs. Its basic tenets — opposition to France and diplomatic and military involvement on the continent — embodied an essentially 'Whig' approach to strategy and diplomacy, in contrast to the 'Tory' policy of non-involvement in Europe and even accommodation with France.[14] In a broader sense, the Old System grew out of the assumptions of most eighteenth-century Englishmen about their political world and the central importance of the Glorious Revolution of 1688 in its creation. For politicians in the age of Walpole and the Pelhams, the Revolution and the subsequent Hanoverian Succession had made the world safe for Whigs. In a more general sense, the Old System was part of the Williamite myth.[15] The men who exercised political power and controlled British policy in the middle decades of the eighteenth century had been born and brought up during the decisive generation after 1688, and this shaped their thinking and actions.[16] Their frame of reference and their political language remained that of the age of the Stadtholder-King and the Dual Monarchy. A central preoccupation of George II was his desire to emulate the soldier-king William III, in whose palaces he lived and whose actions he often followed closely: as, for example, in marrying his eldest daughter to the Prince of Orange, with its obvious echoes of the earlier dynastic marriage between Princess Mary and the Stadtholder and future King.[17]

Newcastle's own links with that age were both personal and political. Born into the Whig tradition, he had married Marlborough's grand-daughter and had entered the Whig establishment in the early years of the Hanoverian dynasty.[18] Like many of his contemporaries, he always saw the glorious quarter-century after 1688 as a storehouse of precedents to guide later generations. His own indebtedness to that age could be remarkably direct: he declared on one occasion that his support for the Dutch alliance and the Barrier had been strengthened by reading a book published in 1712, Bishop Hare's *Barrier Treaty Vindicated.* It is revealing that, casting round for a strategy in 1746, the duke should fix on that adopted during the earlier conflict over the Spanish Succession: an invasion of Provence in southern France from Italy, carried out by Austrian and Savoyard troops. In a more general sense, his ideas as to how the Austrian Succession War might be fought and ended were obviously inspired by Marlborough's strategy: an army was to be sent to Flanders, France was to be defeated in the field and forced to accept a negotiated settlement.[19] For Newcastle, as for his great friend Lord Chancellor Hardwicke and for the King, Britain's actions should be guided, measured and even vindicated by the great struggle against Louis XIV's France: in September 1744, the duke commented peevishly that the Dutch *'absolutely renounce the precedents of former wars'.*[20] For his part, George II was anxious to avoid signing a separate peace at the end of the War of the Austrian Succession and thereby deserting his allies: this, he believed, was the iniquity of the Tory ministers at the end of Queen Anne's reign, who had abandoned England's partners in the Spanish Succession struggle.[21]

Newcastle was convinced that the enduring validity of Williamite ideas had been demonstrated by Britain's difficulties during the 1740s. Though the Old System was rooted in Whig soil, the more immediate stimulus for growth was provided by the War of the Austrian Succession. That conflict had seen the revival of French hostility towards Britain, the operation of a Bourbon axis linking Versailles and Madrid, and a notable resurgence of French military power on the continent. Together these developments represented a serious challenge to Britain, and the duke believed that this threat was the consequence of mistakes in foreign policy at least since the 1720s.

France's re-appearance as an open and formidable enemy came after a generation during which relations had significantly improved. Indeed, particularly during the 1720s, Austria had actually replaced the French as Britain's principal enemy. In the decades between the War of the Spanish Succession and that of the Austrian Succession, Anglo-French diplomacy had been surprisingly harmonious. There had been periodic tension and one or two serious diplomatic crises, and old antagonisms died hard. Nevertheless, the French threat during the age of Walpole generally appeared to be less than at any other period in the eighteenth century, and the two states had actually been allies between 1716 and 1731. This changed dramatically after 1740, as opposition to France once again became the main theme in British policy. An Anglo-Spanish war had begun in 1739 and France, though nominally at peace with Britain until 1744, had not hesitated to throw her naval and diplomatic weight behind her Bourbon ally. The existence of this Franco-Spanish axis and the conclusion of a Second Family Compact in 1743 (the first had been signed a decade earlier) was one source of Newcastle's anxieties. For the allies, the overriding purpose of the Spanish Succession War had been to prevent either a union of the French and Spanish crowns or a Bourbon prince ascending the throne in Madrid, although this attempt had ultimately failed. For two decades after the Peace of Utrecht, Franco-Spanish tension had usually been more apparent than Bourbon unity. From the 1730s, however, co-operation between the two states had increased, and in the Austrian Succession War the 'united House of Bourbon' represented an acute and direct threat to Britain.

Newcastle was even more alarmed by the revival of French military expansion after 1740, which seemed a return to the great days of Louis XIV's military imperialism. The duc de Belle-Isle's motive in propelling France into the continental war had been to destroy finally Habsburg power, and there were certainly moments during the 1740s when Austria's territorial and even political survival appeared in jeopardy. One reason why the military balance on the continent had tilted so sharply against Britain and her allies was the role played by Prussia under her young and ambitious King, Frederick the Great, with his formidable army. Prussia's remarkable emergence after 1740 had provided a second — and notably sharp — edge to the French sword. France now possessed what she had hitherto lacked: a formidable military power as an ally capable of playing a major part in the fighting and winning victories of her own.[22] Frederick the Great's successes were viewed in England as having diverted Austria from her historic role of fighting the French monarchy. Prussia's contribution to France's successes preoccupied Newcastle now and in the future, and this led him to make an unsuccessful bid for Frederick's alliance in the final stages of the Austrian Succession War.[23]

The revival of French power caused even more concern. It reached its peak during the second half of the war when the Marshal de Saxe won a brilliant series of victories and all but destroyed the Barrier in the Southern Netherlands, effectively negating British gains overseas. This anxiety had been strengthened by Hanover's evident vulnerability to French attack. It had been made clear in 1741 when, for the first time during the Personal Union, France had sent an army against the Electorate and immediately compelled George II to conclude a neutrality convention for his German lands. The 1740s had also seen some revival of French naval power, which had been destroyed during the wars of 1688-1713 but which again seemed a rival to Britain during the Austrian Succession conflict. The Jacobite rebellion in 1745 provided the most direct threat. It provoked a panic in England and, for a time, appeared to endanger the Protestant, Hanoverian succession. Newcastle was particularly alarmed in 1745-46, less by the Jacobite clans themselves than by the way their rebellion distracted British attention from the formidable danger now posed by France.[24]

The duke believed that this threat had been exacerbated both by Britain's policies in the past and by her current mistaken strategy. The cumulative effect was to hand over the continent to the French and magnify the direct threat to Britain herself.[25] The duke's analysis was based on the Whig doctrine that France must be fought primarily in Europe. The reasons were outlined by Hardwicke in 1743 when he told the House of Lords:

> . . . if we examine the history of the last century, we shall easily discover that if this nation had not interposed, the French had now been masters of more than half of Europe, and it cannot be imagined that they would have suffered us to set them at defiance in the midst of their greatness.[26]

French hegemony had to be challenged and defeated on the continent, lest a triumphant France strangle Britain's trade and even attack the British Isles. Newcastle had been continuously in office as Southern Secretary since

1724 and might be thought to have had some responsibility for decisions which he now excoriated. But he had always occupied a subordinate role, first to Townshend and then to Sir Robert Walpole. In any case, the duke's views on foreign policy were less consistent than he subsequently proclaimed and he had not always been guided by 'the true principles of the Revolution'. He was certainly not a life long supporter of an Austrian alliance; indeed, in 1742 he had 'the strongest prepossession that the house of Austria was not worth supporting'.[27] A generation before, he had admired Stanhope and in the 1720s he had supported Townshend, though both had co-operated with France to preserve peace. Newcastle had refused to accept the latter's hostility to the Habsburgs, and he always believed that the Bourbons were by far the greater threat. This was why he later became so critical of the 1725 Alliance of Hanover (an alignment he had supported at the time) which had united Britain and France against Austria and Spain. This the duke believed had been an infamous agreement, the source of many later difficulties. In 1752, Newcastle declared that 'The Dread of the Politics of 1725, I have always had before me'.[28] He had encouraged the *rapprochement* with Austria after 1727 and welcomed the Second Treaty of Vienna in 1731 which appeared to restore the traditional alliance.[29] But Anglo-Austrian co-operation soon broke down, as Walpole instead pursued a policy of peace and conciliation of France. This had been facilitated by Fleury's shrewd diplomacy, which was careful not to challenge British — or Dutch — interests in the Southern Netherlands. The absence of obvious French aggression ensured that the slow disintegration of the alliance of the Maritime Powers continued during the final phase of Walpole's ascendancy.

In the 1730s, Newcastle became more and more sceptical of French good-will and increasingly favourable to co-operation with Vienna. During the War of the Polish Succession after 1733 he had been part of that group, headed by Harrington, which feared the Bourbon recovery and urged aid be sent to Austria.[30] The duke appreciated that Fleury's real purpose was to weaken Habsburg power, but he had been unable to deflect Walpole and George II from their policy of non-intervention, which had further alienated Vienna. Involvement in the conduct of British policy for two decades had persuaded Newcastle that France was a hostile power and that her enemy, Austria, should therefore be Britain's friend. The neglect of these principles, he believed, had undermined Britain's interests and influence on the continent and was the real source of her difficulties after Charles VI's death in 1740.[31] Although Britain had acknowledged her obligations to the beleaguered Habsburgs, her support had been half-hearted, while the parallel failure to send prompt and effective aid to Hanover, and the neutrality convention which followed, were seen by

Newcastle as a further abandonment of Austria.[32] Walpole's final years had thus seen an effective continuation of the earlier policy of forsaking the continent and conciliating France, which by 1741 was 'already giving the law to all Europe'.[33] The broad outlines of Carteret's policy were acceptable to the duke and his ascendancy had initially seemed an improvement, since Austria was supported and France vigorously opposed, but the results were less than Newcastle had initially hoped. With the formation of the Broad Bottom at the very end of 1744, he himself became personally responsible for Britain's predicament.

During the first half of the Austrian Succession War, Newcastle had urged the creation of a new Grand Alliance against France and had tried unsuccessfully to bring this about.[34] The duke's response to news of French naval support for Spain in autumn 1740 was in character. He immediately proposed that 'some kind of concert might be set on foot with the Dutch, the emperor, the czarina, the king of Prussia, the king of Poland, the landgrave of Hesse, *etc.*, to form a kind of grand alliance to oppose the ambitious views of the House of Bourbon'.[35] He sought to implement his ideas as soon as he secured control over British foreign policy at the very end of 1744. In the next year, he actually concluded a Quadruple Alliance of Britain, the Dutch Republic, Austria and Savoy-Sardinia, an alignment he later described as 'the best and greatest political system that has been formed this last age'.[36] This coalition superficially resembled the alliance against Louis XIV a generation before, and its purpose was identical: containment of France. But current circumstances only confirmed Newcastle's established preference for a restored Grand Alliance, to which he was increasingly disposed to add Russia and Saxony. Russian participation was sought in the anti-French system on the dubious grounds that she was already an honorary member, through her established hostility to France in eastern Europe and her alliance with Austria; while Saxon involvement was pursued as an ally of Vienna and a subordinate of Russia through her possession of the Polish Crown. But in reality the banner of a Grand Alliance was merely a device for securing the largest number of allies to fight France — not in itself an unreasonable diplomatic strategy. Newcastle's distinctive language and fondness for the precedents of the age of William III and Marlborough made this aspiration a central axiom of British diplomacy.

Until the very end of the War of the Austrian Succession the duke appears to have spoken exclusively in terms of the Grand Alliance.[37] It was only in the summer of that year, during the final stage of the peace negotiations, that he himself was converted to the usage 'old system'. This took place, not in England, but on the continent and it was assisted by the personalities with whom Newcastle now came into contact. During and immediately after the peace negotiations, he visited the Republic and Hanover on three occasions in five years: 1748, 1750 and 1752.[38] These were extended visits and provided the opportunity for lengthy discussions with Dutch and Electoral figures. The final element in the duke's adoption of the Old System was his first-hand acquaintance with European politics and continental statesmen, together with the greater pressure which the King was able to exert in the relative isolation and freedom of Hanover.

One clear influence was that of the Dutch statesman William Bentinck, whose devotion to the Old System exceeded that of Newcastle.[39] Bentinck's whole career was guided by firm opposition to France and equally firm support for the alliance of the Maritime Powers (Britain and the Republic) and for the House of Orange.[40] This was as much a rejection of French absolutism as a system of government as of French military expansion: William Bentinck, like his younger brother, Charles, wanted English Whig ideas to guide the Republic's internal political structure.[41] The elder Bentinck also spoke of 'Revolution principles' and saw the Stadtholder-King as an exemplar and inspiration: as he wrote in summer 1745, at a dark hour for England and for the Republic:

> If King William had been alive, things would not have come to such extremity. And well may one drink to the glorious memory of King William and as *à propos* now as ever.[42]

The Old System had deep roots in Dutch soil and, while it would be too much to claim that it was a Dutch idea, the Dutch contribution was substantial.

The unity of the Maritime Powers and, to a lesser extent, the utility of co-operation with Austria were securely established in Dutch thinking about foreign affairs. The Republic's politicians were also aware of the need to maintain good relations with France, which remained a formidable and direct threat to its security. The value and even necessity of the Old System were always evident to Orangists.[43] English and Austrian alliances had sustained the Republic in the wars of 1688-1713; indeed, political co-operation with both states was of even longer standing, dating from the 1670s, and dynastic links with England went back still further. The Republic's apparent weakness, by the middle decades of the eighteenth century, was seen by Orangists in particular as an incentive to restore a full and active English alliance, which could provide much-needed security. This was certainly the view of William Bentinck, their leading spokesman, during the 1740s. Bentinck was himself a monument to the Anglo-Dutch partnership. Born in England in 1702 and brought up in that country, he was the son by a second marriage of William III's closest political adviser, William Bentinck, Earl of Portland. The younger Bentinck had returned to the Republic in 1719 to make his career and, in the later 1730s, he had emerged as an influential member of the Orangist party.

The situation facing the young William Bentinck was far removed from that during his father's lifetime. The Republic was governed — as it had been since 1702 — not by the House of Orange, but by the Regents, under whose direction Dutch foreign policy had come to be guided principally by a search for peace. Trade, neutrality and even an accommodation with France had become the yardsticks of Dutch policy, and in the 1730s the Republic — like Britain — had remained neutral in the War of the Polish Succession. The principles embodied in the Old System, and its supporters too, were in eclipse on both sides of the North Sea when Charles VI's death precipitated the War of the Austrian Succession. That conflict saw a fundamental transformation in Dutch as in British policy, and in the Republic's political system as well.

Bentinck's advocacy of the Old System was based both on his support for the House of Orange and his wish that it should again rule the Republic, and on his desire to advance his own career. His appreciation of the Republic's weakness, even after the Revolution of 1747, added urgency to his pleas: only a secure British alliance and co-operation with Austria over the Barrier along with a strengthening of the Republic's own military establishment could provide necessary protection in the future. Orangist ascendancy had usually been linked with periods of warfare, first against Spain and then against France after 1672. Successive Stadtholders had been the military leaders of the Republic and Bentinck intended that this should again be so. During the 1740s, when Dutch foreign policy once more sought neutrality in a European conflict, Bentinck pressed the idea of a restoration of the House of Orange not merely on leading Orangists but on the British government as well.[44] His thinking here coincided exactly with that of Newcastle, who believed that an Orangist restoration would restore the Republic to its rightful place in an anti-French alliance. Britain therefore supported the Revolution of 1747, orchestrated by Bentinck, which restored the Stadtholderate in the person of William IV.[45] British agents and British money assisted the restoration, which happened when sweeping French victories on the Republic's southern border menaced its neutrality, destroyed the Barrier and threatened further French conquest.

Bentinck's crucial role in the Dutch Revolution of 1747 made possible the Republic's revived role in British diplomacy.[46] But his contribution to the development of the Old System was far greater, if more elusive. The extent to which Newcastle appropriated other people's ideas is well established. William Bentinck, through his contribution to closer Anglo-Dutch co-operation, certainly assisted in the evolution of the doctrine of the Old System in the later 1740s. The two men met on several occasions at this time, particularly during Bentinck's visit to London in 1747; they corresponded freely on the political questions of the day and — remarkably enough — Newcastle sent his Dutch friend copies of British diplomatic documents.[47] Bentinck's precise role cannot be fixed with certainty. The Old System had roots in British as well as Dutch history and politics. But the Dutch statesman had considerable influence over Newcastle, and his ceaseless advocacy of Williamite ideas — which were already central to the duke's own thinking — was clearly part of the genesis of the Old System. It may even be — though the evidence is fragmentary — that either Bentinck or his close friend, the new *Greffier* Hendrik Fagel, also contributed to the adoption of the name now applied to these ideas by Newcastle.[48] The phrase 'Ancient System' or 'Old System' seems as firmly established in Dutch usage as in British, at least until the mid-point of the eighteenth century.[49]

The duke's adoption of the term 'old system' occurred in the summer of 1748. During the final stage of the peace negotiations he found it prudent to accompany George II on a visit to Hanover. Overcoming his celebrated fear of sea travel and his dislike of foreign places and strange beds, Newcastle set off for the Electorate. He stopped off at The Hague for talks with William Bentinck, the new Stadtholder William IV, other leading members of the Dutch government and the duke of Cumberland. The creation of a Grand Alliance dominated Newcastle's peacetime agenda and formed an important part of these discussions.[50] By that time he reached the Electorate, he had been converted wholeheartedly to the term 'old system'.[51] Indeed, Newcastle's extravagant use of the phrase in his correspondence from Hanover in that summer smacks of the zeal of the new convert, and his brother, Henry Pelham, found the usage novel.[52] The duke latched on to the phrase 'old system' and made it a synonym for 'grand alliance', and it is clear that he meant the same thing: an anti-French alliance, containing as many continental states as possible.[53]

Newcastle's conversion was assisted and encouraged by the influence of two other individuals with whom he had frequent discussions during that summer and over the next few years. The first was the leading Electoral minister G.A. von Münchhausen, whom he met for the first time in 1748.[54] Münchhausen was already devoted to the principles of the Old System and the two men quickly became political allies. His influence on the duke's foreign policy is established.[55] Hanoverian fear of the rising power of Prussia, when added to established anxieties about France, was one factor — and perhaps the predominant one — in convincing Newcastle that an Anglo-Russian alliance could protect the King's Electorate against Prussia and contribute to Britain's own security on the continent. What has not been noticed is Münchhausen's role in confirming and strengthening the duke's adherence to the Old System.[56] Both in correspondence and in conversations during Newcastle's visits to Hanover, the Electoral minister supported and, in some measure, advanced the ideas to which the duke was now devoted. The basic tenets of the Old System — opposition to France and support for Austria — were established principles of Hanoverian policy and they coincided exactly with Newcastle's aims: the close relationship with Münchhausen which developed after 1748, like that with William Bentinck, was self-reinforcing. Münchhausen's fear of the new power of Prussia, Hanover's immediate neighbour to the east and to the south west, was one reason for Newcastle's abandonment after 1748 of all idea of adding Frederick the Great to the Old System, though Anglo-Prussian relations were, in any case, notably poor at this point.

George II's role is less clear-cut, and he was certainly not a consistent supporter of Austria. In the longer term, however, he was usually hostile towards Versailles and friendly to Vienna, and he was certainly convinced of the value of the alliance of the Maritime Powers, which he had sought to uphold and reinvigorate, notably by marrying his eldest daughter to the leading member of the House of Orange. His precise influence on British foreign policy in general and on Newcastle in particular is uncertain, but it was clearly considerable.[57] After the Peace of Aix-la-Chapelle, Newcastle gradually became the minister of the closet as much as the cabinet: this was the source of Bedford's later charge that George II had turned the duke from an Englishman into a German.[58] He accompanied the King on several visits to Hanover, and his interventionist style of diplomacy, which promised alliances to defend Hanover, was more to royal taste than to that of some of his colleagues, above all his brother, Henry Pelham. Royal support was critical in securing the dismissal of the duke's rival, Bedford, in 1751, and the King's wishes would seem to have been a significant influence on Newcastle's foreign policy after 1748, confirming, though certainly not creating, the broad lines of Britain's diplomatic strategy.[59]

III

By the end of 1748, Newcastle's plans for Britain's future foreign policy had assumed their mature form. The influence of Münchhausen, George II and, in particular, William Bentinck had encouraged and developed the duke's own ideas into a coherent diplomatic strategy, now known as the Old System.[60] Its components had been familiar for decades, but they had been mobilised and given new coherence and direction at the end of the Austrian Succession War. Above all, the ideas had been given a novel and enduring label. Newcastle's remorseless advocacy made the Old System the central element in British foreign policy and gave it a life of its own. Some established notions, and the potent myth of the Grand Alliance, had come together to provide a clear purpose for Britain's diplomacy. This was now labelled the 'old system', which soon became a code for any anti-French alliance. 'System', in this context, was employed as a shorthand for a diplomatic alignment. It also conveyed the sense of a political combination which was ordered and proceeded according to rational principles rather than simply being another shifting alliance thrown up by the state of nature in which the European powers had always lived. This reflected the unusual coherence possessed by the idea of the Old System. Once the premise of hostility towards France was accepted, the logic of particular alliances was established and their conclusion seemingly pre-ordained, both in terms of previous history and present necessity. In a broader sense, the adoption of the word 'system' conveyed the more rational approach to international relations encouraged by the Scientific Revolution and early Enlightenment.

The phrase 'Old System' soon became securely established in British diplomatic documents, though only exclusively after 1756. For eight years after the Peace of Aix-la-Chapelle, 'Old System' or 'Ancient System' was the predominant usage, though ministers also spoke of the 'present system'. In negotiations designed to breathe new life into Britain's Austrian and Dutch alliances, it was essential to talk of 'present system' or 'Système actuel', to assert continuing obligations rather than admit that the alignments had already collapsed or were breaking down.[61] This was tactical, and the phrase 'Old System' was becoming a diplomatic commonplace during these years. It was universally employed after the spring of 1756 when, with the signature of the Franco-Austrian alliance, British ministers recognised that their own links with Vienna, like those of the Dutch, were no more.[62] Thereafter, 'Old System' was the established usage, sometimes simply abbreviated to the 'System', the 'True System' or the 'Great System'.

The full restoration of the Old System was Newcastle's aim between 1748 and 1756, when he effectively ran British foreign policy first as Northern Secretary and then (after Henry Pelham's death in 1754) as First Lord of the Treasury. This diplomatic strategy was pursued in partnership with Bentinck and Münchhausen, whom he met on his visits to Hanover. Though he was to be less influential after William IV's death in 1751, William Bentinck brought Dutch policy into step with that of Britain. There is a sense — not fully appreciated by British historians — in which after 1748 there was a common Anglo-Dutch foreign policy, inspired by the Old System:[63] Bentinck referred to this as 'our system' in letters to the duke and to Cumberland.[64] The objective of both Newcastle and Bentinck was the same: that of reviving and strengthening the alliance of Britain, the Republic and Austria. The means to this end were also identical: the King of the Romans scheme and negotiations to restore and, perhaps, re-define the Barrier in the Southern Netherlands, objectives which Bentinck himself pursued vigorously though unsuccessfully during a private mission to Vienna in 1749-50.[65] Britain's failure by the mid-1750s was the Republic's failure as well.

The objections to this grandiose strategy have been as obvious to historians as they were to Newcastle's more acute contemporaries. They were vividly formulated by Horatio Walpole in late 1751 when he wrote:

> I am no enemy to the former grand alliances; I am sensible they saved Europe and this country . . . Neither would I desert or disoblige those powers who joined so zealously and usefully with us in these grand alliances for the common cause. But the misfortune is, that the powers who composed those alliances are so reduced and exhausted as to be incapable of making the same vigorous efforts against France, now as formidable as ever.[66]

Walpole's familiar nostrum — an immediate Prussian alliance — gave point to his critique, but his charge cannot easily be rebutted. Newcastle's plans flew in the face both of the rapidly changing diplomatic alignments of the mid-eighteenth century and of adjustments in the relative standing of continental states.

The Old System was becoming an *idée fixe* of British foreign policy and of its director at exactly the point that its constituent elements were weakening and even dissolving. It is recognised that, whatever its earlier tensions (and these were considerable), the Anglo-Austrian alliance was breaking up in the 1740s and 1750s. The principal solvent was the rise of Prussia as a formidable rival to the Habsburgs in Germany and a more serious threat than France. This led to a fundamental realignment in Vienna's foreign policy which, under Kaunitz's direction, came to aim not at co-operation with Britain against France, but at a *rapprochement* with Versailles, secured in 1756. In a similar way, the feebleness of the Dutch Republic during the War of the Austrian Succession, even after the Revolution of 1747, made clear the extent of its decline to British observers. Relations with both Vienna and The Hague were thus being transformed at exactly the point that the Old System was acquiring definition. Yet this is not the paradox it may appear. Indeed, the very weakening of these historic links may itself have encouraged the concept's development, particularly against a background of poor relations with France. The Old System always rested less on present reality than on past history viewed through the gummy eyes of hindsight.

The Anglo-Dutch alliance was being further changed in the early years of peace in a way that strengthened Britain's devotion to the Old System. The return of the Stadtholderate in 1747 had superficially appeared to restore the traditional alliance, particularly as this office now became hereditary in the House of Orange. But William IV's early death in 1751, together with the fact that his son and successor was three years old, shattered such expectations. The problem was more acute because William IV's widow was George II's daughter, and family duty thus reinforced political obligation. The Republic's evident decline had created an unequal partnership, and the Stadtholder's death made this worse. Britain came to feel that she was the defender of the ascendancy of the House of Orange and of the continuation of the Stadtholderate, a logical extension of her role in the 1740s.[67] Here again William Bentinck's influence was considerable. Britain's new minister at The Hague, Joseph Yorke, who took up his post in 1751, was chosen after close consultation with Bentinck.[68] Yorke's detailed instructions envisaged that he would intervene, though not openly, in the Republic's domestic affairs[69] and this symbolised the increasingly one-sided nature of the Anglo-Dutch partnership, which now resembled Frederick the Great's famous simile of a Dutch cock-boat tied to an English man-of-war. There was a sense of historic obligation in Britain's acceptance of responsibility for the maintenance of Orangist rule.[70] The very choice of Yorke was itself significant, for he was the son of Lord Chancellor Hardwicke, Newcastle's great friend and political confidant. The new minister at The Hague was to become a particularly influential advocate of the Old System during the next generation.

Newcastle's diplomatic strategy after 1748 was inspired by the Old System as well as being expressed in its rhetoric.[71] Britain sought to rebuild and consolidate the fundamental alliances with The Hague and Vienna, and eventually aimed to add a secure alignment with Russia. The restoration of the Old System was to be achieved by means of the 'King of the Romans' scheme and the less familiar, though no less important, negotiations over the Barrier, which was viewed in London as 'the cement of the whole alliance'.[72] The attempt to elect Maria Theresa's eldest son, Joseph, 'King of the Romans' and therefore successor to his father as Holy Roman Emperor was intended to restore the flagging Austrian alliance and also to prevent any further challenge to the imperial succession itself, which Newcastle believed had diverted the Habsburgs during the 1740s from their more important function of fighting France. The duke's original scheme was unpromising and, after much futile diplomacy, it foundered on its own impracticality, Henry Pelham's reluctance to provide subsidies on the scale needed, Austria's half-hearted support and the opposition of France and Prussia. The extended discussions over the Barrier were equally unsuccessful. Newcastle and Bentinck believed that the ideas enshrined in the Barrier Treaty of 1715 were the very foundation of the Old System. Even before Saxe's victories in the final stages of the Austrian Succession War, the military vulnerability and political collapse of the Barrier system were becoming apparent. Anglo-Dutch efforts to rebuild this after 1748, and in particular to persuade Austria to shoulder the prime responsibility both in terms of money and men, foundered on Kaunitz's realism and on the new direction of Habsburg foreign policy. Since Prussia was now Austria's principal foe, the Barrier against France was an irrelevance, and the failure of Anglo-Dutch diplomacy had become evident by 1755.

The collapse of these discussions indicated that the Old System was rapidly ceasing to be practical politics. In 1755-56, Newcastle's grand design was totally destroyed. Though Britain finally secured Russian military support (Convention of St Petersburg, September 1755), this treaty was never ratified and was an immediate casualty of the Diplomatic Revolution. It was precipitated by an Anglo-Prussian agreement in January 1756 to neutralise Germany in a future Anglo-French war (Convention of Westminster). Kaunitz skilfully exploited this to secure the *rapprochement* with France which he had been pursuing unsuccessfully. The First Treaty of Versailles (1 May 1756) ended two-and-a-half centuries of rivalry and hostility between France and the Habsburgs and was the truly revolutionary component in the celebrated 'reversal of alliances'. The Seven Years' War which followed ranged Austria, Russia, France and Sweden against a loose partnership of Britain and Prussia.

The Diplomatic Revolution struck at the heart of the alignments upon which the Old System rested. Austria was now allied to France, and this *rapprochement* in its turn affected the Anglo-Dutch partnership. The Southern Netherlands were ruled by a French ally, rather than an enemy, and together with the Republic's evident weakness and growing commercial opportunism, this led it to remain neutral in the Seven Years' War. That conflict superficially appeared to be the death-knell of the Old System. The pattern of international relations upon which it was founded seemed to be destroyed forever by Pitt's war for empire and Frederick the Great's struggle for survival. The rise of Prussia and Russia to the front rank of European powers by 1763 transformed continental diplomacy. Since the later seventeenth century, this had usually been dominated by fear of French hegemony, but there were now five great powers whose rivalries were more complex, as were the possible diplomatic permutations. The very simple alignments on which the Old System had been based, and principally the rivalry between France and Austria, had disappeared. Yet in a curious way the Seven Years' War in Europe and overseas had the effect of vindicating the principles of the Old System. This was partly due to Britain's refusal to admit that the Diplomatic Revolution was a permanent change to the established political pattern. For decades to come, British observers were slow and even reluctant to acknowledge the transformation which had taken place. In a more fundamental sense, however, the fighting after 1756 emphatically confirmed the basic premise of the Old System: the need to fight France on the continent.

Britain's triumph in the Seven Years' War was based on a strategy which, in effect if not in intention, involved tying France down in Europe and defeating her overseas.[73] America, in Pitt's immortal formulation, had been conquered in Germany. He meant by this that while British resources had been concentrated on the war overseas after 1756, the effectiveness of this strategy had been due to France's residual commitments on the continent and to the role of Britain in sustaining Prussia and thus the European Seven Years' War. Britain's decisive victory owed much to factors over which the cabinet could exert little control: to Prussia's resilience, to Spain's neutrality until 1762 and to France's inability to break free totally from the continental war. But this did not reduce the importance of the successful British strategy. That strategy rested on principles adumbrated in the Old System. Pitt's celebrated ideas resembled Newcastle's muddy formulation of the strategic imperatives more closely than might be imagined. The duke gave a higher priority to the war in Germany, but this was a difference of emphasis. Pitt also saw the necessity of continental operations, both to divert France and to protect Hanover. In November 1761, Newcastle explicitly endorsed Pitt's celebrated remarks about conquering America in Germany.[74] However, the duke went on to argue that colonial conquests would also have to be defended on the banks of the Elbe. This was not merely a plea for the continuation of the 'German war', then coming under increasing attack, but was also an assertion of the need for continued diplomatic involvement on the continent once peace had been concluded. Newcastle believed that this was the principal lesson of the Seven Years' War. The duke had been genuinely alarmed by the threat of invasion in spring 1756. He believed that it was the consequence of the failure of his own diplomacy, which had left Britain isolated and vulnerable to French attack; as he wrote at this time, 'We are not singly a match for France'.[75] Alliances were therefore essential since, if France were not kept occupied in Europe, she would invade Britain and menace the Protestant succession itself.[76] Though Newcastle's wartime work at the Treasury and the increasing difficulties he encountered in raising loans made him doubt whether a protracted worldwide war could either be financed or won, his commitment to the continent was never seriously in question.

The Seven Years' War was — paradoxically — both the death-blow to the diplomatic alignments on which the Old System had been founded and a vindication of its basic principle: fighting France in Europe. Indeed, the costs of such continental operations were strikingly low after 1756 when compared to earlier wars. Precise figures are hard to find, but it seems as if the 'German war' never consumed more than 25 percent of Britain's annual expenditure during the conflict.[77] A subsidy of £670,000 for four years to Prussia and the considerably higher cost of the 'Army of Observation' in western Germany were the principal items in this expenditure, and the sums spent on the navy and the war overseas were far greater. This reversed the pattern in earlier periods of warfare when continental operations had been the principal outlay. The same reversal was apparent where manpower was concerned. British soldiers were sent to fight in the 'Army of Observation', but far fewer than in the wars of William III and Marlborough: in 1761, only 18,000 British soldiers were fighting in Westphalia, and this was the highest figure in the war.[78] Indeed, Newcastle advanced the startling proposition early in 1758 that 'money has always been looked upon as the proper and most effective contribution that England could make to a war upon the Continent'.[79] This may have accorded with the duke's own experiences during the 1740s and it underlines the formative impact of that decade on his thinking, but it would have amazed the Stadtholder-King and the Captain-General. Nevertheless, it remains true that, in terms of British soldiers and even British gold, the 'German war' provided value for money, despite the storm which it provoked after 1760.

It was one reason why Britain's partnership with Prussia during the Seven Years' War was justified and defended in terms reminiscent of the Old System.[80] Indeed, Prussia's Protestantism and the victories won by her armies made her a more attractive partner against Catholic France than Catholic Austria had ever been.[81] Newcastle, though certainly not reconciled to the loss of the traditional alliances with Vienna and The Hague,[82] accepted and defended co-operation with Prussia after 1756.[83] Support for any major continental state against France was coming to be seen as a validation of the Old System. Britain's dramatic victories overseas, however, exacerbated the familiar difficulties of peacemaking. For the same problem which had arisen in earlier conflicts — that of concluding a peace settlement satisfactory to her wartime partners — returned at the end of the Seven Years' War. Austria had considered herself abandoned in the field by the settlements concluded in 1697, 1713 and 1748; Prussia believed herself 'deserted' in 1762 and signed a separate peace at Hubertusburg the next year. The Seven Years' War thus followed the precedents of previous struggles against France more closely than might be imagined and — at one level — confirmed the basic principles of the Old System.[84]

The final year of that struggle saw a remarkable, though unsuccessful, attempt to revive the links with Vienna and The Hague. In the early months of 1762, George III, Bute and Newcastle were involved in a determined effort to restore the Austrian alliance and to rouse the Republic, but the Habsburgs would not abandon their French alliance nor the Dutch their neutrality.[85] The duke's participation proceeded from general and specific concerns. The signature of the Third Family Compact in August 1761 intensified all his ingrained fears of the 'united force of the two branches of the House of Bourbon',[86] while Spain's entry into the war early the next year was accompanied by a threatened invasion of Portugal, Britain's established ally and one to whom support would have to be sent. This in turn fuelled demands for an end to the 'German war', while it also increased the threat from France. Newcastle was concerned that withdrawal from Germany would hand over the continent to France, one of his recurring anxieties.[87] Once again, the figure of William Bentinck can be glimpsed in the background, advocating a restoration of the Old System even though he himself now had 'neither credit nor power in the Republic'.[88]

Newcastle's precise role in The Hague overtures remains unclear. He certainly ensured that the approach was made in the idiom of the Old System and embodied its aims. The language of the overtures to the Republic would seem to be entirely his work. An appeal was made 'to a remembrance and imitation of that glorious stand which she (*sic:* the Dutch Republic) formerly made in conjunction with England against the destructive ambition of the Bourbons', while the threat to 'the Protestant Religion, the Public Liberties of Europe, and the Independence of every particular state' was also proclaimed.[89] But there was more to it than rhetoric. Newcastle saw the rumours about Austrian dissatisfaction with France and the new Family Compact as an opportunity to restore the Old System, and even envisaged excluding Bourbon influence from Italy, which would then be partitioned between Austria and Savoy-Sardinia.[90] The Hague overtures demonstrate the duke's direct and indirect influence and reveal the extent to which the ideas of the Old System now shaped British diplomacy. Newcastle's distinctive approach was, by the early 1760s, becoming a central part of British thinking.

IV

During the two decades after the Seven Years' War, support for the Old System remained an important dimension of British foreign policy. Newcastle was soon to pass from the scene (the duke died in 1768), but the ideas which he had assembled and championed influenced diplomatic strategy throughout the age of the American Revolution and even beyond. British policy continued to be expressed in the language of the Old System, while both the general direction and particular objectives of official diplomacy were influenced by its ideals and expressed in its rhetoric for a generation to come. The persistence of such thinking primarily testified to the continuation and, indeed, intensification of Anglo-French rivalry, for the Old System was essentially a means of opposing France and her ally, Spain. The threat from France appeared more serious after the Seven Years'

War because of the existence of a firm Bourbon alliance, the Third Family Compact of 1761. The Spanish king, Charles III, was hostile towards Britain and, at least until the great confrontation over the Falklands in 1770-71, Bourbon unity was complete.

A clear majority of those responsible for the formulation and execution of British foreign policy between the 1760s and 1780s were supporters of the Old System.[91] They were headed by George III. The King was, perhaps, the most consistent influence on British diplomacy, and his support for the Old System, in which had been 'born and bred up', was unquestioned.[92] In 1763, he startled the new Austrian ambassador by urging its advantages at his first — and purely unofficial — audience, and this was a recurring royal theme in the years ahead.[93] The Earl of Sandwich, who as British plenipotentiary at Breda and Aix-la-Chapelle in 1746-48 had so alienated the Austrians, unsuccessfully sought new alliances with Vienna, The Hague and St Petersburg while he was Northern Secretary in 1763-65. His successor, H.S. Conway, was another celebrated supporter of a revived Austrian alliance, while the Austrophil Earl of Egmont left office in 1766 because of his opposition to Pitt's projected Prussian alliance. Sir Joseph Yorke, who served at The Hague from 1751 until the outbreak of the Fourth Anglo-Dutch War in 1780, never ceased to preach the virtues of the Old System and to urge its revival on his superiors. William Bentinck was now in political eclipse in the Republic, but even after the death of his old friend Newcastle he continued to advance its utility, corresponding with Grafton as late as 1769.[94] Suffolk, the influential Northern Secretary from 1771 to 1779, was an enthusiastic supporter of the Old System, which he actively sought to restore, while his successor, the career diplomat Lord Stormont, could declare in 1781 that he 'must plead guilty to the accusation, of being a man tainted from my earliest youth with Austrian principles; As such that is as a friend to the old and only true system'.[95]

The continuity of support from the Old System at the Northern Department, formally responsible for relations with Austria, Russia and the Dutch Republic, was particularly striking. Only the duke of Grafton and the Earl of Rochford, of all the ministers who held this post between 1763 and the creation of the Foreign Office in 1782, were other than enthusiastic supporters of a revived Austrian alliance, and both were prepared to pay lip-service to its restoration. More generally, control of British foreign policy for two decades after 1763 was exercised predominantly by advocates of the Old System: men who believed in the necessity of opposition to France and Spain and therefore in continental alliances, particularly with Vienna and St Petersburg. The only important supporters of renewed links with Prussia were Pitt, his disciple, the Earl of Shelburne, and Charles James Fox, while in unusual circumstances in 1778 both Suffolk and George III were prepared for a reconciliation with Frederick the Great. In the early 1770s the King, briefly, and Rochford, more consistently, were anxious for a *rapprochement* and even an alliance with France. Better relations with the Bourbons were also sought by the duke of Bedford in the 1760s, while one aim of Shelburne's conduct of the peace negotiations in 1782-3 was eventual co-operation with France. These were exceptions to the rule. British diplomacy usually embodied the doctrines of the Old System during the age of the American Revolution. In three distinct ways its ideas were reflected in official policy: in the enduring concern with the Barrier, in the search for alliances and in the particular strategies pursued towards Austria and the Dutch Republic. There was, of course, far more to British diplomacy after 1763 than the Old System, but many of its assumptions and aims were rooted in ideas championed by Newcastle.

This was particularly evident where the Barrier in the Southern Netherlands was concerned. This had been destroyed by the Diplomatic Revolution, but for the next quarter-century British ministers believed otherwise.[96] During the 1760s joint Anglo-Dutch negotiations took place at Vienna in a futile attempt to persuade Austria to reinforce her garrisons there, while as late as 1774 Suffolk referred to the need to maintain a military barrier in the Southern Netherlands in order to protect the Republic.[97] The security of this area against France was an enduring British and Dutch preoccupation and the Republic's troops remained in the forts in the Southern Netherlands. Yet the continuing concern with the Barrier was rooted in an earlier epoch and was principally a legacy of Newcastle's dominance.

This was even more true where Britain's search for alliances was concerned. This directly reflected the ideas of the Old System and was conducted in its language and based on its assumptions.[98] One main theme of British diplomacy throughout the age of the American Revolution was a protracted but unsuccessful search for one or more allies on the continent, to supplement the existing links with the faded powers of Portugal and the Dutch Republic. Negotiations with Russia continued intermittently for a decade after 1763 and were renewed during the War of American Independence; formal bids were made for the Austrian alliance in 1763-64 and 1780-81, and throughout these decades official policy was based on the premise that the centrepiece of the Old System would one day be restored and sought to achieve this; while brief attempts were also made to secure a treaty with Prussia in 1766, 1778 and 1782. These sustained efforts were in themselves unusual, though not unique. Indeed, previous British practice over peacetime alliances was more ambiguous than was realised during the 1760s and 1770s. Ministers believed that alliances in peace had always been pursued, but this principally reflected Newcastle's decisive influence.

During the two generations after 1688 Britain had sought and concluded such alliances, but these were not as regular or as frequent as was generally assumed after the Seven Years' War. The efforts to secure peacetime allies during the decade after 1763 primarily reflected Newcastle's attempt to conclude new treaties after 1748 and the way in which his ideas became central tenets of British policy. The search for allies was less traditional than ministers realised and is to be explained by their adherence to the doctrines of the Old System.

This is particularly evident where relations with Austria were concerned. The search for a revived alliance with the Habsburgs was usually an aim of British diplomacy during the quarter-century after 1763, and several efforts were undertaken to achieve this end. This in itself is surprising, given the firm, if polite, rejection which British overtures invariably received at Vienna and the apparent stability of the 'friendship between the elephant (Austria) and rhinoceros (France)', the Habsburg-Bourbon alliance of 1756.[99] Nominally this remained in operation until 1792, though in the 1780s it probably existed only on paper since the Russian alliance was the foundation of Austrian foreign policy after its conclusion in 1781. Good relations with Britain were sought by Austria because these could contribute to the broader objectives of Habsburg foreign policy and particularly its desire for continued peace. But it was improbable that Vienna would ever return willingly to the discredited English alliance. At most, there was a possibility that a further reversal of alliances might force a *rapprochement* with London as the alternative to diplomatic isolation.

Britain's pursuit of the mirage of Austria arose mainly from the lack of obvious alternatives. The celebrated and acrimonious break-up of the wartime partnership in 1762 poisoned Anglo-Prussian relations for a generation; while the Russian alliance proved elusive and was, in any case, viewed as an addition rather than as an alternative to Vienna. But the assumptions of Anglo-Austrian diplomacy remained those established by Newcastle.[100] In two distinct ways, the duke's ideas were central to Britain's Austrian policy at least until the 1780s. The first was the avowed nostalgia for an earlier golden age in relations. In fact, the previous history of co-operation had been a chequered one. The exigencies of the struggle against their common enemy, France, had led to several wartime alliances. Such co-operation seldom survived the conflict which produced it, and on three occasions Britain had abandoned her ally by concluding a separate peace. Yet the rhetoric which Newcastle had lavished on the Habsburgs had helped to transmute the 'Allies of Convenience' into Britain's 'natural and traditional ally'. The assumptions behind British policy at Vienna down to the 1780s were exactly those of Newcastle, whose reaction to the First Treaty of Versailles had been to pronounce it 'unnatural' and to prophesy its early demise. The passage of time, and the apparent stability of the Franco-Austrian Alliance, weakened but did not destroy such thinking: British realism took the form of admitting that the restoration of the Old System would be a longer process than at first anticipated, rather than acknowledging that its revival was intrinsically improbable.

Here, too, Newcastle made a decisive contribution to enduring Austrophilia. The duke was inclined to explain Britain's loss of the alliance primarily and even exclusively in terms of the malign influence of Kaunitz. This distrust went back to the Austrian minister's conduct when plenipotentiary at Breda and Aix-la-Chapelle and intensified after 1748, when he became the leading proponent of a *rapprochement* with France and then the architect of the Diplomatic Revolution. Believing that the Anglo-Austrian alliance was natural and even pre-ordained, Newcastle reacted to its final collapse in 1756 by pouring all the blame on Kaunitz. This was accompanied by an exaggerated insistence on the support for the English alliance at Vienna. These two beliefs were carried forward into British policy after the Seven Years' War. They came to be accompanied by an expectation that Joseph II would one day be the agent of a revival of the Anglo-Austrian alliance. It, too, built on ideas which had become ingrained during Newcastle's supremacy. Joseph's father, the Emperor Francis Stephen, filled a place in British thinking before the Seven Years' War similar to that which his son was to occupy during the late 1760s and the 1770s. Francis Stephen had been duke of Lorraine before he became Habsburg Emperor and he never forgave the French for evicting him from his beloved duchy at the end of the 1730s. This made him a supporter of the English alliance — and of Austria's own 'old system' — which he championed during the crucial Conference debates in 1749.[101] It was assumed after his death in 1765 that his son, Joseph, was of similar mind and would restore the 'old and natural system' when he secured full authority in Vienna. This was a serious miscalculation and was shown to be unfounded in 1780-81 when the Emperor rejected the offer of a British alliance early in his personal rule. But this assumption guided British diplomacy at Vienna for over a decade. The language in which British policy was conducted was also that of the Old System: common cause, liberties of Europe, and so on and so forth. Such rhetoric had little meaning for Habsburg observers: 'grosse aber leere Worte' was the dismissive verdict of an exasperated Kaunitz.[102]

Such continuities in language and in basic perceptions were also strikingly apparent in Anglo-Dutch diplomacy.[103] The Republic's evident weakness and neutralism made Anglo-Dutch relations a dark corner of British diplomacy for a dozen years after 1763. In the early months of peace, Sandwich had made an ill-fated attempt to renew the Anglo-Dutch treaties (as has usually been done at the beginning of a new reign), but thereafter relations passed into cold storage. The principles of the alliance were sustained by the influential Yorke from The Hague, and they re-emerged in the quite different situation created by the American colonial rebellion after 1775.[104] This immediately revived Britain's need for support. The political, military and economic weakness of the Republic by the 1770s was apparent to London and it was not expected that the Dutch would now provide either the men or the money specified in earlier treaties. But Britain did expect Dutch aid in her campaign, first to deny the colonists a chance to trade, and then to prevent naval stores being shipped to France in neutral Dutch ships after the Anglo-French war began in 1778.

British requests for such assistance were couched in the language and based on the assumptions of an earlier period. Here again the duke of Newcastle was the link — and also a distorting mirror — between the age of William III and that of William V. From the mid-point of the eighteenth century, ministers believed that the Republic had become a client and dependant of Britain and the ruling House of Orange the agents of their political control. Britain's experiences after 1775, and particularly after 1778, proved very different from her expectations. At first, the Republic was willing to prohibit munitions exports to America. These prohibitions, however, could not always be easily enforced, while the Dutch government also responded to a British request for the loan of the legendary 'Scots Brigade' by prescribing terms which amounted to a refusal. Problems increased after 1778, when the Anglo-French war revived the familiar and sometimes acute problems over neutral commerce. Tension increased sharply in 1779-80, and at the end of that year Britain declared war on the Dutch Republic.

The Fourth Anglo-Dutch War was not caused solely — or even principally — by the serious clashes over wartime commerce created by the American and European conflicts. It was, rather, a desperate attempt to restore the Anglo-Dutch alliance, which Britain believed had been destroyed by Dutch conduct since 1775, and with it British control over the Republic, objectives that were based upon the Old System. Central to this stategy was the position of the House of Orange. The American War had highlighted the growing weakness of William V's *régime,* both against its traditional Regent opponents and, increasingly, against the new political force of the Patriots, who challenged the oligarchical basis of Dutch political life. Though the Orangist government was disposed to follow a mildly pro-English policy and itself supported the Old System, it was unable and occasionally even unwilling to enforce British demands within the Republic. Britain's belief that the alliance had broken down by the mid-point of the American War was the origin of a startling change in London's strategy, albeit one that sought to restore the Old System. Under the influence of Yorke, the ambassador at The Hague, and with the support of the new Northern Secretary, Stormont, British policy came to be directed primarily by a desire to restore the authority of the Orangist *régime* and with it Britain's control over Dutch policy.[105] Believing that a foreign war had usually increased the stadtholder's authority and had twice — in 1672 and 1747 — brought about an Orange restoration, Britain declared war at the very end of 1780 with the aim of reviving William V's crumbling authority. The principal divergence from historical precedent — and an important one — was that hitherto such wars had been principally against France, but the new conflict was to be with Britain alone.

The result was the opposite of what Britain wanted. William V's domestic difficulties were exacerbated rather than resolved by the Fourth Anglo-Dutch War of 1780-84. Nevertheless, it remains true that this conflict, far from being the end of a century of co-operation that had been one foundation of the Old System, was in intention a desperate attempt to restore the Anglo-Dutch alliance and the principles on which it had rested since the mid-eighteenth century.

V

It seems clear that the Old System was a more direct influence on British policy after the outbreak of war with France in 1778 and Spain's entry the next year. Its ideas inspired the attempt to shore up William V's government and thereby revive the Anglo-Dutch alliance through a war with the Republic. They contributed to the bid for the Austrian alliance in 1780-81 and, more generally, to the efforts to secure allies against the Bourbons: Russian support was sought — unavailingly — on several occasions in terms of the French threat to the liberties of Europe. This provides one important key to the persistence of Williamite ideas, as filtered and distorted by Newcastle. The Old System was a means of opposing and defeating France by means of alliances on the continent, and the need for such opposition appeared clearer than ever after the Seven Years' War.

When viewed from London, the threat from France and Spain was considerable and potentially very serious after 1763, and it was perfectly natural for British statesmen to seek to counter it in the familiar way by securing continental allies. The problem was that such rivalry was no longer the dominant political concern of all Europe. Newcastle's diplomacy after 1748 had foundered on Austro-Prussian rivalry and, to a lesser extent, on Russia's new ambitions. These two developments accelerated during and after the Seven Years' War, and together undermined the Old System as a practical diplomatic alignment. It had always depended on an actual or imaginary threat of French hegemony, but such a spectre had disappeared by 1763. The continental Seven Years' War had been the first major European conflict since the mid-seventeenth century (with the sole exception of the Great Northern War of 1700-21) which had not primarily concerned France's power and her place in Europe. The principal foundation of that power, the French army, now seemed far less menacing. The shattering defeat by Prussia at Rossbach (November 1757) destroyed France's military reputation for a generation. Simultaneously, France's strategic priorities were becoming more exclusively colonial, as the struggle with Britain became her principal strategic concern. After 1763 French policy, in Choiseul's capable hands, came to aim primarily at neutralising the continent during any future Anglo-French conflict, and this was actually achieved by Vergennes during the American War.

France's reduced status and her changed objectives made it very difficult for Britain to build an alliance system on the spectre of French power. Talk of a threat to the 'liberties of Europe' or the 'balance of power' had a particularly hollow ring after 1763, at the end of a war when France had been so decisively defeated both on the continent and overseas and when Britain's own conduct had seemed, in some respects, a greater threat. Indeed, if any state threatened to become preponderant after the Seven Years' War it was Britain herself, now 'the terror of Europe' as Charles Jenkinson told the Commons in January 1771.[106] The resulting problems were occasionally glimpsed, but their implications were never fully realised, far less integrated into official policy.[107] Britain's rivalry with France continued and had even increased, and to British ministers and diplomats this suggested the enduring validity of the Old System. But that same system had been undermined by the new international situation. The changes in European diplomacy in the mid-eighteenth century removed the fear of French hegemony and with it Britain's ability to manipulate continental alignments in her own interest. This is part of the larger problem of the failure of British diplomacy to adjust to the new international realities of the 1760s and 1770s, a failure which is much clearer with hindsight than it was at the time. The persistence of the ideas encapsulated in the Old System was both a cause and a consequence of the outdated thinking behind British policy throughout the age of the American Revolution.

The continued threat from the Bourbons and the assumption that France still posed a direct military threat to the Low Countries and to Hanover were obvious reasons for the Old System's persistence. Two further explanations can be suggested. The first is an argument about the men who controlled foreign policy and the impact of their background and political education. Many and probably most of the men who conducted Britain's diplomacy after the Seven Years' War had grown up during the acute phase of Anglo-Bourbon rivalry between 1739 and 1763, and had been in the military or diplomatic front line against France and Spain.[108] H.S. Conway, Secretary of State in the mid-1760s, had a distinguished military career. Sandwich, Stormont and the influential Yorke had all occupied their first diplomatic posts during the 1740s and 1750s. All three men had owed their appointments partly to Newcastle's influence, and the duke's distinctive ideas had contributed to their political education. This was particularly true of Sandwich, who had handled the peace negotiations at the end of the Austrian Succession War, and Yorke, sent to the Dutch Republic to consolidate and uphold the traditional alliance after earlier military service against French armies on the continent. Such men had been exposed, at first or second hand, to the central tenets of the Old System: military operations and continental alliances against France, at a time when the threat of French hegemony was still very real. They thought naturally in terms of Anglo-Bourbon rivalry, and assumed this should be pursued by an anti-French alliance system as well as by a strong navy.

The enduring appeal of the Old System was partly a product of political generations. But its ideas were also transmitted in a rather different way. The survival of Williamite thinking came about through administrative routine. Particularly during the 1760s, Secretaries of State came and went with some frequency, and for the incomers — who often lacked experience and even knowledge of foreign affairs — an obvious guide was the abundant previous despatches kept in their offices. It is clear that the more conscientious of British diplomats prepared for their missions by reading the relevant previous correspondence, and it seems likely that some of their superiors did so too. The formal instructions and orders given to British ambassadors frequently echoed or even repeated those given years or even decades before. Such continuity was, at one level, useful and necessary. Bureaucratic conservatism and inertia may be part of the explanation, producing a simple reiteration of phrases and formulae with scant regard for changing external circumstances. Yet there is more to it than this. A sustained reading of British diplomatic correspondence from the 1760s (and even earlier) to the 1780s reveals the persistence of outdated thinking about foreign policy. The persistence of a set of ideas and assumptions established in an earlier, rather different, age was one source of the problems Britain's foreign policy encountered after the Seven Years' War. It was principally the result of Newcastle's sustained and successful advocacy of the ideas of the Old System and his habitual use of its rhetoric during the two decades after 1744.

The Russian foreign minister, Nikita Panin, remarked on one occasion to the British ambassador, Cathcart, that 'by endeavouring to patch and mend old Projects (Britain) had lost sight of the present state and connections of the Powers of Europe', with consequent problems for her foreign policy.[109] His arguments have a more general validity. The kind of mental rigidity and static thinking which was one dimension — but only one — of British diplomacy in the second half of the eighteenth century and of which the Old System was the most glaring example, was peculiarly, but not uniquely, British. There was a sense in which all foreign policies were likely to have a retrospective dimension. Diplomatic strategies would be influenced and even determined as much by precedent, by a recollection of what had happened in the past, as by the realities of the present international situation or an assessment of future probabilities. In a similar way, mid-eighteenth century British policy was certainly far from unique in labouring under the oppressive weight of the past. Much the same could be written on how eighteenth-century French foreign policy was shaped — and even wrecked — by the traditions and precepts of the age of Louis XIV. But British foreign policy was unusual for the extent and importance of such continuities. The Old System was a far more direct and potent influence on Britain's diplomacy than the Sun King's shadow upon France. It constitutes an essential dimension of British foreign policy from the later 1740s to the 1780s, and was principally a delayed and unappreciated legacy of the old duke of Newcastle.

NOTES

1. I am grateful to G.C. Gibbs, Derek McKay and the editor of this volume for their helpful comments on a draft of this chapter.

2. Quoted by R.E. Abarca, 'Bourbon "revanche" against England: the balance of power 1763-70' (unpublished Ph.D. thesis, University of Notre Dame, 1965), 14.

3. Quoted by Richard Pares, 'American versus continental warfare 1739-63', in *The historian's business and other essays* (Oxford, 1961), 130-72, at p. 138. This article is fundamental for the strategic context within which the concept of the Old System took shape.

4. *Ibid.*, 132.

5. *The Correspondence of King George III from 1760 to December 1783*, ed. Sir John Fortescue (6 vols.,London, 1927-28), ii. 204.

6. This was particularly emphasised by the leading Hanoverian minister, G.A. von Münchhausen, a firm supporter of the Old System. See his views in October 1756: Uriel Dann, *Hannover und England 1740-1760: Diplomatie and Selbsterhaltung* (Hildesheim, 1986), 123. By the mid-eighteenth century, the Personal Union itself was believed to depend on the maintenance of the Old System: Hermann Wellenreuther, 'Die Bedeutung des Siebenjährigen Krieges für die englisch-hannoveranischen Beziehungen', in *England und Hannover/England and Hanover*, eds. A.M. Birke and K. Kluxen (Munich and London, 1986), 145-74, esp. p. 171. For the assumptions which long underlay co-operation with the Habsburgs, see Derek McKay, *Allies of convenience: diplomatic relations between Great Britain and Austria 1714-1719* (New York, 1986), and Jeremy Black, 'When "natural allies " fall out: Anglo-Austrian relations, 1725-1740', *Mitteilungen des Österreichischen Staatsarchivs*, 36 (1983), 120-49.

7. Newcastle to Bentinck, 8 June 1762, BL Add 32939, fo. 224.

8. Hugh Dunthorne, *The Maritime Powers 1721-40: a study of Anglo-Dutch relations in the age of Walpole* (New York, 1986), 9-10.

9. E.g. Newcastle's 'Considerations, relating to the present situation of affairs', 5 Jan. 1762, BL Add 32999, fo. 363.

10. BL Add 32931, fo. 234.

11. For example, the Flemish nobleman, the duc d'Ursel, in 1727: Jeremy Black, 'When "natural allies" fall out', *Mitteilungen des Österreichischen Staatsarchivs*, 36 (1983), 120-49, at p. 142.

12. P.C. Yorke, *The life and correspondence of Philip Yorke, Earl of Hardwicke* (3 vols., Cambridge, 1913), i. 679-80, ii. 13.

13. Jeremy Black, *Natural and necessary enemies: Anglo-French relations in the eighteenth century* (London, 1986), 56.

14. In summer 1763, Newcastle declared that 'a proper connection with the Continent' had been made impossible by the 'Tory principles' which then prevailed: to Devonshire, 20 July 1763, BL Add 32949, fos. 381-2. This distinction between 'Whig' and 'Tory' approaches is necessarily imprecise: the Whigs when in power had pursued what is arguably a 'Tory' foreign policy between 1716 and 1731.

15. S.B. Baxter, 'The myth of the Grand Alliance in the eighteenth century', in *Anglo-Dutch cross currents in the seventeenth and eighteenth centuries*, eds. P.R. Sellin and S.B. Baxter (Los Angeles, 1976), 43-59.

16. Newcastle had been born in 1693; Hardwicke in 1690; George II in 1683; Henry Pelham in 1696.

17. Baxter, 'Myth of the Grand Alliance', 44-6.

18. The standard biography is Reed Browning, *The Duke of Newcastle* (New Haven, Conn., 1975).

19. Jeremy Black, 'British foreign policy in the eighteenth century: a survey', *Journal of British Studies*, 26 (1987), 26-53, at pp. 50-1; Browning, *Newcastle*, 144-5.

20. William Coxe, *Memoirs of the administration of the Rt. Hon. Henry Pelham* (2 vols., London, 1829), i. 175.

21. Yorke, *Hardwicke*, i. 369.

22. Newcastle subsequently referred to 'the late danger, that England and all Europe were in of being swallowed up by the superiority of the arms of France and Prussia': to Hardwicke, 17 Nov. 1748, printed in *Archives ou Correspondance inédite de la Maison d'Orange-Nassau*, 4th series, ed. Th. Bussemaker (3 vols. and Supplement, Leyden, 1908-17), i. 193.

23. See, e.g., the duke's 'Draft of a paper relating to the State of the War', 1 Nov. 1744, printed in Yorke, *Hardwicke*, i. 332-5.

24. Browning, *Newcastle*, 132-3.

25. Newcastle to Carteret, 31 May 1743, printed in Coxe, *Pelham administration*, i. 74.

26. Quoted in Yorke, *Hardwicke*, i. 296.

27. Quoted in *New Cambridge Modern History, vii: The Old Regime*, ed. J.O. Lindsay (Cambridge, 1957), 440. Cf. D.B. Horn, 'The Duke of Newcastle and the origins of the Diplomatic Revolution', in *The diversity of history: essays in honour of Sir Herbert Butterfield*, eds. J.H. Elliott and H.G. Koenigsberger (London, 1970), 245-68, at pp. 247-8.

28. Quoted by Black, 'British foreign policy in the eighteenth century', 51. Hardwicke believed that the Alliance of Hanover was 'the fundamental source of all the mischief': Yorke, *Hardwicke*, ii. 30.

29. Jeremy Black, *British foreign policy in the age of Walpole* (Edinburgh, 1985), 58, 178.

30. Jeremy Black, 'British neutrality in the War of the Polish Succession, 1733-1735', *International History Review*, 8 (1986), 345-66, at pp. 358, 361.

31. See Yorke, *Hardwicke,* i. 318-19, for the duke's long retrospect on the disasters of the early 1740s, drawn up in October 1743.

32. Coxe, *Pelham administration,* i. 20.

33. Yorke, *Hardwicke,* i. 268.

34. E.g. *ibid.,* i. 259, 260, 269; cf. his view in 1749 that support to Austria on Charles VI's death might have avoided or at least reduced many of Britain's problems during the 1740s: *ibid.,* ii. 23.

35. Quoted by Pares, 'American versus continental warfare', 134.

36. Yorke, *Hardwicke,* i. 679.

37. This generalisation is based on an extensive reading of such of Newcastle's correspondence as is in print, and some work in the voluminous unpublished papers; but it may be undermined by further work on the manuscript material.

38. Browning, *Newcastle,* 177.

39. See the comments of the Prussian resident when he died in 1774: *Dépêches van Thulemeyer 1763-1788,* ed. H.T. Colenbrander (Amsterdam, 1912), 133.

40. H. Dunthorne, 'Prince and Republic: the House of Orange in Dutch and Anglo-Dutch politics during the first half of the eighteenth century', *Studies in History and Politics,* 4 (1985), 28-9; A.C. Carter, *The Dutch Republic in Europe in the Seven Years War* (London, 1971), xiv, 12, 27. On William Bentinck and his brother, Charles, see more generally *Briefwisseling en Aanteekeningen van Willem Bentinck, Heer van Rhoon (tot aan de Dood van Willem IV 22 October 1751),* eds. C. Gerretson and P. Geyl, vol.I (Utrecht, 1934).

41. Margaret C. Jacob, 'In the aftermath of revolution: Rousset de Missy, Freemasonry and Locke's "Two Treatises of Government" ' in *L'età dei Lumi: studi storici sul settecento europeo in onore di Franco Venturi* (2 vols., Naples, 1985), i. 492-3, 500. Yorke subsequently described the supporters of the Old System in the Republic as 'the old Dutch Whigs': to Newcastle, 9 Mar. 1762, BL Add 32935, fo. 254.

42. *Briefwisseling en Aanteekeningen,* 130; cf. 123, 145.

43. As it was for William Bentinck and for the old *Greffier* (secretary to the States-General) Fagel who, when he retired in 1744, had been in this important office for over fifty years and provided a personal link with the Stadtholder-King: *ibid.,* 8-9, 25, 51, 59-60, 116, 145, 152, 201. François Fagel and his nephew, Hendrik Fagel, who succeeded his uncle as *Greffier,* were clearly important influences on Bentinck's outlook and political education.

44. In late January 1744 he sent a long memorandum on this subject to Carteret and he continued to press this idea: *ibid.,* 76-83, 84-90.

45. Dunthorne, 'Prince and Republic', 29-30.

46. For Newcastle's real enthusiasm at this change, see *Archives . . . Orange-Nassau,* 4th series, i. 61-2.

47. *Ibid.,* 4th series, i. viii; ii. 152.

48. *Correspondence of John, Fourth Duke of Bedford,* ed. Lord John Russell (3 vols., London, 1842-46), i. 380.

49. In November 1747, e.g., Bentinck referred in a letter to the duke to 'the true system . . . that of King William': *Briefwisseling en Aanteekeningen,* 310.

50. See the 'Points to be considered with the duke of Cumberland and the prince of Orange', The Hague, 28 June 1748, summarised in Coxe, *Pelham administration,* i. 427.

51. Newcastle to Henry Pelham, 10 July 1748, printed in *ibid.,* i. 431.

52. The duke's letter to his brother of 14 July 1748, printed in *ibid.,* i. 438, speaks of the *'old and great system'* twice in successive sentences and then of the 'old system' in the next; Pelham's surprise can be glimpsed on his letter of 18 July 1748, *ibid.,* i. 434. On the 26th, Hardwicke wrote discreetly commenting that 'It has been observed that Your Grace repeats

over and over *the old system*': to Newcastle, 26 July 1748, printed in Yorke, *Hardwicke*, i. 659; *Bedford Corr.*, i. 406; Newcastle to Robert Keith, 29 Aug. 1748, PRO SP 80/181, fo. 20.

53. This is clear from Newcastle to Henry Pelham, 14 July 1748, Coxe, *Pelham administration*, i. 438-9.

54. Dann, *Hannover und England*, 89-91.

55. W. Mediger, 'Great Britain, Hanover and the rise of Prussia', in *Studies in diplomatic history: essays in memory of David Bayne Horn*, eds. Ragnhild Hatton and M.S. Anderson (London, 1970), 199-213, and, more generally, W. Mediger, *Moskaus Weg nach Europa* (Brunswick, 1952).

56. For the partnership between the two men after 1748, see Dann, *Hannover und England*, 96-120.

57. Cf. Black, *British foreign policy*, 35-45.

58. R.R. Sedgwick, ed., *Letters from George III to Lord Bute 1756-1766* (London, 1939), 109. Immediately after 1748, Bedford enjoyed real favour, but he was eclipsed by Newcastle, and here again the duke's visits to Germany with the King were crucial.

59. Another influence on the duke at ths time may have been George II's son, the duke of Cumberland. Newcastle was clearly consulting him on political questions, both in the final stages of the Austrian Succession War and in the early years of peace, but more research is needed to establish his precise influence.

60. The best statement of this is Newcastle to Hardwicke, 17 Nov. 1748, printed in *Archives . . . Orange-Nassau*, 4th series, i. 190-5.

61. For example of this usage, see Yorke, *Hardwicke*, ii. 33; Coxe, *Pelham administration*, ii. 443; Newcastle to Kaunitz, 19 Jan. 1753, BL Add 32842, fo. 189.

62. E.g. Newcastle to Yorke, Very Private, 11 Jun. 1756, ibid., 32865, fos. 257-8.

63. This is clear from the documents in *Archives . . . Orange-Nassau*, 4th series, i-ii, *passim*.

64. E.g. *Bedford Corr.* i. 469, 474.

65. For this, see: *Aufzeichnungen des Grafen William Bentinck über Maria Theresia*, ed. A. Beer (Vienna, 1871).

66. 'Observations upon the present System of Foreign Affairs', November 1751, printed in William Coxe, *Memoirs of Horatio, Lord Walpole* (London, 1802 ed.), 386-96, at p. 392.

67. Dunthorne, 'Prince and Republic', 31-2.

68. Newcastle to W. Bentinck, Very Private, 9 Dec. 1751, BL Add 32832., fo. 21.

69. In PRO SP 84/458: see, in particular, the 'Private and very secret Instructions', 2 Dec. 1751.

70. E.g. Newcastle to W. Bentinck, Very Private, 9 Dec. 1751, BL Add 32832, fo. 24; cf. PRO SP 84/426, fo. 41.

71. Cf. Horn, 'The Duke of Newcastle', 252.

72. Holdernesse to Yorke, Most Secret, 23 Dec. 1755, PRO SP 84/471; cf. the 'Instructions' for Solomon Dayrolle, 7 Mar. 1752, SP 77/88, fo. 7.

73. The latest study, which modifies the traditional view in some important respects, is Richard Middleton, *The Bells of Victory: the Pitt-Newcastle Ministry and the conduct of the Seven Years' War 1757-1762* (Cambridge, 1985).

74. Newcastle to Hardwicke, 15 Nov. 1761, BL Add 32931, fos. 46-7; ibid., 32919, fo. 133.

75. Quoted by Browning, *Newcastle*, 232.

76. The threat of invasion was also worrying Newcastle in August 1761, as a Franco-Spanish alliance was on the point of being signed: 'Some hasty thoughts upon the French answer', 7 Aug. 1761, BL Add 32926 fo. 279.

77. This is suggested by the figures in Browning, *Newcastle*, 276.

78. Sir Reginald Savory, *His Britannic Majesty's army in Germany during the Seven Years War* (Oxford, 1966), 311.

79. Quoted by Middleton, *The Bells of Victory*, 60.

80. Manfred Schlenke, *England und das friderizianische Preussen 1740-1763* (Munich, 1963), 218-25.

81. As Newcastle immediately noted: to Yorke, Very Private, 11 June 1756, BL Add 32865, fos. 257-66.

82. E.g. Newcastle to Hardwicke, 1 Aug. 1761, ibid. 32926, fos. 126, 128.

83. Newcastle to W. Bentinck, 10 Feb. 1756, ibid. 32862, fo. 434; P.F. Doran, *Andrew Mitchell and Anglo-Prussian diplomatic relations during the Seven Years War* (New York, 1986), 34, 51.

84. See Newcastle's comments in early 1762: to Yorke, 8 Jan. 1762, BL Add 32933, fos. 112-18.

85. There is a scrupulous account of these initiatives which corrects some established errors by K.W. Schweizer, 'Lord Bute, Newcastle, Prussia and the Hague Overtures: a re-examination', *Albion*, 9 (1977), 72-97. I believe that the approach to the Republic was slightly more important than is there suggested and Newcastle's role rather greater. The key figure may be neither Bute nor Newcastle, but George III.

86. BL Add 32933, fo. 298; cf. ibid. 32999, fo. 368 (7 Jan. 1762). This makes clear that Newcastle at least was thinking in terms of a much wider alliance system, extending to Russia, the Savoyard state and even other powers. His hopes of Russia were encouraged by the death of the Empress Elizabeth early in 1762: ibid. 32934, fo. 66.

87. Newcastle to Yorke, 8 Jan. 1762, ibid. 32933, fo. 113; same to same, 16/17 Nov. 1761, ibid. 32931, fo. 60.

88. Yorke to Hardwicke, 8 Sept. 1761, ibid. 35358, fos. 203-4; Bentinck to Newcastle, 9 Dec 1761, ibid. 32932, fos. 70-1.

89. Bute to Yorke, Most Secret, 12 Jan. 1762, PRO SP 84/495. Neither of these phrases was in the draft of this despatch and they indicate his direct influence: Bute to Newcastle, 7 Jan. 1762, enclosing a copy of Bute to Yorke, 8 Jan. 1762, BL Add 32933, fos. 80-1, 82-3.

90. Newcastle to Yorke, 15 Jan. 1762, ibid. 32933, fo. 299; cf. same to same, 8 Jan. 1762, ibid., fo. 116.

91. For all aspects of Britain's diplomacy after the Seven Years' War, see H.M. Scott, *British foreign policy in the age of the American Revolution* (forthcoming).

92. George III to Stormont, 12 Nov. 1780, Stormont Papers, Scone Palace, Perthshire, Box 16. I am grateful to the Earl of Mansfield for permission to consult and cite these papers. For the King's belief that the career of William III should be an exemplar, see *The Grenville Papers*, ed. W.J. Smith (4 vols., London, 1852-53), ii. 533.

93. Seilern to Kaunitz, 31 Oct. 1763, Österreichische Staatsarchiv (Vienna), Abteilung Haus-, Hof-, und Staatsarchiv, England — Korrespondenz 110. Several British ministers subsequently echoed the King's arguments in conversations with the new ambassador: 8 Nov. 1763, ibid.

94. 8 Sept. 1769, Grafton Papers, West Suffolk Record Office, no. 320. I am grateful to the Duke of Grafton for permission to consult and cite these papers.

95. Stormont to R.M. Keith, Private, 20 Jan. 1781, PRO FO 7/1.

96. PRO FO 90/12, pp. 6-8 (Instructions for James Porter, 8 Sept. 1763); SP 104/240, pp. 2-4 (Instructions for William Gordon, 4 Dec. 1765) and pp. 311-12 (Instructions for Lord Torrington, 14 Apr. 1783). For Newcastle's view of the Barrier, see, e.g., his letter to Yorke, 1 Feb. 1752, PRO SP 84/458.

97. To Yorke, 30 May 1775, PRO SP 84/546. This was occasioned by rumours that Austria might try to exchange these possessions for Bavaria when the last Wittelsbach elector died.

98. A particularly good example is the anonymous but officially inspired 'State of the Negociation for a treaty of Alliance between Great Britain and Russia from 1763 to 1771', PRO SP 103/63, fo. 41.

99. The description was Stormont's: to Phelps, 11 Aug. 1764, BL Stowe 259, fo. 37.

100. For a particularly clear example of the duke's influence, see Stormont to Sandwich, 23 Jan. 1765, Stormont Papers, Letter-Book 506, fo. 45.

101. See, e.g., the view of Sir Charles Hanbury Williams in 1753: Coxe, *Pelham administration,* ii. 469.

102. Instructions for Seilern, 3 Sept. 1763, *Österreichische Staatsverträge: England,* ed. A. F. Pribram (2 vols., Vienna, 1907-13), ii. 132.

103. See, e.g., Conway to Yorke, 25 Nov. 1766, PRO SP 84/511.

104. For a fuller statement of the arguments that follow, see H.M. Scott, 'The American Revolution and the disintegration of the Anglo-Dutch alliance', (forthcoming).

105. See H.M. Scott, 'Sir Joseph Yorke, Dutch politics and the origins of the Fourth Anglo-Dutch War', *Historical Journal,* 31 (1988), 571-89.

106. BL Egerton 224, fo. 43.

107. Yorke to Gunning, 22 Dec. 1773, ibid. 2702, fo. 265; cf. Yorke to Suffolk, Most Private, 25 Aug. 1778, PRO SP 84/561.

108. Black, *Natural and necessary enemies,* 68-9.

109. Cathcart to Suffolk, 19 May 1772, PRO SP 91/90, fo. 31.

CHAPTER 5

Lord Rochford at Turin, 1749-55:
A Pivotal Phase in Anglo-Italian Relations
in the Eighteenth Century

Geoffrey Rice

This chapter reviews Britain's relations with the Italian court which had greatest significance for British foreign policy in the mid-eighteenth century, at a time when patterns of diplomacy established at the start of the century were changing profoundly. It also gives an insight into the range of routine business and interacting themes of commerce, politics and religion confronting a British diplomat in Italy at this time, and is of interest as the apprenticeship of a career diplomat who later became ambassador at Madrid and Paris after the Seven Years' War, and Secretary of State in the difficult years 1768-75.

Down to the mid-1750s, the court of Savoy-Sardinia at Turin was politically by far the most important of the Italian states for British foreign policy. Good relations were actively sought by successive British ministers throughout the 1730s and 1740s, for several obvious reasons. Savoy's strategic position provided a potential barrier to French military penetration of the Lombard plain. Strong pro-British sentiment had existed at Turin from the late seventeenth century, and the acquisition of Sardinia by the House of Savoy together with its elevation in status to a kingdom had enhanced its value as an ally. Austria was beyond doubt the dominant power in Northern Italy at this time, and was Britain's ally until the Diplomatic Revolution of 1756, but British statesmen were anxious not to let this dominance become total. Turin's independence, with British support, could help restrain Austrian influence as well as provide a useful buffer between French and Austrian interests in the region.[1]

Britain's support was twofold: diplomatic and naval. Carteret's 1743 Treaty of Worms brought about an Anglo-Austrian-Sardinian alliance which succeeded in pushing Bourbon armies out of Northern Italy during the War of the Austrian Succession, causing French forces to be diverted from other theatres. British fleets prevented the movement of Bourbon reinforcements to Italy by sea, and at times effectively controlled the waters off the Ligurian and Provencal coasts. Leghorn and Villafranca were useful friendly ports of call for British warships and merchantment alike, and the King of Sardinia's desire for a wider corridor to the Mediterranean, partially recognised in the Treaty of Worms at the expense of Genoa's claims to Finale, held out the possibility of a longer-term British naval presence close to the great French base at Toulon. There were good reasons, therefore, behind Britain's cultivation of friendship with Savoy-Sardinia. Close military and diplomatic cooperation between London and Turin from 1743-8 marked the highpoint of Britain's naval strategy in the Mediterranean before the French Revolutionary wars, and also, as it turned out, of Anglo-Italian relations in the eighteenth century.[2]

Compared with Turin, the other Italian courts at mid-century were of much less importance to British foreign policy. The closure of the British legation at Genoa in 1722 meant that Britain was represented continuously in only three Italian cities for the whole of the century, namely Turin, Venice and Florence. Venice was notoriously pro-French and anti-Sardinian, though glad of British imports, and Britain's diplomatic role there was limited. Business was overwhelmingly consular and commercial. At Florence, Sir Horace Mann's long residence from 1738 to 1786 was taken up largely with entertaining British noblemen on the Grand Tour, not to mention his voluminous correspondence with Horace Walpole, but the Tuscan port of Leghorn was vital for British trade with Italy, as a clearing house to channel smaller cargoes to other ports, enabling, for example, British textiles to compete with Lombard and Venetian cloth. The British consul at Leghorn, and his colleague at Genoa, were at times far more important for the protection of British commercial interests in Italy than the diplomatic representative in Florence, apart from occasions when a formal diplomatic protest or request was required. Further south, Britain had neither consulate nor legation in the Papal States, and relied on the services of Cardinal Albani until the 1770s for any official dealings with the central Italian territories. At Naples, the British consul was on his own, often fulfilling diplomatic as well as consular functions, until the establishment of a legation in 1753.[3]

Britain's need for an able diplomat of high social rank at Turin was indicated by the bungling performance of the elderly Resident, Arthur Villettes, during the negotiations for the Treaty of Worms in 1742-3. Soon after, Villettes requested a transfer to his native Berne, and Sir Charles Hanbury-Williams, fretting at Dresden, asked for the Turin post in February 1748.[4] Instead, the Duke of Cumberland persuaded George II to name a novice as Envoy to Turin, an ambitious young courtier whose wife was one of the acknowledged court beauties of the day. William Henry Nassau de Zuylestein, 4th Earl of Rochford (1717-81), was of Dutch descent, and though his seat was at St Osyth in Essex, he still possessed various estates in the United Provinces, near Utrecht. Though he was the first English-born holder of the title, his recent forebears were all half-English, and he combined Whiggish patriotism with an understanding of European affairs which was unusual among English aristocrats of this period. His education had been completed in Geneva, where he acquired fluency in French which was likewise unusual amongst British statesmen of the mid-century.[5] When appointed to Turin, Lord Rochford was alone in the British diplomatic service in holding the rank of Envoy Extraordinary and Minister Plenipotentiary, the highest rank short of Ambassador. Since Britain maintained only two full embassies at this time, at Paris and Madrid, Rochford started high in the service. In addition, there were only two other peers in the service, Albemarle at Paris and Holdernesse at the Hague, and the latter was made Secretary of State in June 1751. Rochford had more than one reason for wanting to do well in his first diplomatic post. His motives for entering diplomacy were disarmingly frank; he saw it as the best training for a future statesman, and as a more honourable path to Cabinet than the uncertain corridors of political patronage.[6] He was certainly not in it for the money; most peers regarded service abroad as a form of indirect taxation. In fact, Rochford had accepted his high rank on the secret understanding that he would be paid only as an ordinary envoy. Turin was to prove an expensive post, and he was soon asking for his full emoluments, but it needed a direct appeal to George II to secure this in 1752. If he were to use Turin as the stepping-stone to a more important embassy, he would need to display exceptional zeal and diligence.[7] Rochford's instructions for Turin were brief and formal. Clauses 1 and 7 contained the heart of his duties, namely the cultivation of a 'close and cordial friendship' between the two allies, and close observation of the court and the influence of its various ministers upon the King of Sardinia. Clauses 6 and 8 reminded him to correspond regularly with other British diplomats, and to obey all further instructions from the Secretary of State. The only specific matters of concern were the protection of Savoyard Protestants and the preservation of good relations between Turin and Geneva; both were of personal interest to Rochford.[8] These formal instructions would have been amplified by the verbal briefing which Rochford received from the Duke of Bedford before setting out, and he spent several weeks in Paris during which he held useful discussions with his predecessor, Villettes, before arriving at Turin on 9 September 1749.[9]

Turin was not an easy post for a fledging diplomat, as there were few of the traditional avenues for intrigue or gaining secret information. Charles-Emmanuel III had been a widower since 1741, and led as solitary and secluded an existence as his court duties allowed. There were no favourites or mistresses to retail gossip, and the King's reticence made for a very secretive atmosphere. Rochford's earliest impression was of 'the Custom of this Court which seems to like making a Secret of the merest Trifles'.[10] The lack of a Queen meant that the social life of the court was much less glittering than the Rochfords had been accustomed to in London, but they were delighted to find that English country dances were much in vogue, and Rochford's own love of music and dancing enabled him to make an easy entrée into the social round at Turin.[11] He also found a way to penetrate the King's seclusion, thanks to his passion for horses and riding. Charles-Emmanuel spent much of his time hunting from his country retreat at Venaria, a few miles north-west of the city. In the summer, the court spent weeks on end here, provoking the usual grumbles from the diplomatic corps that hunting took precedence over business. Rochford quickly became an accepted member of the King's regular hunting party 'as I am willing to embrace every opportunity of paying my court, I never fail attending him a-hunting, at which times I have the honour of Breakfasting with him & of being received in a particular gracious manner'.[12]

By such means, Rochford built up a closer working relationship with the King than his precedessor had ever managed to achieve, and at no time during his residence at Turin was Rochford ever *persona non grata,* as Villettes had been on more than one occasion. Even during the most delicate phase of the negotiations for the Treaty of Aranjuez, Rochford was favoured with several private conversations which he was able to use to good advantage.[13] Charles-Emmanuel was known to be extremely jealous of his power, forbidding any member of the royal family to dabble in politics or intrigue. He was also reputed to be one of the shrewdest and best-informed of all Italian rulers.[14] Though the King professed in public his unswerving devotion to the British alliance, Rochford was under no illusion that he would pursue anything other than his own interests if at all possible, so he took care to cultivate other sources of support to maintain pro-British attitudes at court. One of his first such friendships was that of the heir to the throne, the Duke of Savoy, later Victor Amadeus III, who was more openly and enthusiastically Anglophile than his father. Though personally shy, the Duke was intelligent and well-informed, and very ready to discuss European affairs with Rochford, even after his marriage to a Spanish Infanta in 1750. The preparations for this wedding were the main preoccupation of the court during Rochford's first few months at Turin. When Spain conceded the *alternat* demanded by Charles-Emmanuel as the customary mark of equality between contracting powers — each party should sign first on alternate copies of the treaty — Rochford reported that the other Italian courts sneered at him for 'grasping at Honours' when he could not grasp at territory.[15]

Other influential supporters at court befriended by Rochford within his first months at Turin included the Marquis de Breille, who had spent his childhood in England and been the governor to the Duke of Savoy until 1747. Rochford found him a most useful contact, for he was not only thoroughly versed in the intrigues of court but was ardently pro-British, and his advice carried weight with the King.[16] Count San Vittorio, First President of the Senate, was described by Rochford in 1750 as 'my particular friend,' and was of considerable assistance during the negotiations involving English miners in Savoy. San Vittorio seems to have been Rochford's main source of inside information about the debates within the King's council. In 1754, for example, he was able to reassure Rochford that the Duke of Savoy had strongly defended Turin's British connexion against the opposition of pro-Austrian ministers.[17]

Until his death in June 1750, the *Ministro degli Esteri* whom Rochford saw at least once a week in his official capacity was the aged Marquis de Gorzegno, whose early impressions of the young British envoy were good. At the close of 1749 Gorzegno wrote to the Sardinian envoy in London, Count Perrone, that Rochford 'se conduit depuis son arrivée a notre cour avec beaucoup de prudence et de sagesse.'[18] Gorzegno's successor as foreign minister was Giuseppe Ossorio, a Sicilian by birth but a loyal and trusted career diplomat who had represented the King of Sardinia in London in the 1730s, signed the Treaty of Worms in 1743, and assisted at the signing of Aix la Chapelle in 1748. More recently he had been ambassador at Madrid, and accompanied the Duke of Savoy's new bride to Turin. Rochford was delighted by this appointment, as he had met Ossorio in London, and believed him to be the best possible choice from Britain's viewpoint.[19] However, any hopes Rochford might have had of Ossorio's influence over policy would have faded fairly soon in view of the power struggle which developed between Ossorio and the powerful Secretary for War, Count Bogino, whose sympathies lay with Austria. This struggle came to a head in 1751 over talks with Milan concerning the passage of salt barges on the River Po, and Bogino emerged the winner. For the rest of Rochford's stay at Turin, Bogino was regarded as the leading minister by other foreign diplomats, and Ossorio could not claim a deciding voice even in his own portfolio. Yet the reality, as Rochford reported it, was that none of the ministers had a deciding voice: the King of Sardinia preferred to keep his ministers divided and equal in order to retain his own personal control over policy and decision-making.[20]

French influence at Turin was at a low ebb in the early part of Rochford's residence; he had the satisfaction of seeing the new French ambassador Chetardie fail in all but one of his assigned tasks, and alienate both the Spanish ambassador and the King of Sardinia. Chetardie's instructions had included the removal of a small duty on French shipping at the port of Villafranca, and the establishment of a French postal service at Turin, as well as cultivating closer relations between Turin and Paris. He was also advised to be especially watchful of the British envoy.[21] The talks on the Villafranca duty were held elsewhere, and although Chetardie spent lavishly and paid court assiduously, he failed to make himself liked at court, partly because of his strict insistence on ceremonial. By the end of 1750, Chetardie admitted that his business at Turin was at a standstill, and he was recalled the following year, leaving enormous debts.[22]

Chetardie's successor at Turin lasted only six months, and was ill most of the time, so it was not until the start of 1754 that French interests at Turin at last found a capable advocate in the redoubtable François-Claude Chauvelin, later Marquis de Chauvelin. He had been French minister at Genoa in 1749 and since then had command of French forces on Corsica. Consul Birtles warned Rochford that Chauvelin was an officer of exceptional ability: 'A Man of Great Parts and a Compleat Courtier . . . he will cutt a great Figure at your Place . . . he is a Frenchman, consequently very little sincerity in him'.[23] Chauvelin began his Turin embassy very cautiously indeed, rarely seeing the King or his ministers, and avoiding any contact with the diplomatic corps, until he had made himself acceptable in society. Unfortunately a ceremonial dispute with the new Austrian minister, Count Merci, undid much of this careful preparatory work. In addition he was often embarrassed by the antics of the Genoese minister, Gastaldi, who idolised Chauvelin and went to extreme lengths to assist him, usually with negative results. Despite these problems, Chauvelin at last made his secret offer of an alliance with France before the end of 1754. Rochford's contact within the King's council told him that Charles-Emmanuel remained as cautious as ever, but that Ossorio and the Duke of Savoy had rejected the overture with 'great Warmth'. The proposal came to nothing and Chauvelin glumly reported that the Court of Turin was 'très opposé à toute espèce d'engagement' with France.[24]

Rochford therefore came to the end of his time at Turin confident that his efforts to maintain harmony within the diplomatic corps in order to combat French influence had not been entirely fruitless. He had spent a considerable amount of his time in 1753 and 1754 helping to smooth ruffled feathers and to keep the representatives of friendly powers on speaking terms. Though there were definite limits to the influence that a British envoy could expect to exert over the King of Sardinia or his ministers, Rochford could console himself with the reflection that the influence of successive French ambassadors at Turin had been virtually nil.

Military intelligence was always an important aspect of any diplomat's routine work in the eighteenth century, and Rochford was later to demonstrate considerable zeal and ability in this task during his Madrid embassy (1763-66), but at Turin he had very little to report. The King of Sardinia's forces were, he thought, in a deplorable condition, with regiments incomplete and fortress garrisons seriously undermanned. The only matters of note which he reported were changes in the officers' dress regulations in 1751 and large purchases of muskets and Holstein horses in 1752, accompanying troop reductions to peace-time levels in all the regiments. New uniforms for the infantry took a little longer, not arriving until 1754. Rochford drily remarked to Holdernesse that the military parades in the Valentino Gardens might look more impressive once the infantry all wore the same uniform.[25]

Troop reductions were interpreted by Rochford as a healthy sign of peace for Italy; as he remarked to Villettes: 'I need not tell you that they have good Noses in this country, & that they would not be the last informed if any thing was likely to happen, nor the first to reduce their Troops at such a Crisis'.[26] There was another simpler explanation for the troop reductions, however. Exhausted by the Austrian Succession War, the finances of the kingdom were at an all-time low. The King and his ministers made no secret of the fact, and it was a common topic of conversation amongst the diplomatic corps. Rochford wondered if the frequency with which the King lamented his lack of finance was a smokescreen for foreign consumption, and therefore set himself to find out as much as he could from reliable sources, knowing that information on revenue and taxation was often the hardest of all to uncover after military intelligence.[27] What he discovered was that although there was strict constraint on government spending, even including the King's passion for buildings, the kingdom's revenue was indeed almost entirely consumed by repayments and interest on loans taken out to finance the war effort. The salaries of the army and royal household, pegged at pre-war levels, were always in arrears, and the extraordinary war taxes which were long overdue for reduction or removal were still at wartime levels. This extra revenue was being channelled into a sinking fund modelled on British practice and designed to pay off the major loans over the next decade. Revenue from the small territorial gains made by the King of Sardinia under the terms of the Treaty of Aix la Chapelle failed even to cover the interest payments on his wartime loans.[28]

Relations between Turin and Genoa were of particular interest for British foreign policy towards Italy in the 1750s for two main reasons: French involvement in Corsica, and trade rivalry which might affect British commerce in the region. A revolt against inept Geonese administration at the port of San Remo in 1753 further soured already strained relations between Turin and Genoa, as several rebel leaders found shelter in Piedmont and Turin itself. The revolt was finally crushed by a naval expedition which the Corsican rebels feared might next be sent against them. These events contributed to a quieter phase on the island, enabling the complete withdrawal of French troops assisting the Genoese administration later in 1753.[29] Rochford's regular correspondence with the British consul at Genoa, John Birtles, enabled him to supply London with much detailed intelligence of French activities on Corsica. For example, the arrest of the French commander de Cursay late in 1752 on orders from Paris was known to Rochford even before the first reports reached the King of Sardinia and his ministers at Turin.[30]

Soon after his arrival at Turin, Rochford had heard rumours that the French intended to acquire Corsica for themselves, which would have serious consequences for the exercise of British naval power in that part of the Mediterranean. However, he soon discovered that the King of Sardinia's ministers entirely discredited such rumours, and were convinced that France was exasperated by her expensive commitment to Genoa now that the Austrian Succession War was over, and eager to withdraw completely if a decent pretext could be found. This report corresponded more closely to existing French policy than was believed in London at the time; indeed it was not until the middle of 1751 that Ossorio felt sufficiently sure of it to tell Rochford that a French evacuation was likely.[31] Both the British government and the King of Sardinia saw the opportunity here to undermine French influence at Genoa by an offer of mediation between the republic and the Corsican rebels. Ossorio suggested to Rochford that Britain ought to intervene, demand immediate French evacuation, and offer Genoa a peacekeeping force for the island. Consul Birtles was optimistic that the Genoese would listen to such a proposal.[32] But Rochford rightly guessed that the British government would baulk at the expense of keeping troops on Corsica, and the subsidies which would be necessary to persuade Genoa to accept British mediation. He saw Turin as a likelier mediator, given its position as neighbour to the two parties, but doubted whether the King of Sardinia would lift a finger to help solve the problems of Turin's ancient rival. Ossorio then lost interest in the issue, and tried to pass it off as being of no great importance, but Rochford thought his own government should take a closer interest in the fate of Corsica: 'if I may be allowed to differ in my politicks from some of my correspondents, I think the French having or not having a port so near Italy, of the utmost consequence in time of war'.[33] France's involvement in Corsica was the price she had to pay for the use of Genoa as a doorway to mainland Italy. This was why France had provided finance for the development of new ports at Massa and Spetia, and built a new road linking Spetia to the Val de Taro, enabling French troops to reach Parma from the coast in three days.[34]

Rochford's later handling of the Corsican crisis of 1768 when he was British ambassador in Paris needs to be seen in the light of his earlier interest in the problem and the views he had formed of French strategic interests in the region during his diplomatic apprenticeship at Turin.[35]

Ports on the Ligurian coast were of mutual interest to London and Turin for commercial as well as strategic considerations. The King of Sardinia's 'new' port at Villafranca was Turin's principal outlet to the Mediterranean, and he was eager to enlarge this corridor by developing other smaller ports, as the Genoese were attempting to do with French finance. Compared with Leghorn, Villafranca handled only a small fraction of British trade in the region, but its potential as a port was obvious should British trade with Piedmont continue to expand. Perhaps the most significant of Rochford's tasks as an advocate of British commercial interests at Turin concerned the removal of a discriminatory duty on British ships calling at Villafranca: an obvious obstacle to further trade development between the two allies. Though it cost him a great deal of time and effort (almost as much as the scandalous behaviour of the British consul at Cagliari), the removal of the Villafranca duty must be counted as one of Rochford's outstanding successes as British envoy at Turin.

Since the details of this negotiation are available elsewhere,[36] it will be sufficient here to notice that the Villafranca duty forms a recurrent theme in the correspondence between Turin and the Sardinian envoy in London through the early 1750s, from which it is plain that Rochford had to overcome considerable reluctance and opposition to have the matter considered at all. He was frequently fobbed off with the claim that he was poorly informed, or did not understand the legal aspects, but the real reason for the Turin government's delaying tactics was the fear that any concession to British shipping would force them to review privileges enjoyed by ships from Gibraltar and Port Mahon, and give the French a pretext for avoiding other duties. As we have seen, Rochford's initiative on behalf of British shipping forced Turin to open negotiations with the French as well on duties at Villafranca. It was a nice dilemma for Rochford: his efforts to improve conditions for British trade might cause irritation and harm for Anglo-Sardinian relations. It is characteristic of Rochford as a diplomat that he thought the risk worth taking, and despite many delays and frustrations, he maintained pressure to bring the matter to a settlement in Britain's favour in 1754.[37]

Rochford was justified in anticipating an expansion in trade between Britain and Piedmont, because the 1750s saw several projects promoted by the energetic Intendant de Commerce at Turin, Count Chavannes, with this end in view. In 1751 Rochford remarked to Sir Horace Mann that Chavannes was 'putting every Iron in the Fire to make Commerce flourish'.[38] Money was spent to improve the port facilities at Villafranca, and in 1753 Chavannes unveiled a grand scheme to establish a Chamber of Commerce at Nice, with a special fund to boost trade.[39] Of particular interest to Rochford was Chavannes' determination to increase wine exports to Britain to pay for imports of woollen cloth. Rochford thought their red wines tolerably good when allowed to stand long enough 'in Taste

& Quality . . . not very different from the Claret we drink'. If such a trade could be developed successfully, Piedmontese wines might in time reduce Britain's dependence on French claret. As one of the consuls observed, 'what moneys we spend in France in whatever shape is certainly furnishing arms against ourselves'.[40] This trade was not without its teething problems, however. In 1753 a shipment which Rochford helped organise through the British consul at Genoa was a total disaster. Not only had the suppliers used poor-quality casks, but the shippers in their ignorance had carefully nailed tin plates over the fermentation vents, so that all the casks landed at Genoa were leaking copiously. Consul Birtles found only 29 sound casks out of 133. As there is no further reference to this trade in Rochford's correspondence from Turin, the venture may have collapsed.[41]

The case of the English Mining Company in Savoy was Rochford's earliest piece of advocacy in Turin, the only unfinished business left by his predecessor Villettes. This company had been set up in 1738 to develop lead and silver mines for the King of Sardinia, who granted letters patent in 1740 and 1741 giving the English miners exclusive rights on all royal lands for forty years. Unfortunately, the Austrian Succession War seriously disrupted their activities, and several mines were plundered by marauding Spanish troops. More seriously, some of the smaller mines abandoned at this time were taken over by local interests in defiance of the Royal patents, and the war ended with the English company enmeshed in a welter of law suits.[42] Most of these were settled fairly soon, but one proved more complicated and potentially more serious. This case concerned a group of rich silver mines at Peyrey on land belonging to the Marquis de St Maurice, which had been developed by local contractors named Deriva. The mines had been abandoned during the war, and in 1745 the Marquis signed over the rights to the English company, which worked the mines so profitably for the next three years that it was able to pay the Marquis his seigneurial dues several years in advance. However, in 1749 a younger brother of the Marquis, Baron Chabo, procured a fresh title for the Derivas, and declared that the English company should confine its activities to royal lands. The Deriva partners then sued the English company for the return of the mines at Peyrey, together with damages for equipment lost during the war. Though the English company promptly lodged a counter claim, it was vital that the two cases be heard together for the full facts of the case to be made plain. Villettes had secured a joint hearing on 4 September 1749, but as soon as he had left Turin, Baron Chabo pulled strings to have the Deriva hearing brought forward by itself to 25 August. Before a sympathetic magistrate, they won their case easily, and the English company was ordered to surrender the mines and pay damages.[43]

When Rochford arrived at Turin on 9 September he was greeted almost immediately with a desperate plea from the English miners to help them appeal against this decision. Despite a hectic round of audiences and formal visits which filled the next few weeks, he set himself to master the details of the case, and once he was satisfied that the decision was unjust, he asked the company for a detailed summary of their case which he translated into French and submitted to Gorzegno.[44] He was somewhat alarmed to find that the affair was much talked about, and treated almost as a matter of national honour at Turin. When it was obvious that Gorzegno would do nothing to help, Rochford asked for an audience with the King, and by late November he had secured suspension of the lower court decision pending the appointment of a royal delegation to consider the whole dispute afresh.[45] When named early in 1750, the delegation was packed with Chabo's cronies. Rochford protested, and a new delegation was appointed with the First President of the Senate as its chairman. If anything, the bias had now swung to the opposite extreme, for Count San Vittorio was openly Anglophile and already one of Rochford's best friends at Court. The King had even offered Rochford free choice of the members of this second delegation, but Rochford had seen the trap and declined. By September 1750 a compromise had been reached which satisfied all parties: the Derivas yielded their claim to the Peyrey mines in return for a settlement of 5,000 livres, and the King granted the English miners a higher price for their silver, together with various additional safeguards designed to prevent their skilled workers from being tempted into local employ.[46]

This case reveals Rochford as an energetic advocate, careful to master the details of a complex affair, and wary of such traps as naming the second delegation. He told Villettes in reply to the latter's congratulations that he had only done his duty, but regretted that it might have made him some enemies among the Savoyards, 'who will I suppose look on me as their declared enemy, whereas I have really done no more than every Minister must have done who would have obeyed his Master's orders'. This was a modest disclaimer for a novice diplomat who had seen his first piece of advocacy on behalf of British nationals meet with complete success. An indolent or indifferent envoy would have been content with much less.[47]

As British envoy at Turin, Rochford had a special responsibility towards the Protestant subjects of the King of Sardinia, who had enjoyed Britain's protection since the late seventeenth century. As we have seen, Rochford's instructions on this head were quite specific. The Vaudois of Savoy, or 'Protestants of the Valleys' living in the foothills of the Alps west of Turin, were in touch with Rochford soon after his arrival with appeals for permission from the King to repair two churches. This he obtained without any difficulty.[48] In September 1750 he spent two weeks touring the villages in this district, meeting their pastors and listening to their complaints of harassment by Catholic neighbours. He judged that a formal protest at this time would do more harm than good, but he was soon obliged to intervene in a case of alleged abduction of two Protestant children and their incarceration in a Catholic hospice near Pinerolo. Once again, he ran the risk of making himself unpopular at Court, and was undoubtedly relieved when the episode was resolved without a formal protest.[49] That he made an impact, however, is clear from the proclamation issued by the King in April 1751 to all inhabitants of the valleys that they were to desist from harassing their neighbours, and that the Protestants should make any future complaints direct to the authorities at Turin, and not to the representatives of any foreign power![50]

More serious for relations between Turin and Geneva was the dispute which arose over the jurisdiction of two villages named St Victor and Chapitre near the Genevan border, where numbers of Protestant silk weavers had settled during the Austrian Succession War. This was an old bone of contention, and an earlier attempt at a negotiated settlement had collapsed in 1741. The presence of the Protestant weavers now added a religious dimension to the jurisdictional dispute.[51] The first approach came from Turin. In May 1750 Count Bogino informed Rochford that the King wanted to revive the 1741 negotiation and settle the matter, but Rochford rightly suspected that Bogino only wanted to steal a march on his rival Ossorio. Fearing that Bogino's anti-Genevan attitudes would wreck the new negotiation, he counselled delay. But Newcastle replied that this was 'a Matter of Consequence' in which George II had taken a personal interest, and Rochford was instructed to support their proposal.[52] The King of Sardinia wanted to broaden the negotiation to gain something useful in return for the concessions which it seemed likely Geneva would ask of Turin, and proposed an alliance of the Protestant Swiss cantons to guarantee his kingdom against a future French invasion through the Swiss passes by threatening to withdraw their regiments from French service. Newcastle was delighted by this broader scheme, but Geneva insisted that the local dispute over St Victor and Chapitre be settled before the idea of a wider treaty could be discussed, and on this rock the initative of 1750 quickly foundered.[53]

In March 1752, however, the Senate of Savoy suddenly ordered all foreign Protestants living in St Victor and Chapitre to remove themselves within three months or be forcibly expelled. The weavers promptly appealed to Rochford for British protection, and for the next six months he laboured for the suspension of the order, exchanging detailed notes and memoirs with Ossorio. He was finally authorised by London to make a formal demand in February 1753, which gained an indefinite suspension, and he set off on his Grand Tour in March hoping to have heard the last of the affair.[54]

By the end of that year, however, Geneva agreed to resume serious negotiations with Turin, and Rochford was delighted to find his old friend Mussard named as the Genevan commissary. Talks proceeded smoothly, and a treaty was signed on 3 June 1754. The most continuous issue was settled in a secret clause: the King of Sardinia yielded his claims to sovereignty over St Victor and Chapitre for compensation of 3 million livres.[55]

Implementation of the agreement was not without its problems, however, and Rochford was obliged to intervene again on behalf of the Savoyard Protestants later in 1754; Ossorio remarked to Perrone that he was always speaking out on their behalf.[56]

Jacobitism was another problem combining religious and political issues which gave occasional anxiety to British ministers over the 1750s. In the decade following the rebellion of 1745, much effort and expense was devoted to watching the movements of the Young Pretender, Charles Edward Stuart, and his attempts to drum up support for his cause at various European capitals. Though the Young Pretender kept a household at Avignon, his father's 'court' at Rome was still regarded as the real home of the Jacobite movement, and in the absence of any British diplomatic representative there, Rochford and Mann had been briefed to report whatever they heard of the Young Pretender's movements. Not content with waiting for news, Rochford sought it from the British consul at Naples, James Allen, and was rewarded with a report that the Young Pretender had been at Ancona on the Adriatic coast early in 1750, which contradicted the assurances of the King of Sardinia's ministers that he was nowhere in Italy.[57]

In June 1751 Rochford was visited by one John Phillips who claimed to be a government agent working inside the Jacobite movement. His story was that he had been in the Guards before volunteering to infiltrate the rebel army in 1745. Having gone to Lisbon to recover a debt and been greeted by a group of Jacobites as one of their own, he had accompanied them to Avignon where he obtained letters of introduction from the Young Pretender's secretary, Kelly, to visit Cardinal York at Rome. He had then managed to miss his ship at Marseilles in order to travel overland and deliver a progress report to the British envoy at Turin, and a letter which he had copied in Kelly's room when left unattended. Rochford decided he was genuine, agreed to send the letter to London, and gave Phillips money to continue his journey to Rome.[58] Within a month, Rochford had a report which justified his trust. Phillips had gained interviews with both Cardinal York and the Old Pretender, confirming rumours that Charles Edward had recently been in Berlin seeking Prussian support for his cause. He had been so well disguised that even the French ambassador, an old personal friend, had failed to recognise him.[59] From Rome Phillips went to Naples where he approached Consul Allen for assistance, using a note signed by Rochford to convince Allen of his credentials. Rochford later reimbursed Allen the money he had advanced to Phillips. Though this was the last Rochford heard of Phillips, Consul Allen continued to be a useful source of news about the Young Pretender's movements.[60]

In addition, Rochford employed his own agent in Rome from early 1752, who gave him early notice of the breaking up of the Young Pretender's household at Avignon, and the quarrel between the Old Pretender and Cardinal York which caused the latter to set up his own separate establishment. At Turin people recalled that the Young Pretender had broken up his household just before the rebellion of 1745, and speculated whether another rising was being planned. Rochford himself doubted that Charles Edward was ready to run 'such foolish risques' again, but there was in fact a plot by British Jacobites for November 1752, now known as the Elibank Plot, which was largely uncovered that winter; its failure was symbolised by the execution of Archibald Cameron in 1753. This period was therefore one of considerable anxiety for the British government, in which every piece of intelligence about the Jacobite cause had potential value.[61]

When he made his Grand Tour of Italy in 1753, Rochford spent several weeks in Rome using his agent there (as yet unidentified) to make discreet enquiries about the Jacobite 'court'. The results were disappointingly meagre, but he was able to report on sources of support for the Jacobites amongst the College of Cardinals. Their most open supporters, Cardinals Lante and Valenti, were regarded quite simply as French pensionaries, and their other supporters took care not to be openly identified with their cause. From a contact in Valenti's household, Rochford's agent heard that when the Young Pretender broke up his household at Avignon, the Papal Legate absolutely refused to store his furniture or effects in the Palace. This report from Rochford was one of the first indications British ministers had that papal support for the Jacobites was on the wane after the failure of 1745.[62]

Such brief glimpses as Rochford had of the eighteenth-century underworld of plots and secret agents contrast vividly with his involvement in the most important piece of formal diplomatic business of his apprenticeship at Turin, the negotiations leading to the Treaty of Aranjuez of 14 June 1752. Though Madrid was the scene of the main negotiation, where Sir Benjamin Keene was Britain's chief negotiator, Rochford's role at Turin was not unimportant, for it was his task to help persuade a reluctant court to join the treaty project against its inclinations, then when difficulties and ill-feeling arose between Turin and Vienna, to help reconcile their differences.[63] Originally intended as a simple guarantee by Spain and

Austria of Bourbon and Habsburg territories in Italy as they had been fixed by the Treaty of Aix la Chapelle, the project was widened by the Duke of Newcastle to include Britain and Savoy-Sardinia. There was good reason for this; the Austrian project named only Naples, Parma and Tuscany as acceding courts, yet as Newcastle pointed out, unless it included Turin as the Italian state most directly threatened by future French aggression, and militarily the most considerable of the Italian states, the mutual guarantee would not be worth much. Newcastle therefore offered to act as mediator for the inclusion of Savoy-Sardinia, and Rochford conveyed this first offer to the King of Sardinia on 19 September 1751.[64]

Charles-Emmanuel III was at first very reluctant to become involved, complaining that he saw no particular advantage in it for himself. Rochford privately thought that Turin would not join 'without being well paid for it'.[65] The amended treaty project, including Britain and Savoy-Sardinia, arrived on 26 October and Rochford's task was to persuade the King of Sardinia to join either as a contracting or acceding power under British mediation, and to press for full powers to be sent to the Sardinian ambassador at Madrid. The buoyant optimism of Newcastle's instructions contrasted with Rochford's own gloomy pessimism after his first conversations with Ossorio.[66] Austria and Spain predictably resisted Newcastle's proposal, on the very reasonable grounds that Britain had no territories in Italy, and if Britain was included, then France might demand to be included as well. Newcastle therefore ordered Keene to withdraw Britain's bid and to insist all the more strongly upon Turin's inclusion as a full contracting party. This changed the situation dramatically for the King of Sardinia, who now saw some advantage in joining as a full contracting power, gaining further recognition of equality as a crowned head from the courts of Madrid and Vienna.[67]

Though the Spanish were quite ready to admit Turin, the Austrians took several more months to agree, raising the objection that the guarantee of territories covered only mainland Italy and should not include the island of Sardinia. Another difficulty arose over precisely the point which now made the King of Sardinia eager to join: the *alternat* or customary privilege in treaties between equals that each party should sign first on alternate copies of the treaty. Count Esterhazy had been ordered not to sign as an equal without making a formal declaration that this was not to be taken as a precedent: Maria Theresa regarded the Kingdom of Sardinia as a 'mushroom crown' and not as an equal. The Austrian chargé d'affaires at Turin absolutely refused to discuss the treaty proposal without fresh instructions from Vienna.[68] Rochford here played a useful part in helping to thaw the Austrian minister's coolness, and persuaded him to give a more favourable view of Turin's attitude to the treaty project. April saw the breakthough; Vienna agreed to concede the *alternat* to Turin with a milder private Reservation, and the problem of Sardinia was resolved by an agreement to use Austrian troops in ships provided by Turin, should the need arise to defend the island. This latter concession was the result of a frantic round of talks at Madrid, speeded by the provisional signing of a separate treaty between Madrid and Vienna alone, which was then replaced by the main tripartite treaty once agreement was reached.[69] News of the agreement reached Turin on 28 May, and a day's festivities were proclaimed in celebration. Rochford immediately wrote to congratulate Keene on the successful conclusion of a rather trying negotiation, and a week later, in the Valentino Gardens, the King of Sardinia thanked Rochford for his assistance with 'this curious Treaty, which had given more trouble than a ten times more important one'.[70]

Contemporaries greeted the Treaty of Aranjuez as a reassuring affirmation of Aix la Chapelle and a harbinger of peace for Italy. They were right; there were no major wars in Italy for the next forty years, until the Revolutionary-Napoleonic era. Newcastle could justifiably regard the outcome as something very close to that which he had hoped for, a major peace treaty which included Britain's principal Italian ally, the Court of Turin. Yet he must also have recognised that the negotiation had demonstrated with great clarity the limits to British influence over that ally. It must have been as galling for Newcastle as it was for Rochford to find that the King of Sardinia listened politely to their advice but went ahead and did exactly as he pleased. Once Britain had withdrawn as a contracting power, her influence at Turin was drastically reduced. The real triumphs of British mediation lay elsewhere, especially at Madrid, where Keene laboured mightily to keep Savoy-Sardinia in the treaty project. Yet it must also be remembered that Anglo-Italian relations had a low priority in British foreign policy at this time, and that Aranjuez was a minor negotiation compared with the effort expended on Newcastle's great project of the 1750s, the Imperial Election plan.[71]

Though it would be too strong to speak of a cooling of relations between London and Turin after the signing of the Treaty of Aranjuez, there is clear evidence from the affair of the Modena Marriage Contract of 1753 that Britain would not automatically pander to the interests of the King of Sardinia. Duke Francis III of Modena had married his only son Ercole to a Malaspina Duchess, Maria Teresa of Alberigo, but after producing a daughter in 1750 the couple separated and thereafter lived apart. Anxious to secure his lineage, Francis set about finding a suitable future husband for his infant granddaughter. He even made secret overtures to George II in 1751, but when these proved fruitless he turned to Austria. The result was a secret marriage convention, signed on 11 May 1753 and ratified in June, which betrothed the infant Princess of Modena to the young Archduke Leopold. As part of the deal, which marked a further increase in Austrian influence in Northern Italy, Francis III became governor of Milan and commander of Austrian forces in the north.[72]

Rochford was instructed in April 1753 to say nothing about this treaty at Turin, even though it was widely rumoured there. On his return from his tour of Italy in June, Rochford ingeniously asked Ossorio whether these rumours were true, and Ossorio merely grumbled that the Duke of Modena might have considered the King of Sardinia's youngest son, the Duke of Chablais, instead of an Austrian archduke. But Rochford knew that such a match would have alarmed all the smaller courts of Northern Italy and was quite unthinkable.[73] It was not until August 1753, after it was safely signed and sealed, that Rochford was instructed to make formal notification of the Modena Marriage Treaty at Turin. His unenviable task was to explain to an ally why that ally had been pointedly ignored during a negotiation which was of very considerable interest to them. Newcastle suggested making the excuse that this was seen in London as something of a 'Personal & Family Nature' in which George II had not wished to interfere. Ossorio grudgingly accepted this thin excuse, but complained to Rochford at some length that they 'should not have been kept so long in the Dark' by their principal ally.[74] The French ambassador's secretary told Rochford that he knew the King of Sardinia was 'extremely disgusted at this Affair', as was the French government. Britain's silence had been necessary simply to prevent the King of Sardinia from finding any pretext to upset the negotiation, as Rochford was sure he would have done, had he known about it in time.[75]

Rochford's appointment to Turin turned out to be the last in which this post held real importance for British foreign policy in Italy. Though his successor matched his rank, there was little for him to do, and the post changed hands frequently with long periods of non-residence in the 1760s, until the decade of Sir William Lynch as envoy, 1768-79.[76] By his share in the negotiations for the Treaty of Aranjuez, Rochford had himself helped to curtail the strategic value of Savoy-Sardinia as Britain's ally in Italy. While the mutual guarantees between Madrid, Turin and Vienna were designed to contain future French interference in the region, they also effectively reduced any need for British involvement. From 1752 on, and especially after the 1756 Franco-Austrian alliance, 'the Italian Question' ceased to be a source of instability in European diplomacy; it was a stable region for the rest of the eighteenth century. Overshadowed by greater powers, Turin might have been forgiven for throwing in its lot with one or the other of them. Yet at the outbreak of the Seven Years' War, Turin opted for neutrality and a precarious independence. According to Benjamin Keene, the Court of Turin stood 'as firm as a Rock', resisting tempting offers from Frederick II, and William Pitt later wrote of the King of Sardinia as a 'firm and affectionate' ally in a time of great crisis.[77] This was hailed as a direct consequence of the careful preservation of friendship between the British and Sardinian crowns over the previous decade, and for this Lord Rochford deserves at least some of the credit.

As Jeremy Black has pointed out, the Italian settlement of 1752 and subsequent Austro-Bourbon dominance in Italy destroyed the King of Sardinia's freedom of manoeuvre, and decisively curbed his expansionist ambitions on the Ligurian coast, thus making a Sardinian alliance much less attractive for Britain.[78] Where the prospect of naval assistance was irrelevant, it is hard to see how Britain could expect to influence (much less control) an Italian ally after the mid-century. The Court of Turin found that Britain took less and less interest in Italian affairs after the Seven Years' War, despite repeated warnings about French designs on Corsica. This lack of interest resulted in a state of ignorance and apathy on the part of British ministers in the 1760s which encouraged Choiseul to move boldly to acquire the island in 1768. By then Rochford was British ambassador in Paris. His warnings were not heeded either, partly because the Chatham administration's bungling of the Manila Ransom and first Falkland Islands crisis in 1766 had made him overly cautious, and partly because he was seriously ill for two weeks just at the critical juncture when greater diplomatic pressure from Britain might have made Choiseul pause. The French acquisition of Corsica finally convinced the Court of Turin that Britain was no longer capable of effective intervention in Mediterranean or Italian affairs; a far cry indeed from the heady days of close military cooperation earlier in the century.[79]

ABBREVIATIONS

AST	Archivio di Stato, Torino, Lettere Ministri Inghilterra
BL Add MSS	British Library, London, Additional Manuscripts.
DNB	*Dictionary of National Biography,* London.
FO	Foreign Office Papers, Public Record Office, London.
RDL	Rochford Diplomatic Letters, Bodleian Library, Oxford, MSS Eng. Lett., C. 336-340.
SP	State Papers Foreign, Public Record Office, London.
TRHS	*Transactions of the Royal Historical Society.*

NOTES

1. D.B. Horn, *Great Britain and Europe in the Eighteenth Century*, Oxford, 1967, p.335.

2. F. Valsecchi, *L'Italia nel Settecento*, Milan, 1959, pp. 177-80; F. Cognasso, *I Savoia nella politica Europa*, Milan, 1941, pp. 235-9; J. Black, 'The Development of Anglo-Sardinian Relations in the first half of the Eighteenth Century,' *Studi Piemontesi*, 12 (1983), 48-59.

3. Horn (1967), pp. 339-41.

4. R. Lodge, *Studies in Eighteenth Century Diplomacy, 1740-1748*, London, 1930, p. 50; D.B. Horn, *Sir Charles Hanbury Williams and European Diplomacy, 1747-58*, London, 1930, pp. 41-6.

5. *DNB* xxi, pp. 1344-6 (under Zuylestein); Collins' *Peerage of England*, 5th edition, London, 1779, iv, pp. 140-4; and my unpublished Ph.D. thesis, The Diplomatic Career of the Fourth Earl of Rochford, 1749-68, University of Canterbury, New Zealand, 1973, pp. 1-26.

6. D.B. Horn, *British Diplomatic Service, 1689-1789*, Oxford, 1961, pp. 47-8; Horn, *British Diplomatic Representatives*, Camden Society, 3rd series, XLVI, 1932, pp. 20, 37, 92, 99, 107, 134, 153, 166; RDL D/18, Rochford to Cumberland, 2 May 1750.

7. SP 92/59, f.48, Rochford to George II, 10 April 1751; Rice, thesis, p. 46.

8. FO 90/40, f.118, 12 June 1749.

9. SP 92/58, f.119, Bedford to Villettes, 9 March 1749 O.S; ibid. f.171, Rochford to Bedford, 17 September 1749.

10. SP 92/58, f.175, Rochford to Bedford, 24 September 1749; RDL D/92, Rochford to Albemarle, 10 November 1751; D. Carutti, *Storia del Regno di Carlo Emmanuele III*, Turin, 1859, II, pp. 174-180.

11. SP 92/60, f.56, Rochford to Amyand, 19 January 1752; *Notes and Queries*, 2nd series, 4 (1856), p. 71.

12. SP 92/58, f.210, Rochford to Bedford, 5 Nov 1749; RDL D/34, Rochford to Yorke, 24 Oct 1750.

13. Lodge, *Studies*, p. 50.

14. BL Add MSS 32821, f.325, Rochford to Newcastle, 13 June 1750.

15. S. Cordero di Pamparato, 'Il matrimonio del duce Vittorio Amadeo III di Savoia,' *Atti della R. Accademia di Scienza di Torino*, 33 (1897-8), pp. 98-120; SP 92/60, f.267, Rochford to Holdernesse, 16 Dec 1752.

16. SP 92/58, f.326 & 347, Rochford to Newcastle, 9 May & 27 June 1750.

17. SP 92/58, ff.293 & 300, Rochford to Bedford, 28 Feb. & 21 Mar. 1750; SP 92/62, f.179, Rochford to Robinson, 21 Dec. 1754, Very Secret.

18. AST 56, Gorzegno to Perrone, 27 Dec 1749.

19. SP 92/58, f.300, Rochford to Bedford, 21 Mar 1750; Carutti, *op. cit.*, II, pp.49-50.

20. SP 92/62, f.155, Rochford to Robinson, 2 Nov. 1754; on Bogino, see G. Quazza, *Dizionario Biografico degli Italiani*, Rome, 1960-, XI, 185.

21. *Recueil des Instructions données aux Ambassadeurs et Ministres de France*, XV, Savoie-Sardaigne, ii, 1748-89, ed. H. de Beaucaire, Paris, 1899, pp. 1-28; SP 92/58, f.303, Rochford to Aldworth, 28 Mar 1750.

22. SP 92/58, f.383, Rochford to Newcastle, 24 Oct. 1750; RDL D/110, Rochford to Mann, 22 Mar 1752.

23. RDL A/83, Birtles to Rochford, 12 Jan 1754.

24. RDL D/133, Rochford to Dickens, 4 Dec. 1754; SP 92/62, f.177, Rochford to Robinson, 21 Dec. 1754.

25. SP 92/58, f.285, Rochford to Bedford, 21 Feb. 1750; SP 92/60, f.167, Rochford to Holdernesse, 23 Feb. 1753; SP 92/62, ff. 19 & 23, Rochford to Holdernesse, 2 & 13 Mar. 1754.

26. RDL D/64, Rochford to Villettes, 17 April 1751.

27. SP 92/61, f. 148. Rochford to Holdernesse, 29 Sept. 1753.

28. BL Add MSS 32823, f.1, Rochford to Newcastle, 22 August 1750; SP 92/59, f.56, Rochford to Bedford, 8 May 1751; SP 92/61, f.148, Rochford to Holdernesse, 29 Sept. 1753.

29. RDL A/76-8, Birtles to Rochford, 16, 23, 30 June 1753; SP 92/61, f. 186, Rochford to Holdernesse, 15 Dec. 1753; R. Boudard, *Gênes et la France dans la deuxième moitié du XVIIIe siècle, 1748-97,* Paris, 1962, pp. 60-64.

30. SP 92/60, f.270, Rochford to Holdernesse, 23 Dec 1753.

31. SP 92/58, f.210, Rochford to Bedford, 5 Nov. 1749; SP 92/59, f.95, Rochford to Bedford, 26 June 1751.

32. SP 92/58, f.300, Rochford to Bedford, 21 Mar. 1750.

33. RDL D/81, Rochford to Yorke, 11 Sept. 1751.

34. RDL D/74, Rochford to Yorke, 9 July 1751; Thadd E. Hall, *France and the Eighteenth Century Corsican Question,* New York University Press, 1971, pp. 64-6, 74-5.

35. Rice, thesis, chapter 16, pp. 484-533; see also N. Tracy, 'The Administration of the Duke of Grafton and the French Invasion of Corsica,' *Eighteenth Century Studies,* 8 (1974-5), pp. 169-82.

36. G.W. Rice, 'British Consuls and Diplomats in the mid-eighteenth century; an Italian example,' *English Historical Review,* 92 (1977), pp. 834-46.

37. AST 56, Gorzegno to Perrone, 6 Dec. 1749; AST 58, Ossorio to Perrone, 27 Jan. 1753 & 18 Aug. 1754.

38. RDL D/83, Rochford to Mann, 28 Sept. 1751.

39. SP 92/60, f.14, Rochford to Holdernesse, 5 Jan. 1752; SP 92/61, f.140, Rochford to Holdernesse, 12 Sept. 1753.

40. RDL D/83, Rochford to Mann, 28 Sept. 1751; RDL A/55, Allen to Rochford, 9 Nov. 1751.

41. RDL A/80, Birtles to Rochford, 18 Aug. 1753.

42. SP 92/58, f.106, Bedford to Villettes, 27 Feb. 1749.

43. SP 92/58, f.181, Rochford to Bedford, 8 Oct. 1749; ibid., f.185, Relation du fait qui s'est passé entre la Compagnie des M. les Anglais et M. le Marquis de St Maurice . . . et les cousins Derive pour les miniers de Peyrey, Sept. 1749.

44. SP 92/58, ff. 218 & 220, Rochford to Bedford, 19 & 29 Nov. 1749.

45. BL Add MSS 32823, f.197, Rochford to Newcastle, 12 Sept. 1750.

46. RDL D/33, Rochford to Villettes, 25 Sept. 1750.

47. RDL D/21, Rochford to Villettes, 16 May 1750.

48. SP 92/58, f.269, Rochford to Bedford, 21 Jan. 1750; see also F. Venturi, 'Il Piemonti dei primi decenni del Settecento nelle Relazioni del diplomatici Inglesi,' *Bolletino Storico-Bibliografico Sub-Alpino,* 54 (1956), pp. 227-271, and J. Black, *British Foreign Policy in the Age of Walpole,* Edinburgh, 1985, p.129.

49. SP 92/59. f.4, Bedford to Rochford, 7 Jan. 1751.

50. SP 92/59, f.52, Rochford to Bedford, 24 Apr. 1751.

51. SP 92/61, f.108, Rochford to Holdernesse, 14 July 1753; Valsecchi, *L'Italia nel Settecento,* pp. 273-5.

52. BL Add MSS 32821, f.325, Rochford to Newcastle, 13 June 1750; 32822, f.1, Rochford to Newcastle, 27 June 1750; f.30, Newcastle to Rochford, 2 July 1750.

53. RDL D/57, Rochford to Villettes, 17 Mar. 1751.

54. RDL D/111, Rochford to Mussard, 19 Apr. 1752; SP 92/60, f.124, Rochford to Newcastle, 22 Apr. 1752; AST 58, Ossorio to Perrone, 6 & 20 Jan. 1753.

55. AST 58, Ossorio to Perrone, 3 Mar. 1753; SP 92/61, f.38, Rochford to Holdernesse, 3 Mar. 1753; SP 92/62, f.93, Charles to Holdernesse, 27 June 1754.

56. AST 58, Ossorio to Perrone, 10 Nov. 1754.

57. C. Petrie, *The Jacobite Movement; the Last Phase, 1716-1807,* London, 1950, pp. 116-159; Black, *British Foreign Policy in the Age of Walpole,* pp. 153-5; RDL A/15, Allen to Rochford, 14 Mar. 1750.

58. SP 92/59, f.75, Rochford to Bedford, 2 June 1751.

59. BL Add MSS 32828, f.151, Rochford to Holdernesse, 13 July 1751.

60. RDL A/49, Allen to Rochford, 3 Aug. 1751.

61. BL Add MSS 32838, f.329, Rochford to Newcastle, 29 July 1752; RDL D/123, Rochford to Dayrolles, 29 July 1752; SP 92/60, f.219, Rochford to Newcastle, 29 July 1753; Petrie, *Jacobite Movement,* pp. 149-55.

62. SP 92/61, f.63, Rochford to Holdernesse, 21 Apr. 1753.

63. R. Lodge, 'Sir Benjamin Keene K.B; a study of Anglo-Spanish Relations in the earlier part of the eighteenth century,' *TRHS,* 4th series, 15 (1932), pp. 16-25; F. Cognasso, *I Savoia nella politica Europa,* pp. 236-7.

64. BL Add MSS 32829, f.214, Holdernesse to Rochford, 29 Aug. 1751 O.S., Very Secret; SP 92/59, f.143, Rochford to Holdernesse, 22 Sept. 1751.

65. RDL D/87, Rochford to Yorke, 9 Oct. 1751.

66. SP 92/59, f.181, Rochford to Holdernesse, 30 Oct. 1751.

67. SP 92/59, f.202, Rochford to Holdernesse, 10 Nov. 1751.

68. SP 92/60, ff.85 & 90, Rochford to Holdernesse, 1 & 8 Mar. 1752.

69. BL Add MSS 32835, f.178, Rochford to Newcastle, 29 Apr. 1752; BL Stowe MSS 256, f.125, Keene to Rochford, 15 May 1752.

70. BL Add MSS 32836, f.237, Rochford to Newcastle, 2 June 1752; RDL D/115, Rochford to Keene, 1 June 1752; RDL D/116, Rochford to Albemarle, 10 June 1752.

71. Black, 'Development of Anglo-Sardinian Relations . . ,' p. 57, see also R. Browning, 'The Duke of Newcastle and the Imperial Election Plan, 1749-1754,' *Journal of British Studies,* 7 (1967), pp. 28-47, and P. Langford, *The Eighteenth Century, 1688-1815, Modern British Foreign Policy,* London 1976, pp. 130-2.

72. Valsecchi, *L'Italia nel Settecento,* pp. 244-7; Carutti, *Storia della diplomazia della Corte do Savoia,* II, pp. 335-6.

73. SP 92/61, f.200, Holdernesse to Rochford, 2 Apr. 1753; AST 58, Ossorio to Perrone, 30 June 1753; A/79, Birtles to Rochford, 14 July 1753.

74. SP 92/61, f.205, Newcastle to Rochford, 19 July 1753; f.130, Rochford to Holdernesse, 8 Aug. 1753; AST 58, Ossorio to Perrone, 11 Aug. 1753.

75. SP 92/61, ff.116 & 156, Rochford to Holdernesse, 21 July & 24 Oct. 1753.

76. Horn, *British Diplomatic Representatives,* p. 126.

77. G. Quazza, 'Italy's Role in the European Problems of the first half of the Eighteenth Century,' *Studies in Diplomatic History,* ed. R.M. Hatton & M.S. Anderson, London, 1970, pp. 138-54; *The Private Correspondence of Benjamin Keene,* ed. R. Lodge, Cambridge, 1933, p. 415, Keene to Castries, 7 July 1755; Horn (1967), p. 336.

78. Black, 'Development of Anglo-Sardinian Relations . . . ,' pp. 57-8.

79. G.W. Rice, 'Great Britain, the Manila Ransom, and the First Falkland Islands Dispute with Spain,' *International History Review,* 11 (1980), pp. 386-409.

CHAPTER 6

The Crown, Hanover and the Shift in British Foreign Policy in the 1760s

Jeremy Black

'The future conduct of states is not the subject of mathematical certainty, and who shall presume to foreknow the resolutions of politicians, a species of men that know their own minds as little as the vulgar world do theirs? All this I do most readily acknowledge, and therefore kingdoms, as well as individuals, must be content to provide against the probable injuries of each other; not waiting for unattainable certainty on the one hand, nor on the other, outrunning the appearance of danger, to bestow vain, impracticable, and endless endeavours, to be secure from mischiefs barely possible.'

Samuel Martin MP, *Thoughts on the System of our Late Treaties with Hesse-Cassel and Russia, in regard to Hanover* (1756), p. 38.

Shortly after the resignation of his favourite, the Earl of Bute, as First Lord of Treasury in April 1763, George III saw the French envoy. The conversation which lasted about an hour, took place without the Secretary of State for the Southern Department, the Earl of Egremont, and in it George spoke of the spirit of fermentation and excessive licence which reigned in England, of the need both to neglect nothing to repress that spirit and to use firmness as much as moderation for that end. George delcared his determination not to be the plaything of factions and announced that his fixed plan was to re-establish his authority without breaking the law.[1] Twenty-four years later Sir John Sinclair MP, returning from a seven months' tour of northern Europe, had an audience with George III in which the two men chatted for one and a half hours. Sinclair wrote, 'I was astonished with the extent of information which the King displayed upon a variety of subjects' and he directly quoted George's remark on Gustavus III's reimposition of monarchial authority in Sweden in 1772: 'I never will acknowledge, said his Majesty, that the King of a limited monarchy can, on any principle, endeavour to change the constitution, and to increase his own power. No honest man will attempt it'.[2]

However, the nature of the British constitution was unclear, especially in so far as some central issues of 'responsibility' were concerned.[3] It was not surprising that George III's views gave rise to often bitter debate, particularly given the tendency to ascribe policies to sinister motives in the hyperbolical and sometimes paranoid political culture of the age. The extent to which the debate over George III's views affected judgements of British foreign policy is far from clear. Compared to the situation under his grandfather, George II, and his great-grandfather, George I, what is striking about contemporary discussion of George III's constitutional and political views is how little of it relates to foreign policy. There were of course bitter debates over foreign policy in the last four decades of the century. Prominent examples include the peace negotiations with France in 1762-3, the Falkland Islands crisis of 1770, the Ochakov crisis of 1791, and British relations with revolutionary France in 1792-3. The views, real and supposed, of George were mentioned during these debates. In Dent's caricature of 30 April 1792, 'Declaration of War or Bumbardment of all Europe', in which the French National Assembly was presented as a battery of bums bombarding Kings with liberty, George III was pictured saying to Pitt, 'You must take care of the Hanoverian Horse'. However, debates over foreign policy were conducted largely with reference to the policies of the ministry of the time. In contrast, under George I and, though to a lesser extent, in part because of the rise of colonial and commercial issues, George II, the position of the monarch had been central in discussions over foreign policy. This owed much to both rulers' determination to protect and enhance the position of Hanover, often at the cost of interests and diplomatic possibilities that could be regarded as 'British', to genuine unease within Britain concerning the monarchs' commitment to Hanover, to a polemical tradition of antipathy to the Georges that derived from Jacobite hostility to the Hanoverian succession, but was not confined to Jacobites, and to the opposition of specific politicians to royal policies. Disquiet over the position of the Crown centred on its alleged preference for Hanover, a charge that could be best demonstrated with reference to foreign policy, though the granting of British pensions to foreigners and supposed foreign cultural preferences at Court were also condemned. Hanover thus served as both cause and demonstration of the perversion of the constitution by the monarch and of the political bankruptcy and craven behaviour of Whig ministers who would not defend the constitution. The constitutional safeguard of the Act of Succession (1701) had placed Parliament at the centre of any active diplomatic relationship between England and Hanover. Entitled programmatically 'An act for the further limitation of the crown, and better securing the rights and liberties of the subject', it had stipulated, 'that in case the crown and imperial dignity of this realm shall hereafter come to any person, not being a native of this kingdom of England, this nation be not obliged to engage in any war for the defence of any dominions or territories which do not belong to the crown of England, without the consent of parliament'.

Therefore, any supposed distortion of British interests for Hanoverian goals was not only brought up in Parliament as a political matter by opposition politicians, but could also serve to illustrate their charge that the ministry was failing to defend the constitution. Negotiations and commitments could be criticised as likely to provoke a situation in which Britain would support Hanover. In the sessions of the early 1740s sustained attacks were mounted on this basis and 'it was publicly, avowedly and expressly maintained that the interests of England and Hanover are incompatible'. Though the impact of anti-Hanoverian propaganda outside the parliamentary world cannot be proved, the large amount of it that was produced, ranging from the printed protests of opposition members of the House of Lords to abusive ballads, such as *The Late Gallant Exploits of a Famous Balancing Captain* of 1741, suggests that it was believed to be worth producing and, in some cases, sponsoring. In December 1742 Sir Mathew Decker, a Director of the East India Company and a former MP, expressed his fear that the decision to hire 16,000 Hanoverian troops for the army designed to help Maria Theresa, the ruler of the Habsburg dominions, against France would cause 'great dissatisfaction all over England'. Again it is unclear how far this extra-parliamentary agitation influenced the ministry and Parliament. On 7 December 1742 an estimate of the ministerial majority in the forthcoming Commons debate on the 16,000 Hanoverians suggested that it would be '100 at least'. In the event the division was 260-193, leading to the conclusion, 'we had greatly the justice of the debate on our side yet pamphlets and popular declamations made several good friends leave us', and, indeed, the published division list revealed that 70 MPs who can be classed as Whigs voted against the motions.[7]

Public discussion of the Hanoverian issue was not restricted to specific points such as whether at Dettingen in 1743 George II had displayed a preference for his role as leader of the Electoral forces. Opposition publications also raised constitutional points in order to create a sense that particular grievances could be explained with reference to a more general problem and tendency. In 1744 the London newspaper *Old England* claimed:

> Should any part of the Electorate be attacked by any power, upon any pretence whatever, I have the authority of the Act of Settlement to assert, that England ought not to be encumbered with the expence of defending it; notwithstanding the late truly British declaration of a late common, and now noble Patriot, that, if the Electorate were attacked upon the account of England, it was the duty of England to defend it.
>
> The Act of Settlement hath no such proviso: and should any such insidious interpretation be admitted, it is obvious Hanover would never be attacked but upon the account of England: consequently England would lose the very benefit of being an island, and become a most wretched part, of a most contemptible particle of the Continent.

The article stated that if the war led to troops in British pay being sent to the defence of Hanover or to territorial gains by the Electorate it would clearly be a Hanoverian war, and later in the year the paper claimed that the 'nation's war' with Spain, the War of Jenkins' Ear, was being neglected in favour of a German one with France.[8]

Hanover was not consistently a major British political issue during the reigns of George I and George II. Though the Anglo-French alliance of 1716-31 could be ascribed in part to Hanoverian concerns,[9] it ensured that relations with France provided the central topic of public debate over foreign policy during the years when it was in force. This was especially the case once the ending of the Great Northern War in 1721 had reduced interest in the Baltic and northern Europe and correspondingly diminished the importance of alleged Hanoverian influence on Anglo-Russian and Anglo-Swedish relations. Thus ministers were criticised for failing to defend British interests against France and for allegedly allowing the alliance to establish the parameters for their relations with other states. Hanover featured primarily in public discussion in the 1720s only after the formation of the Alliance of Vienna in 1725 and, more particularly, the defection to it of Prussia the following year led to its defence becoming a central concern of the ministry and, therefore, a political issue. The negotiation of an Anglo-Austrian alliance in 1731 and the consequent easing of tension in the Empire led to a corresponding reduction in ministerial and public concern with Hanover. This was sustained by British neutrality in the War of the Polish Succession (1733-5) and culminated in 1738-9 in the obsession with Spanish depredations and a neglect of Continental concerns.

Hanover was thrust to the front of British concern with foreign policy in 1741 as a consequence of the disruption of international relations caused by the death of the Emperor Charles VI and the subsequent invasion of Silesia by Frederick II (the Great) of Prussia. In April 1741 Thomas Clutterbuck, a Lord of the Admiralty, moving a Commons' address, declared, 'We ought to pronounce that the territories of Hanover will be considered on this occasion as the dominions of Great Britain, and that any attack on one or the other will be equally represented'.[10] The ministerial view, challenged in the Commons by William Pulteney, who referred to the Act of Settlement, led that summer to the offer of 12,000 British troops for the defence of Hanover against a threatened French invasion.[11] Had the British troops been sent that would have led to a public outcry but, in the event, this arose out of the neutrality negotiated for the Electorate which it was widely believed contained secret clauses affecting British conduct towards Spain. This was denied by George II and the British ministry,[12] and this statement can be confirmed from French sources. According to Amelot, the French foreign minister, George had rejected a French attempt to extend the neutrality to comprehend Spain, stating that he was not the master in Britain, that to give his word would be useless and that he would not be able to sustain what would offend the entire nation.[13]

The Hanoverian neutrality dispute began a period of sixteen years in which the Electorate was frequently a contentious issue in British politics. As a sympathetic account of the Hanoverian position has appeared recently[14] and as it is possible to concentrate on British political and public criticism of the Electorate, it is worth pointing out that such criticism was voiced also by informed British diplomats. For example in January 1741 Thomas Robinson, the envoy in Vienna, sent a letter, endorsed 'most private and secret', to Edward Weston, an Under Secretary in the Northern Department. He wrote, 'You will easily imagine why I trust with you for Lord Harrington's use, rather than to a dispatch, the enclosed papers. One a letter from the Regency at Hanover, without the King's order, to the Elector of Mainz, the other the paper of this court thereupon to the Electoral minister here . . . The King our master has not yet declared his personal view, not even, as appears by the letter, to his own Regency, which makes it the more extraordinary that they should hastily adopt a doctrine, that for what they may know or foresee may thwart his Majesty in quite different views . . . what you will easily perceive is, that the Elector's Minister very often comes across the King's. This is and has been so much the case that I have often seen by one blind and random shot overturned the best endeavours, in an universal capacity, of himself'.[15] It is unclear how far the criticism of experts informed and affected the discussion of Hanoverian issues by other politicians, but it is worth pointing out both that the diplomatic service was not divorced from domestic politics and that several diplomats rose to senior positions. Just as Weston, the recipient of the letter above, was to serve as an Under Secretary in the Northern Department until 1746 and then again from 1761 until 1764, linking the world of Walpole to that of George III, so its sender, Robinson, was to be Secretary of State for the Southern Department in 1754. The ministers and diplomats who negotiated the end of the War of Austrian Succession had to consider a Spanish debt that George sought as Elector, George's interest in the territories of Hildesheim and Osnabrück and his claims to East Friesland.[16]

Though nothing approaching the scale of the disquiet in 1741-44 recurred, Hanover remained an issue in the inter-war period of 1748-55 because of the prominence of the Imperial Election Scheme, the negotiations by which Britain sought to ensure the succession of the future Joseph II to the Imperial throne, hoping thus to preserve the stability of central Europe. Though the leading British minister with responsibility for foreign affairs, the Duke of Newcastle, at this time a keen advocate of 'the old alliance, and the true and solid system of Europe',[17] was a major proponent of the scheme, it owed much to Hanoverian suggestions and those of the Margrave of Ansbach's envoy Baron Seckendorf.[18] In addition, at least according to the French envoy, the people and most of the government saw links with Austria and Russia primarily as though they were Hanoverian connections.[19] The extent of public concern about Britain's negotiations on the Continent is unclear, but those who commented on it assumed public disquiet and the consequent political vulnerability of the ministry to events abroad was readily apparent. Joseph Yorke, the envoy in The Hague, wrote of Frederick II in 1752, 'his view seems evidently to provoke the King, and to alienate as far as in him lies, the affections of the English from their sovereign, by mixing the affairs of the Electorate with those of England'. Fears in 1753 that Anglo-Prussian commercial disputes and the mutual distrust of George II and Frederick II would lead to a Prussian attack on Hanover were not realised. The British ministry intended to support Hanover in the event of hostilities and likewise sought Dutch assistance, but, just as anxiety was expressed over the Dutch response, so it is unclear what the reaction within Britain would have been.[20]

As in the case of Carteret in 1742-4, the aggressive and interventionist diplomacy of Newcastle aroused disquiet and hostility in ministerial as well as in political circles and in public discussion. Newcastle's brother, Henry Pelham complained in November 1748:

> all this proceeds only from this active spirit, he wants to be doing, and the many interested parties he has been lately with, have found out that, and of consequence flatter him into their own measures. He always had a partiality and regard for the late Lord Stanhope. I know he thinks no minister has made a great figure but him in the two reigns: he will therefore imitate him as far as he can, and I doubt, if he is not checked by somebody, will bring himself if not his country into the same distress that fertile but well intentioned Lord did before him.[21]

Pelham's prescient letter reveals the historical perspective of so many of the politicians of the period, one not of distant history but of the experience of their own lives. This provided both the basis upon which ideas could be judged and the canons of fame that must be matched. Like Carteret and Stanhope, though it is important not to ignore the role of the monarchs whose responsibility the ministers assumed, Newcastle not only divided the ministry in pursuit of the foreign policy he supported, but also made the policy a contentious political issue. As in the earlier episodes, the supposed nature of Hanoverian interests and influences was criticised. Discussion of the Electorate both served as a surrogate for debate about the influence of the monarch and related clearly to it.

The legacy of both ministerial division and political and public disquiet over Hanover led to serious difficulties in the international crisis of the mid-1750s, when the British government sought to take diplomatic measures for the protection of the Electorate, and in the early stages of the

Seven Years' War when its vulnerability was exploited by France. The note of popular hostility was set by the response to the Hanoverian troops brought to Britain at the beginning of the war to protect her against a possible French invasion. The vast bulk of the printed comment was hostile, the themes of greed and rape being prominent. One pamphleteer claimed that the foreign troops had 'furnished so copious a field for our ballad-makers, print-sellers, and newswriters to display their talents for satire and ridicule'.[22] The situation abroad was more contentious politically than at the beginning of the decade and in late 1755 a major parliamentary attack was mounted on subsidy treaties with Hesse-Cassel and Russia which, it was fairly claimed, were essentially for the defence of Hanover. On 10 December 1755 in the House of Commons Thomas Potter declared that the treaties were 'illegally concluded, as being made for the defence of Hanover without consent of Parliament, in violation and defiance of the Act of Settlement, and charged besides, the payment of the Hessian levy money in the summer as a criminal misapplication of the public money. And without entering into the expediency or tendency of the Treaties, thought for these reasons, the House should not give them so much countenance as to refer them'.

In the same debate Henry Fox attacked William Pitt and the attempt to create 'the fatal distinction . . . of Englishman and Hanoverian'.[23] Samuel Martin MP, who had followed Henry Legge into opposition over the treaties, produced a pamphlet that admitted that Hanover was endangered by British policy but, nevertheless, insisted that the measures taken to defend it were excessive, not for the purpose, but with reference to British interests and resources. Crown and country were clearly differentiated in the shape of George's conception of the interests of Britain and Hanover as opposed to those which Martin, like other writers, advanced for Britain:

> I will ingeniously acknowledge, that there could be no room to apprehend any project from France, to hurt his Majesty's Electoral dominions, except in consequence of the quarrel between that Kingdom and Great Britain. Nay, I will own that we are bound in generosity as well as respect for our sovereign to exert all reasonable endeavours to shelter those dominions from injury, intended upon our account. But I condemn the treaties, as they aim at the defiance of Hanover, by a system which is absolutely impracticable, surpassing the utmost stretch of Great Britain's ability to accomplish . . . The two treaties in question must be considered as parts of a vast comprehensive system, to gather and combine the powers of the European Continent into a defensive alliance, of magnitude sufficient to withstand the utmost efforts of France and her adherents against the Electorate; and all this to be effected at the expence and charge of Great Britain . . . foreign nations are not bound to distinguish between the Royal and Electoral functions of our Sovereign, and may think it lawful to retaliate upon his Electoral dominions for any affront received from him in the capacity of King of Great Britain.[24]

Jonathan Clark, in his recent detailed political study of this period, has suggested that 'even stock issues like those of subsidy treaties and the threat of invasion, which both concerned MPs and could be used to stir passions without doors, had no necessary impact on parliamentary politics independent of the tactical context within which, and the party vehicles by which, they were given political significance'.[25] This is a cogent argument, but it is worth noting that the politics of the period did not proceed simply in terms of parliamentary arithmetic. The extent to which the discussion and political context of issues influenced the attitude of politicians is a difficult one, but a sphere in which it is possible to suggest a connection is that of Hanover. A link can be traced between the criticism of Continental involvement and specifically of commitments entered into for the sake of Hanover in the 1750s, and policy in the 1760s. This link is most apparent in the case of George III. As heir, he had written to Bute in August 1759: 'as to the affairs on the Weser they look worse and worse; I fear this is entir'ly owing to the partiality (the King) has for that horrid Electorate which has always liv'd upon the very vitals of this poor Country; I should say more and perhaps with more anger did not my clock show 'tis time to dress for Court'. As king he showed his determination to end Britain's involvement in the German part of the Seven Years' War, 'though I have subjects who will suffer immensely whenever this Kingdom withdraws its protection from thence, yet so superior is my love to this my native country over any private interest of my own that I cannot help wishing that an end was put to that enormous expence by ordering our troops home . . . I think if the Duke of Newcastle will not hear reason concerning the German war that it would be better to let him quit than to go on with that and to have myself and those who differ from him made unpopular'. Conscious of the importance of popularity, George informed Bute in 1762 that he would 'never wish to load this country with' subsidies.[26]

In the 1760s George III was not conspicuous as an advocate of Hanoverian interests and of British commitments to aid the Electorate. As a result the king's views on foreign policy were not as politically contentious as those of his grandfather and great-grandfather had been. This owed much also to the dominance of colonial, commercial and maritime issues in both British foreign policy in the 1760s and in the political and public discussion of it. In addition, after 1763 foreign policy ceased to be such a consistently contentious sphere for and source of political debate. Domestic and American constitutional, fiscal and political issues helped to divert attention from foreign policy, with which it was difficult to link them. Those who challenged George III or his ministers did not need to refer to foreign policy. The collapse of Jacobitism and the attenuation of certain political themes in the late 1750s and 1760s, as political groupings reformed, helped further to create a new agenda on which Hanover and the royal role in foreign policy played little part. This argument must not be pushed too far: foreign policy was not forgotten and reference was made to George III's views, but a substantial change followed his accession.

George III has been described as 'the first English king in the age of nationalism' and 'the patriot king'. It was certainly the case that the views of the new monarch and the aspirations engendered by his accession created disquiet in some from the outset, as the dispute over his address to his first Privy Council revealed. Five days after the death of George II on 25 October 1760, one of Newcastle's supporters, the Marquess of Rockingham, displayed concern over the terms of a likely address from Yorkshire: 'I could wish that the words *(Native Country)* and *(Truly English)* were not echo'd back from Yorkshire — as indeed it strikes me as carrying with it a signification that that was wanting in his late Majesty . . . Queen Anne on the death of King William in her declaration set forth that *Her Heart was entirely English* which gave great offence to the Whigs at that time'.[27] The break with his grandfather's ministers was intertwined with the break with the policies of the 1750s. It was not only that the alliance with Prussia was lost, but that the gap was not filled by an alliance with another major continental power. The motive for such a course of action, royal anxiety about Hanover,[28] ministerial concern about this anxiety and the sense that defensive arrangements for Hanover could and should serve as the basis for a British alliance system, had been largely lost. So also had the interventionist habit of mind and the concomitant diplomatic assumptions. George III might be very gracious to Carteret soon after his accession,[29] but he had little interest in the views that that minister had once stood for. In March 1761 Baron Haslang, the Palatine envoy in London, pointed out that the prince-bishopric of Hildesheim, which the neighbouring Electorate of Hanover had long sought, was both vacant and actually occupied by George III's forces. George II had wished to gain the territory but George III did not share his grandfather's views. Three weeks after reporting that Hildesheim was vacant, Haslang observed that the predilection for Hanover was no longer so strong and suggested that there would be no territorial cessions elsewhere in order to make gains for the Electorate.[30] This was at a time when the Electorate of Saxony was seeking territorial gains from the Archbishopric-Electorate of Mainz.

When in June 1761 Francois de Bussy began peace negotiations with the British ministry, he was told by Carteret that the British had little interest in Hanoverian affairs. When Bussy told Pitt that France would expect compensation for her Hanoverian conquests, on the grounds that in order to pursue her operations on the Continent, France had diverted resources from the defence of her colonies, Pitt replied that the argument would have had a great effect during the reign of George II, but that the situation had changed. This was a position that Choiseul found difficult to accept, though he had already commented in February 1760 that it would not matter to Pitt if France devastated Hanover.[31] Bussy returned to the subject when he saw Pitt on 23 June 1761. He claimed that the Electorate should be regarded as a province of England, because George II, as King, had broken the 1757 Convention of Klosterseven for the disbandment of the Hanoverian Army of Occupation, and because the army commanded by Prince Ferdinand of Brunswick for the defence of Hanover acted in accordance with George's orders and for 'the cause of England'. Bussy reiterated the charge that French losses in the colonies were due partly to their operations on the Continent. Choiseul was determined to establish the principles of compensations and equivalence.[32] Pitt was willing to moderate his attitude and offer the return of Guadeloupe and Martinique as compensation for the French evacuation of her gains in Hanover and the territories of the latter's allies. He also insisted that France evacuate Prussia's Rhenish territories and Frankfurt. However, in the end the negotiations failed as a result of the Franco-Spanish Family Compact signed on 15 August, the deterioration of Anglo-Spanish relations and the British delay in offering acceptable terms to France. Though Pitt had shifted his ground on Hanover, it was clear that George III and his leading ministers were not willing to allow Hanoverian concerns to play a major role in the negotiations. Haslang had noted in July 1761 that whatever happened in the Empire would have little effect on British government policy, adding, 'Ce n'est plus le temps de George II'. Bute told the Sardinian envoy, Viry, in October 1761 that France would not gain better terms if she took Hanover. A month later Newcastle wrote to Rockingham, 'There are *many* who are for abandoning the German war, and giving up Hanover, and our allies. That is what I can never consent to, nor, I believe, any of our friends, I have talked very plainly to the King, and My Lord Bute upon it'.[33]

Pitt's resignation and the collapse amidst recriminations of the Anglo-Prussian alliance helped to ensure that in 1761-2 commitment to the Continent was discussed in terms of shifting British political alignments. The alliance with Prussia had served during the Seven Years' War to legitimate such commitment for Pitt and many others. It had diverted attention from the issue of Hanover and provided a plausible basis for policies that would have been condemned had they been linked only with the Electorate. Frederick II also had an aura of success to commend him, one that the Hanoverians did not gain with the British public. George II did not fight the French in 1741, while his victory at Dettingen was compromised by accusations of prejudice in favour of the Hanoverian troops. Cumberland's defence of the Electorate in 1757 was a humiliating failure with serious political consequences. Fame was only gained by Ferdinand of Brunswick, a German but not a Hanoverian. In contrast, Providence could be found at work in Frederick II's victories and even in the more surprising sphere of British foreign policy. The London periodical the *Monitor* claimed in 1758 that:

> under the direction of Providence, this nation has after a course of sixty years bad policy in the support of the popish house of Austria, been forcibly driven by her natural enemies to an alliance with the only power upon earth that is capable of assisting us in the defence of the Protestant faith, and by his military capacity, to reduce the common enemy . . . to an incapacity of disturbing the peace of his neighbours for the future. Such alliances are agreeable to the constitution and interest of these kingdoms. They are according to that model of sound politics, which were laid down by the ministers of our Elizabeth, who could never be persuaded to take any further share in the troubles on the continent, than was necessary to facilitate the schemes of their own government. But it is very wide of those continental measures, which of late years have loaded this nation with heavy debts for the support of armies in the time of peace, and for taking upon us the greatest burden in every quarrel raised by the house of Austria.

Such comments might be regarded as an example of what Richard Rigby MP, the secretary to the Lord Lieutenant of Ireland, referred to as 'all the trite nonsense of popularity'.[34] However, they also demonstrate the extent to which the Prussian alliance provided the possibility for bridging the traditional antithesis of pro-Hanoverian ministerial continental interventionalism and 'patriot' isolationism, a bridging that Pitt represented and helped to popularise. By 1762 the defence of the alliance was no longer easy. War-weariness and the greater popularity of 'blue-water' policies sapped public support for the British commitment to Prussia. Pitt's intransigence and the obvious preferences of George III reduced political support, and in so far as the cause of allies commanded favourable attention, it was that of Portugal, threatened by Spain, rather than Prussia. The reassessment of the Prussian alliance was linked to renewed criticism of Hanover. Having served to distract attention from Hanover and to limit antagonism towards continental engagements, the disintegration of the alliance was linked with both. However, in obvious contrast to earlier periods of marked hostility towards continental commitments, in 1762 Hanover played only a minor role and the king was not criticised. The move to restrict British commitments and to limit policy to recognisably British goals came from the monarch. It was the *Briton,* a weekly newspaper established by Bute, that admitted in July 1762 that there was a danger of Hanover being invaded if Britain refused to assist Prussia. However, the paper added:

> it is the duty, the interest of the Germanic body to see justice done to any of its constituent

members that shall be oppressed: but should they neglect their duty and interest on such an occasion, I hope the elector of H . . . r will never again have influence enough with the K . . . g of G . . . t B . . . n, to engage him in a war for retrieving it, that shall cost his kingdom annually, for a series of years, more than double the value of the country in dispute.

The paper calculated the annual cost of the 'herculean task' of the defence of Hanover as £6 million.[35]

At the same time as George III and the government sought to disentangle themselves from the 'German war', there was an interesting sign that George was not without concern for the position of the Electorate, albeit a concern in which territorial aggrandisement played no role. The Hanoverian minister, Baron Behr, suggested to Haslang that once a general peace had been made, a German league, of at least the leading Electors, should be formed so that the participants were not always at risk of being invaded on the slightest pretext. He added that George III would seek agreement first with the Elector of Bavaria. The same month the Duke of Nivernais, the French envoy sent to London to negotiate peace in the autumn of 1762, was reporting that George III and his British ministers wished to make the fewest links possible in the Empire and to spend no money there and that peace was likely to be followed on the part of Britain by 'un sistême d'indifférence' towards the Empire.[36] There was no real contradiction between Behr's approach and Nivernais' report, given that George both seemed determined to retain the distinction between Britain and Hanover and revealed little interest in territorial acquisitions for the latter. Furthermore, Newcastle's charge that the British government was intent on 'abandoning the Continent'[37] was true only in so far as the war in the Empire was concerned. The personal, indeed emotional, attachments to Hanover of George II and to continental interventionism of Newcastle were not matched by their successors but, once freed of the incubus of the war, George III and his British ministers were willing to consider a revival of the search for allies. This was not intended to repeat the subsidy-offering diplomacy of Newcastle after the War of the Austrian Succession, but the major powers whose alliance were sought were the same: Austria and Russia.

Nivernais had been struck by the hostility expressed towards Austria, but the British ministry in fact sought improved relations and there was hope that the Austrian Chancellor, Count Kaunitz, who was generally regarded as hostile to Britain, was losing influence. In February 1762 the French envoy in Madrid had discussed with Charles III the possibility of Britain sacrificing Prussia in order to unite with Austria, though he claimed that there was no sign of such a development at that moment. James Porter, who had represented Britain in commercial negotiations with Austria and was soon to be sent as envoy to Brussels, urged the negotiation of an alliance with Austria. He argued that if France was sure of Austria she would be able to reduce her army and within five years have a fleet of 100 of the line, whereas 'if you are in friendship merely with that house, that of Bourbon will not be secure under such a reduction but be obliged to keep up their land army and they cannot supply for both'. The diplomatic Joseph Yorke hoped that the end of the war would be as traumatic for the Austro-French alliance as it had been for that of Britain and Prussia: 'it is very clear that court (Austria) cannot long subsist without some connection, and it is a little difficult to suppose that France will be her object much longer'. Viscount Stormont was named as the British envoy to reopen the diplomatic relations broken in 1757. Baron Steinberg, who had represented Hanover at Vienna before the war, resumed his mission. The Earl of Buckinghamshire had already arrived in St. Petersburg in September 1762.[38]

This attempt to resume negotiations with two states whose conflict with Prussia had kept them distant from Britain was in part a reaction to the end of the Anglo-Prussian alliance and a natural response to the sense of reopened diplomatic possibilities that every peace brought in this period. There was, however, no comparable attempt to use British diplomatic assistance to support Hanoverian interests in north-western Germany where the death of the Wittelsbach episcopal pluralist Clement-Auguste, Archbishop-Elector of Cologne and Prince-Bishop of Hildesheim, Münster, Osnabrück and Paderborn, on 7 February 1761 had produced a tremendous opportunity not only for ecclesiastical place-seekers and the advocates of secularisation, but also for those who wished to enhance their influence in this region. However, George made little attempt to intervene in the elections in marked contrast to the position in the 1720s when they had last been conducted. In 1753 a Dutch approach for British support in elections to vacant positions in the chapters led Newcastle to reflect, 'it is certainly of consequence, to have a well-intentioned person chose Prevot of the Cathedral Chapter of Munster'. In 1763 the Hanoverian attitude to the position in Osnabrück gave rise to some concern about Hanoverian intentions, but this proved to be exaggerated.[39]

Haslang was told that George would go to Hanover in the summer of 1761 and he suggested that this would be not only a great consolation for his subjects but also an opportunity to arrange many things for the general good of the Empire.[40] Haslang's suggestion draws attention to an obvious difference between George III and his two predecessors. Their often lengthy trips to Hanover had served as the basis not only for the reinvigoration of Hanover diplomacy, but also for the development and implementation of interventionist British schemes, for example Townshend's negotiation of the Alliance of Hanover in 1725, his negotiations with the Wittelsbachs in 1729 and Newcastle's pursuit of the Imperial Election Scheme. During these trips British ministers, as well as the monarch, met high-ranking continental statesmen whom they were unlikely to ever meet in London. Negotiations were facilitated and time was gained, which was vital in any discussions involving more than two powers. While British ministers were in Hanover it was natural for them both to think of an active Continental diplomacy, in part in terms of Hanoverian interests, and to be aware of Hanoverian vulnerability. Leaving aside the important question of how far George III sought to foster Hanoverian interests, it is appropriate to note that his failure to visit Hanover ensured that it was more difficult in the course of British foreign policy to further these interests. In addition, because George did not visit the Electorate, his British ministers did not go there and thus Hanover ceased to be the episodic focus of British foreign policy. The possible importance of royal visits was indicated by the role of Frederick Duke of York, George's second son. Prince-Bishop of Osnabrück from shortly after his birth in 1763, he went to Hanover in 1781 and from 1783 his presence and actions helped to improve relations between George III and Frederick II. It is open to speculation as to whether a visit by George to the Electorate would have served for the negotiation of an improvement on earlier occasions. Imminent visits to Hanover by George were reported on a number of occasions, for example by *Owen's Weekly Chronicle* on 17 and 31 March 1764, but he never went.

Stormont was instructed to give 'proper assurances of our sincere desire to return to the ancient system of union, intimacy and communication of counsels, for our mutual benefit, and for the public good'. However, the response was not especially warm, envoys not being exchanged with Austria until the Autumn of 1763. On 1 July 1763 the Earl of Halifax, Secretary of State for the Northern Department, observed, 'What may be the present dispositions of The Queen of Hungary towards us, we have no other knowledge than what arises from some vague and general professions of her ministers, at other courts, of her inclination to return to the old system of friendship with England . . . But there is a great reason to believe that the intimacy between the Austrian and Bourbon houses is cultivated as much as possible by France, and still continues'.[41]

Though desirous of better relations with the major continental powers, George III and his British ministry were not willing to bind Britain to extensive diplomatic commitments as was revealed clearly by the unwillingness to accept Russian demands for support in Poland and against the Turks. The Russian minister, Count Panin, told Buckinghamshire on 19 September 1763 that 'with regard to the stipulations, relative to Sweden and Poland . . . when England proposed to enter into an alliance with Russia, it must be with a view of interesting herself in the affairs of the

North, and, in that case, the system of Europe could not be too comprehensive, for, unless we secured Russia against the attacks of her neighbours, she would be very little able, upon any emergency, to assist us'. Buckinghamshire made it clear that in his view Turkey had nothing to do with the affairs of northern Europe. Three months later he received fresh instructions from Halifax's replacement, the Earl of Sandwich, himself a former diplomat:

> Your Excellency will continue the same language with respect to their idea of receiving any pecuniary aid from Great Britain, which neither the present situation of affairs in Europe, nor the state of a country, just at the end of a bloody, and most expensive war, nor the necessities of alliance, give any room to expect or desire . . . nor does the situation of His Kingdoms require, that the King should purchase, or solicit, an alliance, in which the interests of Russia are at least, as much connected as those of Great Britain.[42]

Britain was perceived by foreign diplomats as a state that did not wish to take an active role in Continental disputes.[43] This view was fortified by the British response to two issues that were to cause greater concern within a decade, Poland and Corsica. Responding in July 1763 to the movement of Russian troops into Lithuania, Kaunitz suggested that the leading European powers, namely Austria, Britain and France, should co-operate in preventing Russia and Prussia from dominating Poland. The French envoy Chatelet replied by suggesting that Britain's position was equivocal and he subsequently argued that British policy might be affected both by ministerial instability and by the need for Russian support in the event of a quarrel between George III, as Elector, and Frederick II. The government was opposed to taking any role in the Polish royal election that followed the death of Augustus III and welcomed signs that it would not lead to conflict. The French envoy pressed Britain to take a stand which France was to seek again in 1772-3 at the time of the First Partition of Poland: 'He spoke of the reports which have lately prevailed concerning the intended dismembering of some parts of Poland and added that any such dismembering ought, if possible, to be prevented, as contrary to the interest of his court as well as ours'. The British government indeed made it clear that it was opposed to any dismemberment, Sandwich himself telling the Russian envoy. However, it was equally clear that the government did not intend to act.[44]

Britain had played a major role in the western Mediterranean in the first half of the century,[45] but this had depended on regional allies as much, if not more, as on naval power. These allies had been, at various times, Austria, Sardinia (previously Savoy-Piedmont and, briefly, the kingdom of Sicily) and Spain. After the collapse of the Anglo-French alliance in 1731 Britain had sought allies among other powers opposed to France, but this number had declined. Though not always sympathetic to her, Spain had not been a member of an anti-French alliance from 1733 nor Austria after 1756. This shift made an Anglo-Sardinian alliance less credible. Sardinian hopes that Britain would take a more forceful role after the Seven Years' War were soon shown to be without substance. On 10 November 1763 the new Sardinian envoy, Count Marmora, pressed Sandwich on Corsica. He stressed the importance of the island and argued that if Genoa was compensated for its loss by territorial gains in Italy this would facilitate a possible Bourbon invasion of the peninsula. Sandwich in his response revealed a lack of interest and Marmora suggested that the government was not really concerned about foreign affairs. Despite the threat to Britain's influence in Italy created by the growing danger of a French acquisition of Corsica, Marmora had no success throughout the winter in eliciting a positive response.[46]

The British government displayed more interest in gaining the alliance of Austria. The new Austrian envoy, Count Seilern, arrived in London on 24 October 1763. George III and his ministers, especially Sandwich, made it clear that they sought a close alliance and the re-establishment of old links. Concern over the position of Hanover also appears to have played a role, though it is not clear how far this was intended to serve as the pretext for an approach to Vienna. Judging from the diary of George Grenville, it was certainly important as far as George III was concerned. He seemed determined to protect the Electorate against a possible Prussian attack, and to resist Prussian demands, which reflected Frederick's strength in northern Germany. George had recently ordered Andrew Mitchell, the British envoy in Berlin, to press Frederick to stop recruiting violently for his army in Mecklenburg-Schwerin and to draw attention to the family links springing from George's marriage. Though Frederick's ostensible quarrel was with Britain, the Electorate appeared the likely victim. The previous September the French minister plenipotentiary, the Chevalier D'Eon, had suggested that it was natural for the Elector of Hanover to fear Frederick. In December 1763 Sandwich wrote to Stormont:

> Situated as this country is, we are, thank God, out of the reach of any molestation from His Prussian Majesty; and therefore, I cannot conceive how He can effect, what He calls doing Himself justice, but by offering some insult upon His Majesty's Dominions in Germany.

Ordered by George to sound Seilern on whether Austria would provide help in such an event:

> I began by telling him, how much it was to be wished, that the union which formerly subsisted with the House of Austria might be reestablished; That we were the Natural Allies of each other; and that, though untoward events had unfortunately made a breach

between us, I still hoped, time, and a good disposition on each side might bring things back to their original state.

Seilern said he was certain that Austria would provide help against Prussia, shrewdly adding 'that Count Kaunitz, and all the well-intentioned people at Vienna, were greatly pleased at the triumph of the present Administration, who were considered there, as persons who knew the true interests of their country, and would have firmness enough to support that system'.[47]

The Austrian government was not interested in abandoning France in order to ally with a British government which made it clear that it was unenthusiastic about continental commitments. Hardwicke's third son, Joseph Yorke who, having served in the War of the Austrian Succession as the Duke of Cumberland's aide-de-camp before representing Britain in Paris (1749-51) and The Hague (1751-80), can be regarded as a member of the mid-century interventionist diplomatic tradition, wrote in 1764:

> The great error which has always struck me in all Englishmens reasoning about the Continent; is that they confound the interest of their country in the general system, with the particular mode of expence which is followed, and the sending a body of national troops abroad at an expence which is insupportable, but which we ourselves are the cause of; I am sure however, that without we do preserve a certain influence upon the Continent, we cannot maintain the peace we always fight for and purchase, and that I always wish Great Britain should appear in the light she can do, and direct the councils of other countries.[48]

This tradition had never excluded alternative views in ministerial circles, Henry Pelham's resistance from 1748 to his brother's subsidy plans being a conspicuous instance. In turn, the different views advanced within the Whig ministries between 1714 and 1735 had indicated the various possibilities that commitment to the Hanoverian Succession, the Whig tradition and the exigencies of office could lead to. In essence a similar difference continued about 1763, but the emphasis was no longer placed so clearly on the search for allies. Instead, the cost and costs of alliances were stressed. In August 1764, for example, Sandwich wrote to the Under Secretary, Richard Phelps, concerning the need to send Buckinghamshire fresh instructions about a possible treaty of alliance with Russia:

> it might not be amiss to hint to him that it is our opinion here that the showing too great eagerness to forward it does more hurt than good, and that in consequence of that idea I had flatly told Mr. Gross that I should not agitate that subject any more till the first motion came from their side. He should also be told that as Count Seilern had assured me by authority that the House of Austria had not acceded to any of the treaties between France and Spain, nor formed any new engagements with them, there was no occasion for us to be very precipitate in forming new alliances, though this consideration would not make us unwilling to renew our old ones when proper attention was paid to us by those whose interest it is to be united with us.[49]

British ministers assured foreign envoys that Britain did not wish to accede to any treaty that entailed aggressive schemes. The envoys themselves saw a general lack of interest in the Continent.[50] The reasons for the shift from the inter-war period were various. In part, success in the Seven Years' War bred in Britain a sense that foreign states needed her and that any alliance would have to be reciprocal, which in foreign eyes could mean an apparent lack of willingness by Britain to offer assistance. The note of optimism concerning national success and capability was not only captured by the British press. William Gordon, on his way via Brussels and Aachen to take up a posting at Regensburg, wrote from Hanau in 1764:

> the joy I felt through the whole course of my route through the Empire is not to be described. Judge what my feelings must be, when in every place through which I passed every man from the highest to the lowest was striving who should do the greatest justice to the character and shining virtues of our most gracious master, and to the nation who has the glory and happiness to be his subjects. The war we carried on with such success and reputation to our arms, the support we gave to those powers with whom we were connected and the finishing the war by so glorious and honorable a peace has struck such an awe upon all foreigners, that they look upon us as a race of people superior to the rest of mankind.[51]

The years after the war can be presented as a period in which a position of and reputation for strength were lost and dissipated by foolish policies, an unwillingness to make the necessary commitments to foreign powers and the effects of domestic political strife. Such claims were indeed advanced by 'Patriot' writers of the period. 'An Occasional Writer', writing in the *St. James's Chronicle* in 1765, contrasted Grenville and Pitt, to the disadvantage of the former:

> it is his opinion, that the saving of half a crown to the Sinking-Fund, is a more important subject, than the credit of the nation and the affection of our allies.
> Mr Pitt thinks that we ought, by well chosen alliances, to prevent the approach of danger, weaken the connections of France, and maintain the Balance of Power in our own hands.
> Mr. Grenville disclaims all knowledge of foreign affairs; and thinks no alliance worth the money paid for engrossing the Treaty.[52]

These views also took pictorial form. In an anonymous caricature, *Picture of Europe for July 1772*, George III was presented as slumbering on his throne, while Austria, Russia and Prussia planned the Partition of Poland and Britain's weight in the Balance of Power did not prevail. This view was unfounded. George was very concerned by the Partition and by the Swedish monarchial *coup d'état* of the same year. However, it was certainly true that many of the ministers in the post-war period lacked a determination to win allies. Nevertheless, rather than presenting this as both a consequence of folly and as the loss of a strong position, it is more appropriate to suggest that Britain had little to offer as an ally, especially to the major powers of central and eastern Europe, Austria, Prussia and Russia. This had been less true when George I, George II and Newcastle had sought to intervene actively with schemes such as the anti-Russian league in the last stages of the Great Northern War and the Imperial Election Scheme, but it would be misleading to suggest that the major western European powers, Britain and France, had wielded considerable influence further east in the first six decades of the century and lost it subsequently. Instead, their influence had been only episodic in the earlier period, as Peter the Great showed when he defied George I. The fate of Poland was plotted by its neighbours before the death of Augustus II in 1733 with as little interest in western Europe views as was to be shown in 1772. Even had Britain allied with Austria, Prussia or Russia after the Seven Years' War, there is no reason to believe that she would have enjoyed much influence with her ally or even been consulted. This had certainly been the case with the Anglo-Austrian alliance negotiated in 1731. British fame in the early 1760s reflected naval and trans-oceanic successes. It did not translate into tens of thousands of troops on the plains of north Germany. The best point of comparison for Britain's continental position after 1763 was not the second half of the Seven Years' War, but 1751-6. Then Britain had found it difficult to win Russia as an ally on acceptable terms, had been badly disappointed by Austrian policy during the negotiations arising from the Imperial Election Scheme and infuriated by Austria's refusal to adopt a sympathetic attitude and supporting position during the confrontation with France in America, and had found that British influence over her new Prussian ally was limited. The centre piece of much British diplomacy in that period had been the defence of Hanover. When this was removed, many British ministers adopted a more circumspect approach to possible commitments. They sought alliances, but with greater caution when events moved from the state of expressions of good will to actual negotiations. A distinct shift had occurred.

NOTES

1. Duke of Nivernais to Duke of Praslin, French foreign minister, 11 May 1763, AE. CP. Ang. 450 f.337.

2. Sinclair to Charles Jenkinson, Lord Hawkesbury, 2 July 1787, BL Add. 38222 f. 90-1.

3. M. Peters, 'Pitt as a foil to Bute', in K.W. Schweizer (ed.), *Lord Bute. Essays in Re-interpretation* (Leicester, 1988), p.111.

4. E.N. Williams (ed.), *The Eighteenth-Century Constitution* (Cambridge, 1965), p.59.

5. Draft possibly of a letter to George II, 1744, Cambridge University Library, Cholmondely (Houghton) manuscripts 90/30.

6. Decker to the 13th Earl of Morton, a supporter of the ministry in the House of Lords, 16 Dec. 1742, Edinburgh, Scottish Record Office, GD 150/3485; Sir James Lowther MP to his agent, John Spedding, 11, 14, 16, 18 Dec. 1742, Carlisle, Country Record Office, D/Lons/W.

7. Anon. to Morton, 7, 11, Dec. 1742, GD 150/3485.

8. *Old England* 28 Apr., 20 Oct. 1744.

9. Black, 'The Anglo-French Alliance 1716-31', *Francia* 13 (1986).

10. W. Cobbett, *Parliamentary History of England from . . . 1066 to . . . 1803* (36 vols., 1806-20), 12, 157.

11. Duke of Newcastle, Secretary of State for the Southern Department, to Lord Harrington, Secretary of State for the Northern Department, 31 July 1741, PRO. 43/101.

12. Harrington to Lord Hyndford, envoy in Berlin, 24 Nov. 1741, PRO. 90/51 f.137; Hon. Philip Yorke MP to his wife (early Dec. 1741), Bedford, County Record Office, Lucas papers 30/9/113/3.

13. Amelot to Bishop of Rennes, envoy in Spain, 19 Feb. 1742, AE. CP. Espagne 470 f.95.

14. U. Dann, *Hannover und England 1740-1760: Diplomatie und Selbsterhaltung* (Hildesheim, 1986). See also A. M. Birke and K. Kluxen (eds), *England und Hannover* (Munich, 1986).

15. Robinson to Weston, 18 Jan. 1741, PRO. 80/144.

16. Earl of Chesterfield to Earl of Sandwich, 17 Feb, 1747, Henry Legge, envoy in Berlin, to George II, 12 May, Newcastle to Sandwich, 13 July, George II to Busch, Hanoverian envoy at the Congress, 6, 27 Aug., Newcastle to Robinson, 21 Sept. 1748, BL. Add. 32807 f.127, 32812 f.133, 32813 f.5-7, 226, 32814 f.1-2, 248.

17. Newcastle to Sandwich, 17 May, 26 July, Newcastle to Robinson, 16 July 1748, BL. Add. 32812, f.209, 32813 f.135, 33.

18. Seckendorf to Hanoverian ministry, undated, 29 Nov. 1748, BL. Add. 32815 f.132, 301-2; Newcastle to Gerlach Adolf von Münchhausen, Hanoverian minister, 29 Nov., 9 Dec. 1748, Hanover, Niedersächsisches Hauptstaatsarchiv, Calenberg Brief Archiv, 24 Nr. 1740 f 1,9; Münchhausen to the Austrian minister Khevenhüller, 23 Mar. 1749, Hanbury-Williams, envoy at Dresden, to Henry Fox, 27 July 1752, BL. Add. 32816 f.247. 51393 f.111.

19. Mirepoix to Puysieulx, French foreign minister, 2 Oct. 1749, AE. CP. Ang. 427 f.126.

20. Yorke to his father the Earl of Hardwicke, the Lord Chancellor, 22 Dec. 1752, BL. Add. 35356 f.107; Newcastle to Yorke, 6 Mar. 1753, PRO. 84/462.

21. Pelham to Hardwicke, 14 Nov. 1748, B.L. Add. 35423 f.80.

22. Anon., *A Serious Defence of some late Measures of the Administration; Particularly with regard to the Introduction and Establishment of Foreign Troops* (1756), p.4; Anon., *German Cruelty: A Fair Warning to the People of Great Britain* (1756).

23. Fox to the Duke of Devonshire, 11 Dec. 1755, Chatsworth House, Devonshire Mss 330/87; Horace Walpole, *Memoirs of King George II*, ed. J. Brooke (3 vols., New Haven, 1985), 2, 95-102.

24. Martin, *Deliberate Thoughts on the System of our late Treaties with Hesse Cassel and Russia* (1756), pp5, 13, 41. Mss text is BL. Add. 41355 f.29-98.

25. J.C.D. Clark, *The Dynamics of Change* (Cambridge, 1982), p.211.

26. R. Sedgwick (ed.), *Letters from George III to Lord Bute 1756-1766* (1939), pp.28-9, 78-9, 177.

27. G. Newman, *The Rise of English Nationalism. A Cultural History, 1740-1830* (1987), p.171; M. Peters, *Pitt and Popularity* (Oxford, 1980), p.180; J. Brooke, *King George III* (1972), p.75; Rockingham to Sir George Saville, 30 Oct. 1760, Oxford, Bodleian Library (hereafter Bodl.), Ms. Eng. Lett. c.144 f.284.

28. K.W. Schweizer, 'The Non-Renewal of the Anglo-Prussian Subsidy Treaty, 1761-

1762; *Canadian Journal of History* 13 (1978); Schweizer, 'Bute, Newcastle, Prussia and the Hague overtures: reexamination', *Albion* 8 (1977); Schweizer and C. Leonard, 'Britain, Prussia, Russia and the Galitzin letter: a reassessment', *Historical Journal* 26 (1983); Schweizer, 'Britain, Prussia and the Prussian territories on the Rhine 1762-63', in Black and Schweizer (eds), *Essays in European History in Honour of Ragnhild Hatton* (Lennoxville, 1985), pp.103-14.

29. Carteret to his daughter Sophia, 30 Oct. 1760, Bodl. Ms. Lyell. empt. 35 f.89.

30. Haslang to Baron Wachtendonck, Palatine foreign minister, 10, 31 Mar. 1761, Munich, Bayerisches Hauptstaatsarchiv, Bayr. Ges. London (hereafter Munich), 238.

31. Bussy to Choiseul, 11 June, Choiseul to Bussy, 19 June 1761, AE. CP. Ang. 443 f. 176, 180, 445 f. 10; Choiseul to Ossun, envoy in Mardir, 19 Feb. 1760, AE.CP. Espagne 527 f.235.

32. Bussy to Choiseul, 26 June, 9 July, Choiseul to Bussy, 27 June 1761, AE.CP. Ang. 443 f.277, 339, 445 f.17; Choiseul to Ossun, 30 July 1761, AE.CP. Espagne 533 f.173; Viry, Sardinian envoy in London, to Charles Emmanuel III, 30 June 1761, Turin, Archivio di Stato, Lettere Ministri Inghilterra (hereafter Turin), 66.

33. Bussy to Choiseul, 26 July 1761, AE. CP. Ang. 444 f.67-8; Haslang to Wachtendonck, 28 July 1761, Munich 238; Viry to Charles Emmanuel III, 23 Oct. 1761, Turin 66; Newcastle to Rockingham, 19 Nov. 1761, Sheffield, City Library, Wentworth Woodhouse Mss (hereafter Sheffield), R1-22.

34. *Monitor,* 22 Apr. 1758; Rigby to Sir Robert Wilmot, 20 Nov. 1759, Derby, Public Library, Catton Collection WH 3457.

35. *Briton* 10, 24 July, 22 Oct., 4 Dec. 1762.

36. Haslang to Wachtendonck and to Count Preysing, the Bavarian foreign minister, 7 Sept. 1762, Munich 239; Nivernais to Choiseul, 24 Sept. 1762, AE. CP. Ang. 447 f.146-8.

37. Newcastle to Hardwicke, 31 July 1762, BL. Add. 32941 f.126.

38. Nivernais to Choisseul, 24 Sept. 1762, AE. CP. Ang. 447 ff.147-8; Ossun to Choiseul, 8 Feb. 1762, AE.CP. Espagne 535 ff.169-70; Joseph Yorke, envoy at The Hague, to Weston, 2 Nov. 1762, 8 Feb., 1 Ap. 1763, BL. Add. 58213 ff.158, 202, 224; Haslang to Wachtendonck and Preysing, 12 Nov., 3 Dec. 1762, Munich 239; Porter to Weston, 29 Jan. 1763, BL. Add. 57927 f.23; Viry to Charles Emmanuel III, 14, 28 Apr. 1763, Turin 68; Black, 'Anglo-Russian Relations after the Seven Years' War', *Scottish Slavonic Review* 9 (1987), 27-37.

39. Nivernais to Praslin, 11, 17 Dec. 1762, 5, 8 Jan., 13 Feb., 21 Apr. 1763, AE. CP. Ang. 448 ff. 268, 325, 449, ff.40, 67, 306, 309-10, 450 f.287; Haslang to Preysing, 11 Mar., Preysing to Haslang, 17 Mar. 1763, Munich 241; Yorke to Newcastle, 5 Jan., Newcastle to Yorke, 16 Jan. 1753, PRO. 84/462; 84/462; Chatelet, French envoy in Vienna, to Praslin, French foreign minister, 3, 25, 31, 11, 21 Sept., Praslin to Chatelet, 16 Sept. 1763, AE.CP. Autriche 295, ff.135, 240-6, 266-8, 303-4, 330-1, 310-11.

40. Haslang to Preysing and to Wachtendonck, 11 Mar. 1763, Munich 241.

41. Instructions for Stormont, 25 May, Halifax to Buckinghamshire, 1 July, Buckinghamshire to Halifax, 5 May 1763, PRO. 80/199, 91/72 f.2, 91/71 f.238; Yorke to Weston, 5 July 1763, BL. Add. 58213 f.264; Viry to Charles Emmanuel III, 21 June 1763, Turin 68.

42. Buckinghamshire to Halifax, 20 Sept., Sandwich to Buckinghamshire, 20 Dec. 1763, PRO. 91-72 f.138, 237-8.

43. Chatelet to Praslin, 16 July, 17 Aug. 1763, E.CP. Autriche 295 f.67-71, 201-2; Viry to Charles Emmanuel III, 26 July 1763, Turin 68.

44. Chatelet to Praslin, 16 July, 17 Aug., 21 Sept., Praslin to Chatelet, 28 Aug. 1763,

AE.CP. Autriche 295 f.67-71, 201-2, 326, 26; Count Guerchy, Nuvernais' replacement as French Ambassador, to Praslin 23, 28 Oct., 4 Nov. 1763, AE. CP. Ang. 451 ff. 456-8, 473, 475, 477, 452 f.41; Marmora, Viry's replacement as Sardinian envoy, to the Sardinian foreign minister, 8 Nov. 1763, Turin 69; Sandwich to Buckinghamshire, 28 Oct. 1763, PRO. 91/72 f.155-6; Sandwich to Stormont, 27 Dec. 1763, PRO. 80/199; W.J. Smith (ed.), *The Grenville Papers* (4 vols., London, 1852-3), 2, 240; H.M. Scott, 'Great Britain, Poland and the Russian Alliance 1763-1767', *Historical Journal* 19 (1976), 53-74.

45 G. Quazza, 'I negoziati austro-anglo-sardi del 1732-33', *Bollettino Storico Bibliografico Subalpino* 46 (1948), 73-92, 47 (1949), 45-74; C. Baudi di Vesme, La politica mediterranea inglese . . . 1741-48 (Turin, 1952); D. Francis, *The First Peninsular War 1702-1713* (London, 1875); G.H. Jones, 'Inghilterra, granducato di Toscana e Quadruplice Alleanza', *Archivio Storico Italiano* 138 (1980), 59-87, and 'La Gran Bretagna e la destinazione di Don Carlos al trono di Toscana, 1721-32', *Archivio Storico Italiano* 140 (1982), 47-82; Black, 'The Development of Anglo-Sardinian Relations in the First Half of the Eighteenth Century', *Studi Piemontesi* 12 (1983), 48-60.

46. Marmora to Charles Emmanuel III, 11, 15 Nov., 13 Dec. 1763, 6, 24 Jan., 7 Feb., 20 Apr., 18 Jun 1764, Turin 69.

47. Précis of Sandwich's overtures to Seilern, 16 Jan. 1764, Vienna, Haus-, Hof- und Staatsarchiv, Staatskanzlei, England, Varia 11 ff.19-20; Smith (ed.), *Grenville Papers* 2, 240-1; Draft to Mitchell, 23 Sept. 1763, BL. Stowe 257 f.107; D'Eon to Praslin, 22 Aug. 1763, AE. CP. Ang. 451 f.109; Sandwich to Stormont, 27 Dec. 1763, PRO. 80/199.

48. Yorke to Weston, 25 May 1764, BL. Add. 57927 f.228.

49. Sandwich to Phelps, 1 Aug. 1764, BL. Stowe 259 ff.1-2.

50. Mitchell, Prussian envoy in London, to Frederick II, 21 Feb. 1764, PRO. 107/97; Marmora to Charles Emmanuel III, 18 May, 15 June, 20 July 1764, Turin 69; Haslang to Count Baumgarten, Bavarian foreign minister, 12 June, 10 Aug. 1764, Munich 242.

51. Gordon to Sandwich, 2 Aug. 1764, PRO. 81/107.

52. *St. James's Chronicle,* 18 July 1765.

CHAPTER 7

George III, Hanover and the Regency Crisis

T.C.W. Blanning and Carl Haase*

The Regency Crisis, which began in the autumn of 1788 when George III was incapacitated by an attack of porphyria, occurred at a critical time in European affairs. The reopening of the Eastern Question in August 1787 by the Turkish declaration of war on Russia had set in motion a chain of events which shook the states-system from one end to the other. The original combatants were soon joined by the Habsburg Monarchy, whose preoccupations in Eastern Europe then allowed Prussia to intervene in the United Provinces, to destroy the power of the French-sponsored 'patriots' there and to restore that of the British-sponsored Stadholder William V. In the North, Gustavus III of Sweden invaded Russia through Finland in July, 1788, thus postponing until the following campaigning season any major Russian initiative against the Turks. That in turn allowed the Turks to concentrate their effort against the luckless Joseph II and to inflict a series of reverses on his scattered forces.

This international turbulence exacerbated existing domestic tensions. In France, the humiliation inflicted on the monarchy by the Prussians and the British over the Dutch imbroglio arguably delivered the *coup de grâce* to the old regime. Joseph II's need to concentrate his armed forces in the Balkans allowed his restless Belgian subjects to revolt and encouraged the numerous dissidents elsewhere in the Habsburg Monarchy to organise sedition. After a generation of peace, prosperity and social order, old-regime Europe was entering a phase of intense upheaval, precipitated initially *not* by the French Revolution but by changes in the international system.

This prolonged agony was just beginning when George III appeared to lose his reason. If evidence were needed that the king was still responsible for the most important affairs of state, the four months of his illness certainly provided it. The conduct of foreign policy simply came to a halt, leaving negotiations in suspension and representatives at foreign courts without instructions. On 6 January 1789 the foreign secretary, the marquis of Carmarthen, told an impatient Joseph Ewart, his man at the Court of Prussia:

> The present situation of this Country renders it impossible for me to send you any particular or precise Instructions. I trust however that the System for supplying the present unfortunate Interruption in the executive Part of the Government will be speedily completed, at least with as little delay as the importance of the Object will admit of, and which being once formed will of Course restore that Part of the Constitution to its usual Energy & Effect.[1]

Quite justifiably, historians have concentrated their attention on the domestic aspects of the Regency Crisis — on William Pitt's successful efforts to retain power in the face of a determined if inept challenge from the Prince of Wales and Charles James Fox. Neither of the two most authoritative modern accounts makes any mention of the foreign dimension.[2] Certainly, all of the important action took place in and around Westminster, but there was one foreign episode occasioned directly by the Regency Crisis which is worth recalling. It began with the arrival in London of a letter from a Hanoverian civil servant, Ernst Brandes, addressed to Sir Gilbert Elliot, a friend and supporter of Fox. The letter is of such importance for what follows that it needs to be quoted in full:

Hannover the 20th of January 1789

Dear Sir,

I must rely on your wanted goodness, my dear Sir, for presuming to intrude upon You at a time when all Your Moments are employ'd in the most weighty business You perhaps were ever engag'd in, but the contents of my letter will I hope plead strongly in my favour.

By the melancholy situation His Majesty labours under, the Electorate of Hannover is depriv'd of its regular form of Government. The common business it is true goes on, but the Machine wants the invigorating spring and everything of the smallest moment is postponed. Pernicious as this would be in any state whatsoever, there is yet one reason of the first magnitude which renders the continuance of the present unsettled State of Government in the Electorate of the most dangerous consequence to the indisputable right of the Prince of Wales, of the whole royal family, and even of the King himself if ever he should recover. — I mean an intervention on the part of the Emperor. It is to be dreaded, that as head of the Germanic body, he may venture to send Commissaries to govern in his name the Electorate during the illness of the Sovereign. A similar attempt was made two hundred years ago, when a Duke of Lüneburg — William, the founder of the present English line of the House of Brunswick, was attack'd of a Malady nearly of the same nature as that which afflicts the King. There was then no heir of age at hand. The States resisted the intrusion of the Imperial Commissaries. The nearest relation govern'd the Dutchy, till the eldest Prince was enabled to transact the business of Government during the illness of his father, who remain'd in this melancholy state near twenty years and was only restored to the unimpair'd use of his mental faculties a few months before his death. From the Character of Joseph the 2d a similar attempt seems not at all unlikely to be expected. This would exceedingly perplex our Lords of the Regency, and tho' they may resist any intrusion of the Imperial power in the Electorate itself, what could they do if the Emperor and his party refused to acknowledge the Minister of the Elector of Hannover at the Diet of Ratisbon? A step by which the Prince would be depriv'd of his whole influence in the Germanic Body. The only remedy by which all future claims may at once be cut of (*sic*), would be an explicit declaration of the Prince of Wales to the Ministry and the States of the Provinces here, to take upon himself the business of Government during the illness of his father. By actual possession the Prince will be secured against any attempt, but no time ought to be lost, it being impossible to foretell the consequences of a delay. Nobody *here can* and will dare to dispute the right of the Prince. The Hanoverian ministers should have advis'd this Step immediatly (*sic*) after the incapacity of the King was legally known by the report of the Physicians. Tho' some of them wished that the Prince might take the reins in his hands, they were too fearful to venture to propose anything, leaving all at the discretion of the Hannoverian (*sic*) Minister in England, who seems not to possess the confidence of the Prince, nor desirous of obtaining it, and who amuses his Colleagues with the favourable accounts he receives from Dr. Willis. Our States ought also to have address'd the Prince to the above mentiond (*sic*) purpose, but forming six different assemblies, unconnected in the smallest degree with each other, and dreading to incur the displeasure of the Ministry, the idea, though entertain'd by different persons among them, was not brought forward.

God knows therefore how long we shall remain in this present unsettled state of affairs. The longer it continues, the greater the danger is of the Prince's losing part of his just prerogative, or at least of seeing it question'd by a foreign ambitious and encroaching Court.

Could not You venture to talk to His Royal Highness on this subject, and engage him to step forward? It is unnecessary to observe how much this attention to the wellfare (*sic*) of his Hanoverian subjects would endear the Prince to my country, and be an unequivocal mark of his not neglecting the interest of his ancient patrimony.

The greatest and the most painfull of Your endeavo'rs my dear Sir, have been for the good of a people whom You have never seen. Why would you refuse Your aid to another portion of mankind, who tho' small as it may be, comparatively to the natives of India, is certainly not to be despised. Near a Million of inhabitants, the bravest of the brave German race, want to have their public independance (*sic*) ascertain'd, want to have a regular form of Government of which they are depriv'd. If You have any objection of opening Yourself the matter to His Royal Highness, could You not engage Mr. Fox or the Duke of Portland to do it? Could they, who so nobly have acted for the sake of humanity, refuse to engage in a cause, where the interest of no contemptible portion of the human race is inseparably link'd to that of a Prince to whom they are attach'd. If England must have continental connexions, the Elector of Hannover is the most natural ally. English Ministers cannot see therefore with perfect indifference the independence of the Elector annihilated. No quarrel whatever will arise with the Emperor, if the Prince is but once in the possession of the Electorate, but if that, the taking of the possession, is delayed, every ambitious step is to be expected from the Court of Vienna. The good of the people calls for a Sovereign, and we certainly deserve to be happy here. I know of no people under a monarchical form of Government, besides the English, who merit as much the attention and the good wishes of a lover of mankind than we do. Much good remains to be done, but the spirit of the people under a proper administration will incline much more to forward it here, than it would do in another part of Germany. By taking the reins of the Government of the Electorate in his own hands, the Prince will certainly endear himself to the Majority of the People. It is true that different ideas are entertain'd by some, and that these ideas will gain ground, the longer the interregnum lasts, but by a decisive step the friends of the Prince will see all objection removed. Rational men here can have but very small hopes of the King's full recovery. The first physician of the King at Hanover (*sic*), Dr. Zimmermann, one of the most eminent men in his profession in Germany, thinks it highly improbable, and tho' he may not chuse perhaps to have his opinion publicly known, ascerted (*sic*) in an ironical way, after reading the report of the Physicians, that Dr. Willis by being so positive must know more of the matter than any one of the faculty in Europe of these cases. I dare not encroach any longer upon Your Patience my dear Sir. Your prudence will determine what You can do for the benefit of my country. I have been bold enough to ask this service from a Man, who has sacrific'd his whole life to the well being of humanity, of a Man attach'd to the Prince whose interest is at stake, of a Man whom I glory to call my friend. You will receive this letter through Mr. Meyer as I am not sure of Mr. Tatter's being in town. Should You want any more information, You could ask it from me through one of these Channels.

> Believe me for ever to be with the greatest respect Dear Sir
> Your most obedient humble servant
> and friend
> E. Brandes[4]

Brandes, who was later to become one of the most effective German critics of the French Revolution, had probably made the acquaintance of Elliot during his extended visit to England in 1784-5.[5] His attempt to persuade the Prince of Wales to take pre-emptive action to safeguard his rights in Hanover against possible imperial encroachment was certainly understandable, in view of Joseph II's reputation. Especially since the restraining influence of Maria Theresa had been removed in 1780, Joseph had caused one sensation after another, as he sought to promote the interests of the Habsburg Monarchy at the expense of the Holy Roman Empire. The successful campaign to exclude the jurisdiction of 'foreign' prince-bishops and the unsuccessful attempt to exchange his possessions in the Netherlands for Bavaria were only two of a series of initiatives which had outraged German opinion, both princely and public.

One result of the Bavarian imbroglio had been the formation by Frederick the Great of a League of Princes (*Fürstenbund*) in July 1785. It was a fine irony that the man who had shaken the Empire to its foundation in 1740 and 1756 should now emerge, in the last year of his long reign, as the champion of the imperial constitution. Once Joseph II had abandoned his imperial duties, it was natural, if not inevitable, that Frederick should move gratefully into his place - now that the gamekeeper had turned poacher, the poacher had to become gamekeeper. Frederick's action was entirely cynical: he no more cared for the Holy Roman Empire than did Joseph. But with Prussia isolated and the Habsburg Monarchy apparently in a dominant position, thanks to its recent alliance with Russia, anything was better than nothing.[6]

Some members of the League of Princes, however, took the rhetoric about imperial integrity seriously. Indeed, the first initiative for the formation of a league had come not from Prussia, but from a group of less important princes, anxious to modernise the Empire's laws and institutions.[7] And none took it all more seriously than the Elector of Hanover, George III of England. When first approached about the possibility of a league, in February 1785, George had proved positively enthusiastic, brushing aside the reservations of his Hanoverian ministers with a strongly worded attack on the total inadmissibility of Joseph II's plans and the need for 'the most energetic and most effective action' to frustrate them, both then and in the future.[8]

He was as good as his word. Hanover became a founder-member of the League of Princes and proved to be one of its most active and committed members. It is now realised that the George who had referred to Hanover in 1759 as 'that horrid Electorate which has always liv'd upon the very vitals of this poor Country'[9] was a creature of the past. By the 1780s he was referring to 'my German fatherland' and was sending his younger sons (William and Edward) to be educated at the Hanoverian university of Göttingen.[10] Indeed, when driven to the point of despair in 1783 by the political crisis occasioned by the Fox-North coalition, he even contemplated abdication of the English throne and a permanent removal to Hanover.[11]

This sense of a German identity, enhanced by a feeling that he had been left in the lurch over the American war, prompted George to pursue Hanoverian policies irrespective of their implications for British interests. The predictable result was a bruising collision between his two dominions. From the moment they took office, in December 1783, William Pitt and his foreign secretary, the marquis of Carmarthen, made every effort to secure an alliance with the Habsburg Monarchy. Just when it looked as though success was within their grasp, thanks to Austrian disenchantment with France, Elector George's vigorous opposition to Joseph II's German schemes sent them straight back to square one. To make matters worse, George had left his British ministers 'totally in the Dark with respect to the Progress of the Hanoverian Negotiation', as Carmarthen grumpily put it.[12] He added that there was no prospect that the King would change his mind:

> His Majesty looks upon His own personal Honour as to be engaged in supporting the League, and I much doubt whether the most advantageous connection with the two Imperial Courts in favour of this *Kingdom* would prevail upon Him to retract one iota of His Electoral Stipulations, or even patiently submit to that distinction of Interests which cirmcumstances may one time or another render it, not a matter of Choice but of Necessity to make.[13]

In the three years following the foundation of the League of Princes, Hanover unfolded a vigorous policy in the Holy Roman Empire. This was designed partly to counter growing Austrian influence in North-West Germany (Joseph II's brother — Max Franz — had become elector of Cologne and prince-bishop of Münster in 1784 and it was rumoured that he would try to add Paderborn and Hildesheim to his collection), partly to expand the Hanoverian network of princely clients, but also to defend the imperial constitution against further attempts at encroachment.[14] It is difficult to read Elector George's repeated pronouncements on the subject without concluding that he was sincere.[15] In the course of 1787, the focus of international attention moved East to the Balkans and West to the Low Countries, but George continued to keep German affairs at the front of his mind. Writing to the Princess of Orange, the sister of Frederick William II of Prussia, in June 1788, he made a point of conflating British and Hanoverian interests:

> Je vous prie d'être persuadée que je regarde l'alliance que j'ai faite avec le roi votre frère en ma qualité d'Électeur, comme un garant du maintien de la constitution Germanique; et que je considererois une alliance semblable entre nos deux couronnes, comme un moyen d'obliger les cours de Vienne et de Versailles à désirer le continuation de la paix de l'Europe, et pour cet effet entre autre à travailler à une paix en Turquie.[16]

The result of these royal initiatives was that Anglo-Austrian relations had reached a very low ebb by the time the Regency Crisis broke. In the summer of 1787, an ostensible dispatch from Kaunitz to his envoy in London, Count Reviczky, stated bluntly that the distinction British ministers liked to draw between the policy of the King of England and the policy of the Elector of Hanover was unacceptable: either it was a ploy (in which case any further communication was impossible) or it revealed a contradiction between British and Hanoverian policies (in which case any further communication was pointless).[17] Just three days before it became common knowledge that George III was seriously ill, Reviczky sent a lamentation to Kaunitz about the 'extreme devotion' of the British court to Prussia. Even before Prussia had come to Britain's assistance in the United Provinces, he complained, the King had blindly followed the dictates of Berlin, especially when it was a question of the Holy Roman Empire.[18]

Given the apparent Prussophilia of the King, all that was left to Austrian diplomats was the cultivation of the reversionary interest. When Reviczky first arrived in England, in the summer of 1786, he was told to establish good relations with the Prince of Wales, Charles James Fox and other leaders of the opposition, and to make himself ready to exploit the notorious volatility of the British political scene (a favourite target for Kaunitz's withering contempt).[19] Reviczky did his best, but found it a difficult assignment. He reported dejectedly that the Prince of Wales had retired to Brighton, while Fox divided his time between his mistress and Boodle's — and, as a newcomer, he was finding it very difficult to gain admission to the latter.[20]

By the time the reversionary interest came into its own, two years later, Reviczky had made no discernible progress. His first analysis of his country's prospects under a new regime headed by the Prince of Wales was shrewd but depressing. He predicted that all the existing ministers would lose their positions, with the possible exception of Thurlow. The Prince had opposed everything the existing administration had done at home, as a matter of principle, but his views on foreign affairs were just the same as Pitt's — and that was the one area where there would be no change. Continuity was even more likely if Thurlow remained, for he was a great supporter of the Prussian alliance.[21] A few days later he found a crumb of comfort in the observation that the conduct of foreign affairs had come to a complete standstill and would remain stationary until the form of the regency had been sorted out; at least that meant that Prussia could gain nothing further.[22] Reviczky's analysis was entirely correct. On 2 January 1789, Lord Malmesbury — a close associate of the Prince of Wales and his most expert adviser on foreign affairs — wrote to Joseph Ewart, the British envoy to Prussia. 'Whatever changes may happen here, you will remain in office, that *both sides* equally approved your conduct . . . & that no alteration whatever will take place in our continental system'. Later in the same letter, he stressed again the fact that there was 'no possibility of a change in our system'.[23]

One reason for the Prince of Wales's surprising reluctance to refrain from overturning everything he had inherited was the influence of his younger brother Frederick, duke of York. As the prince-bishop of Osnabrück since infancy, permanently resident at Hanover from 1781 until 1787, and frequent visitor to Prussia, the duke prided himself on his understanding of German affairs. He had played an important part in the negotiations leading to the formation of the League of Princes, in the course of which he had been the recipient of much flattering attention from Frederick the Great.[24] As a result, he was variously described by British diplomats as 'very much attached to Prussia' and by the Hanoverian ministers as 'tout é fait dans les Intérêts de Sa Majesté Prussienne'.[25] As far back as 1784 he had warned his father against Joseph II, who, he predicted with commendable prescience, 'will do everything in his power to augment his German provinces'.[26] This was not the man to advise his brother to carry out a diplomatic revolution. As Reviczky caustically observed, 'having attended the military reviews at Berlin a few times, he believes he is a Prussian and wants to put the British army on a Potsdam footing'.[27]

For the time being, there was nothing the Prince of Wales and his advisers could do. All their energies were concentrated on securing a form of regency which would allow them to take power. That the Hanoverian connection had not been forgotten altogether, however, was shown by a letter of 5 December 1788 from the duke of Portland to Edmund Burke: 'It were certainly much to be wished that little Brandes was here, but the measure must probably be decided before he could come over. A Letter however cannot but be of use, and I should think might be safely written to Him, as his attachment and ability are equally to be depended on'.[28] (Burke had met Brandes during his visit to England in 1784, when the two men began a friendship which lasted until the former's death.[29]) It was not until 23 December 1788 that the Prince of Wales wrote to the Hanoverian minister attached to the King in London, Johann Friedrich Carl von Alvensleben, informing him officially of his father's indisposition and asking how the government of the electorate should be constituted in future.[30] Alvensleben's reply was hesitant; he advised against any 'precipitate' action, urging that nothing should be done until it became absolutely necessary and then only in a form which would win the approval of the King when he recovered.[31]

Meanwhile, in Vienna something began to stir. It might have been expected that Joseph II would have taken this opportunity to improve relations with Great Britain. With his war in the Balkans going badly, his Belgian, Polish and Hungarian subjects becoming increasingly restive and his main allies either paralysed by bankruptcy (France) or diverted by war (Russia), he needed all the friends he could get. Yet he chose just this moment to launch a diplomatic initiative against Hanover which could only achieve the notable feat of alienating both the Prince of Wales and George III (when he recovered). By some uncanny coincidence, on the very day — 20 January 1789 — that Ernst Brandes sent his appeal to Sir Gilbert Elliot, expressing the fear of 'an intervention on the part of the Emperor', Joseph II duly obliged. Instructions were sent to every important embassy in the Holy Roman Empire, spelling out Austrian policy on Hanover's position in the Regency Crisis: 'His Imperial Majesty regards it as settled that He will be solely and entirely responsible for ordering the administration and the regency for the German lands of the incapacitated king and that at the Imperial Diet no envoy from those lands will be recognised unless legitimated by an imperial deed of authorisation'. The envoys were to present this position as non-negotiable and were simply to ignore any attempt by the Hanoverian ministers or the royal house in England to establish a regency unilaterally.[32]

On the following day, the same document was sent to Reviczky in London, although some of the sting was taken out of its uncompromising language by the informal instruction that the British ministers and Alvensleben should be told 'amicably' that if the King should not improve and if a regency for his German lands became necessary, then the Emperor would deem it a pleasure to be able to assist the Prince of Wales.[33] Even that formula made it clear that any arrangement would have to be seen to be dependent on prior imperial approval. That was also the message which reached Hanover from the electorate's envoy in Vienna, Friedrich Alexander von Wenckstern, who reported on 21 January that two senior Imperial officials, the Imperial Vice Chancellor von Colloredo and the Imperial Privy Councillor von Albini, had told him that the Emperor had decided that any regency in Hanover for the Prince of Wales would have to be conditional on imperial 'consent, nomination and confirmation'.[34]

Whether it was the appeal of Brandes or the news from Vienna, or both, the Prince of Wales' response was immediate. On 3 February 1789 he sent the following declaration to Alvensleben:

> I have sent for you, Sir, to acquaint you that the King my father having for some time past been afflicted with a severe & melancholy disorder, which renders him incapable during its continuance of attending to publick business or transacting any affairs whatever, in his own person, and the care of his interests in his Electoral dominions and the administration of the Govt. in these countries on his Majesty's behalf, having for these reasons devolved on me during the interval of his Majesty's incapacity — I feel it my duty not to neglect longer the execution of a trust so important to his Majesty & to the welfare of his Electoral subjects; I have therefore judged it proper to make to you this communication of my intention to take upon me immediately the administration of affairs in the Electorate, & to desire that you will without delay inform the Regency thereof in such a manner as may best prove my personal regard for them and my affection for the interests of Hanover.[35]

The Prince also moved smartly to enlist the support of his Prussian ally. By 15 February his Hanoverian ministers had orders to inform their Prussian colleagues that their new master proposed to open a personal and confidential correspondence with Frederick William II in which he would express 'ses sentiments devoués pour ce monarque, et son zèle de s'acquérir sa confiance'.[36]

Meanwhile, Joseph II had been prosecuting his attempt to take control of Hanoverian affairs. On 4 February his envoy in Mainz was instructed to call on the Elector of Mainz (the arch-chancellor of the Holy Roman Empire) not to accept any communications from the Hanoverian representative at the Imperial Diet until the question of his credentials had been sorted out.[37] In other words, Hanoverian representation at the Imperial Diet was to be suspended. The alarm provoked in Hanover by reports of this démarche was calmed almost at once, however, by the welcome news from London that the Prince of Wales had assumed the regency of the electorate unilaterally and by the even more welcome rumours that his father was on the mend.[38] Nevertheless, the tocsin was sounded by the despatch of pleas for help to all friendly German courts and, of course, London.[39] It was there that the Austrian initiative was dismissed out of hand by a newly resolute Alvensleben. He told Reviczky that the Prince of Wales had taken over direction of the electorate's affairs and that no outside interference would be tolerated.[40] As the Prince of Wales informed his Hanoverian ministers, on 17 February 1789, it could be assumed that this rebuff would put an end to such 'an untimely and unexpected importunity'.[41]

He was right. The prompt counter-action taken by the Prince of Wales, together with assurances of support from other members of the League of Princes (most notably, from Prussia), persuaded the Austrians that there was nothing to be achieved from any further assertion of imperial rights. On

17 February, Reviczky lamented to Kaunitz that Prussia would certainly exploit the whole affair and alienate the Prince of Wales from Austria.[42] In fact, this despatch crossed with fresh instructions dated 20 February, which told him to present the whole affair as an unfortunate misunderstanding, brought about by the Austrian envoy in Mainz exceeding his instructions.[43] The same message was conveyed via 'informal' conversations between the Imperial Privy Councillor, von Albini, and the Hanoverian envoy in Vienna, von Wenckstern.[44] In fact, this smokescreen was entirely spurious — the instructions sent to Mainz were quite explicit and had not been exceeded one jot.[45]

By this time, the likely reactions of the Prince of Wales had become entirely academic, for the recovery of George was now certain. Progress had been rapid since 6 February; a public bulletin on 12 February spoke of 'progressive amendment'; by 17 February this had improved to become 'a state of convalescence'; on 23 February George wrote his first letter to Pitt since his illness began and saw him on the following day.[46] According to the Hanoverian minister von Beulwitz, the newly operational King's thoughts turned at once to his Prussian ally and to the League of Princes; for he had sent a personal letter for immediate forwarding to Frederick William II.[47] Beulwitz did not know the nature of the contents, for the letter was sealed, but there is a copy in the Royal Archives; it runs 'Je ne puis sur tout assez vous témoigner combien je suis sensible à la manière dont Votre Majesté a bien voulu en agir à mon Egard, à l'occasion de la conduite inouie de l'Empereur durant ma maladie'.[48]

That George did inquire about German affairs as soon as he had regained his reason and was impressed by what he heard about the help given by Prussia is also revealed by a letter from Colonel Richard Grenville, aide-de-camp to the duke of York, to Joseph Ewart:

> I have the pleasure to assure you that He [the King] is completely recovered and in every respect the same as ever; He mentioned to me the other morning that He had just received a most affectionate letter from the King of Prussia, and that somebody had told His Prussian Majesty that he had inquired after him the first thing on His convalescence, which the King of Prussia had taken very kindly . . . I have every reason to believe from several expressions which have dropped, that the King is firmly attached to the King of Prussia both *personally and politically*, I flatter myself therefore that the Alliance will be *solid*, and *efficacious*.[49]

That was also the impression gained by the Prussian envoy, Count Alvensleben,[50] who sent encouraging reports on a number of highly satisfactory audiences he had enjoyed with the newly recovered king. He also reported that George was particularly bitter about Joseph II's attempt to take advantage of his incapacity.[51] More informal evidence of George's enhanced Prussophilia reached Joseph Ewart in Berlin from Karl August von Hardenberg (the later Prussian reformer) in Brunswick:

> Les liaisons entre les Cours de Londres et de Berlin semblent avoir été un des prémiers (*sic*) objets de l'attention du Roi. Il a écrit une très belle et bonne lettre à la Duchesse [of Brunswick, George's elder sister], où après avoir beaucoup raisonné sur le néant des Grandeurs humaines, il s'étend sur la reconnoissance qu'il doit à ses amis de l'appui qu'ils ont pris à son désastre et surtout sur *his good friend the King of Prussia*.[52]

The message was clear, from all sources: George was enraged about Austrian conduct and correspondingly grateful to the Prussians for the help given in warding off Joseph's incursion. This news must have been very welcome in Berlin, for there a major diplomatic offensive was being planned by Ewald Count von Hertzberg, Frederick William II's senior adviser on foreign affairs. Hertzberg believed that Prussia could exploit the war in the East to make substantial territorial gains without having to resort to war, thus emulating Frederick the Great's achievement in orchestrating the first partition of Poland in 1772. In return for an international guarantee of the integrity of their remaining territories, the Turks would be induced to cede Moldavia and Wallachia to Austria; Austria would return Galicia to Poland; Poland would cede Danzig, Thorn, the Palatinate of Posen and Kalisch to Prussia.[53]

With three of the major European powers (Russia, Austria and Turkey) embroiled in war and another immobilised by revolution (France), that left in a dominant position Prussia — and Great Britain. Hence the relish with which the Prussians read the reports of George III's gratitude for recent favours. Memory of the decisive assistance given to the British in the United Provinces in 1787 could only strengthen their hope for a joint démarche in Eastern Europe. Yet a little more thought and closer study of the relevant communications should have dampened their optimism. All of George's excited letters in the aftermath of his recovery made it clear that what he really cared about was the integrity of the constitution of the Holy Roman Empire. This can be seen, for example, in his letter to his son Prince Adolphus, who was studying at the Hanoverian university of Göttingen, written on 6 March 1789:

> May Heaven continue to so direct your steps that you may daily become more deserving of the affection of your parents, relations, and of all good men, and that you may never forget that the House of Hanover have ever been famous for their integrity and for true courage when the dictates of justice not of lucre called them forth as assertors of the rights of the Germanick Constitution.[54]

For all the sweet murmurings about affection and gratitude which passed between London and Berlin, in reality George III and Frederick William II, Great Britain and Prussia, and Hanover and Prussia had always been essentially at odds with each other. Elector George had joined the League of Princes in his capacity as a middling prince of the Empire, to maintain the status quo. Frederick the Great had established the League of Princes as a figleaf to cover his isolation. When Prussia's position improved dramatically, with the reopening of the Eastern Question in 1787, the League was no longer necessary.[55] Prussian policy, especially after the accession of the ambitious Frederick William II, once again became assertive. A first request to the British for assistance in furthering Prussia's plans for expansion in the East had been made in the spring of 1788. The evasive reply it elicited provoked anger from the Prussians, who not unreasonably were looking for a *quid pro quo* for their intervention in the United Provinces the previous autumn.[56]

This situation was not changed by the events of the Regency Crisis. When the dust stirred up by Joseph II's clumsy démarche settled, it became clear that George and his ministers were just as opposed as they had ever been to any major restructuring of Eastern Europe. Alvensleben warned Berlin repeatedly that they would do nothing to help the Hertzberg plan and that Prussian policy should be based on the assumption that all the British were egoists — the government even more so than the country at large, in as much as that was possible.[57] This perceptive appraisal of the British national character was soon shared by Hertzberg, who on 12 May told a colleague, 'the English ministers are dead for us'.[58]

It was also clear that George III was no more alive for Prussia than his cabinet, neither in his royal nor in his electoral capacity. Protecting the 'Germanick constitution' was one thing, helping the Prussians to expand was quite another. Like every other Hanoverian, George was well aware that the Electorate was the enticing filling in a sandwich formed by the Prussian territories on the Rhine and the Prussian territories in the East and that what the Prussians did to Poland today, they might well do to Hanover tomorrow. Consequently, British and Hanoverian policy ran harmoniously during the next year or so: the British did all they could to brake Prussian assertiveness in the East, while the Hanoverians did all they could to brake Prussian assertiveness in the Empire. Indeed, George appears to have been more insistent on this point than his ministers, intervening to ensure that the Hanoverian delegate to the imperial election of 1790 was told to exercise caution in his dealings with the Prussians.[59]

It cannot be claimed, therefore, that the Regency Crisis represented any sort of turning-point in Great Britain's foreign affairs. As this chapter has tried to show, however, it did make explicit a number of important features of the British position and of British policy in the period: the importance attached to Hanover (not least by George III), the decisive role still played by the King in the determination of foreign policy, the striking continuity between the attitudes of the King and the Prince of Wales on things which really mattered, the self-destructive clumsiness of Joseph II, and the fragility of the Anglo-Prussian alliance.

It also provided the opportunity for Count Reviczky to write an account of the aftermath of the King's recovery which not only shrewdly identifies the reasons for his huge popularity but which also offers an indictment of the regime of his own master which is none the less penetrating for being indirect. That a senior Austrian diplomat should send such a lightly coded message back to his superiors was an indication of how far the alienation of the elites of the Habsburg Monarchy from Joseph II had gone by this stage. Reviczky reported that George III returned to St. James for the first time since his illness on 26 March. There was a tremendous press of peers at court, with almost all the ladies wearing ribbons on their hats proclaiming 'God Save the King!'. He went on:

> When one observes these manifestations of joy shining out everywhere on this occasion and in so extraordinary a fashion, one cannot help but be somewhat surprised that the King should possess the love and affection of the nation to such a high degree, indeed to an extent that has never been witnessed before, for in itself his reign has not achieved much to boast about but has suffered such calamities as the loss of a large overseas possession and the limitless expansion of the National Debt.

After observing that no one in England now regretted the loss of America, for trade had actually increased while the previous burden of defence had been lifted, he presented the following double-edged analysis which provides a suitably cheering note on which to end:

> It is clear, therefore, that what has really counted in winning for the King the love of his people have been his good personal qualities, which allow them to live under his rule secure in their liberty and their rights, the judicious choice of ministers which the King has made, the economic way of life he follows, so that he can be as light a burden to the nation as possible, despite his numerous family which needs to be provided for, and finally his morals, principles and piety make him more popular with each day that passes, so that for all time he can count on the most forceful demonstrations of devotion from his subjects.[60]

NOTES

* We acknowledge with gratitude the permission of Her Majesty the Queen to use material from the Royal Archives, Windsor Castle.

1. P.R.O. F.O. 64/15 no. 1.

2. John W. Derry, *The Regency Crisis and the Whigs 1788-9* (Cambridge, 1963); John Ehrman, *The Younger Pitt*, vol. I : *The Years of Acclaim* (London, 1969), ch. 20.

3. So far as we are aware, this is the first time that this episode has been discussed in an English publication. The original version of this article was written by Carl Haase and was published in the *Blätter für deutsche Landesgeschichte*, 113 (1977), pp. 432-49. It was always intended that an English version, designed for an English-speaking rather than a German audience, would be written by T.C.W. Blanning, but alas other commitments and a natural procrastination have delayed its composition. He has taken the opportunity to incorporate some new material.

4. This letter is in the papers of Sir Gilbert Elliot, in the National Library of Scotland at Edinburgh. We are grateful to the Trustees for permission to reproduce it and to Dr Paul Kelly, formerly Assistant Keeper at the National Library of Scotland for providing us with a photocopy of the document.

5. Carl Haase, *Ernst Brandes, 1758-1810,* 2 vols. (Hildesheim, 1973, 1974), II, 114-71.

6. There is a good account of the situation in the Empire and analysis of the effects of Joseph II's policies in Karl Otmar Freiherr von Aretin, *Heiliges Römisches Reich 1776-1806,* 2 vols, (Wiesbaden, 1967).

7. Alfred Kohler, 'Das Reich im Spannungsfeld des preussisch-österreichischen Gegensatzes: Die Fürstenbundbestrebungen 1783-1785', *Fürst, Bürger, Mensch, Untersuchungen zu politischen und soziokulturellen Wandlungsprozessen im vorrevolutionären Europa,* ed. Friedrich Engel-Janosi, Grete Klingenstein and Heinrich Lutz (Vienna, 1975), *passim.*

8. Hanover, Hannover 92, LXI, Nr 1 a, fos. 48-9. This was reprinted by K. Gödeke, 'Hannovers Anteil an der Stiftung des deutschen Fürstenbundes', *Archiv des Historischen Vereins für Niedersachsen* (1847), p. 75.

9. George to Lord Bute, 5 Aug. 1759, in Romney Sedgwick (ed.), *Letters from George III to Lord Bute 1756-1766* (London, 1939), p. 28.

10. For references to 'ma patrie germanique' and 'mein deutsches Vaterland', see Wilhelm Adolf Schmidt, *Geschichte der preussisch-deutschen Unionsbestrebungen seit der Zeit Friedrichs des Grossen* (Berlin, 1851), I, 350, and S. Conrady, 'Die Wirksamkeit König Georgs III für die hannoverschen Kurlande', *Niedersächsisches Jahrbuch für Landesgeschichte,* 39 (1967), 190.

11. John Cannon, *The Fox-North coalition: crisis of the constitution 1782-4* (Cambridge, 1969), p. 79. George III's Hanoverian attachment is discussed in greater detail in T.C.W. Blanning, ' "That horrid Electorate" or "ma patrie germanique"? George III, Hanover and the *Fürstenbund*', *The Historical Journal*, 20, 2 (1977).

12. Carmarthen to Thurlow, 5 Aug. 1785, BL, Egerton MSS 3498, fo. 245.

13. Ibid.

14. Aretin, *Heiliges Römisches Reich,* I, 181-2.

15. Blanning, 'That horrid Electorate" or ma patrie germanique', p. 340.

16. Arthur Aspinall (ed.), *The later correspondence of George III,* vol. I: *December 1783 to January 1793* (Cambridge, 1962), p. 377.

17. Kaunitz to Reviczky, 12 July 1787, HHStA, Staatskanzlei, Weisungen, Kart. 129. Reviczky's name was and has been spelt in half-a-dozen different ways; I have preferred the version he used most often himself.

18. Reviczky to Kaunitz, 4 Nov. 1788, Ibid., Berichte, Kart. 126.

19. Kaunitz to Reviczky, 30 Aug. 1786, HHStA, Staatskanzlei, Weisungen, Kart. 129.

20. Reviczky to Kaunitz, 27 Sept. 1786, Ibid., Berichte, Kart. 125.

21. Reviczky to Kaunitz, 28 Nov. 1788, Ibid., Kart. 127.

22. Reviczky to Kaunitz, 2 Dec. 1788, Ibid.

23. National Library of Scotland, Edinburgh, Papers of Monro of Williamwood, bundle 148.

24. Blanning, ' "That horrid Electorate" or "ma patrie germanique" ', pp. 342-4.

25. Joseph Ewart to Sir James Harris, 4 April 1785, James Harris first earl of Malmesbury, *Diaries and Correspondence*, 2 vols. (London, 1844), II, 117; National Library of Scotland, Edinburgh, Papers of Monro of Williamwood, bundle 159.

26. Prince Frederick to George III, 15 October 1784, Aspinall (ed.), *The later correspondence of George III*, p. 103.

27. Reviczky to Kaunitz, 17 March 1789, HHStA, Staatskanzlei, Berichte, Kart. 127.

28. Thomas Copeland (ed.), *The correspondence of Edmund Burke*, 7 vols. (Cambridge, 1958-70), V, 431.

29. Stephan Skalweit, 'Edmund Burke, Ernst Brandes und Hannover', *Niedersächsisches Jahrbuch*, 28 (1956), 15.

30. Hanover, Hannover 92, Nr. 87.

31. Ibid.

32. HHStA, Reichskanzlei, Weisungen ins Reich, Kart. 49. The instructions were sent to Austrian envoys in Prussia, Saxony, the Bavarian, Swabian, Electoral Rhenish, Lower Rhenish-Westphalian and Upper Rhenish Circles, and the Electorate of Mainz.

33. Ibid., Weisungen nach Braunschweig-Hannover, Kart. 7.

34. Hanover, Cal. Br. 11, Nr. 3528.

35. A. Aspinall (ed.), *The Correspondence of George, Prince of Wales, 1770-1812*, 8 vols. (London, 1963-71), I, 394. Aspinall printed a copy he had found in the Royal Archives but was unable to date it, suggesting November-December 1788. The original is in Hanover, dated 3 February 1789-Hann. 92, Nr. 87.

36. Ludwig Friedrich von Beulwitz to Joseph Ewart, Hanover, 15 February 1789, Papers of Monro of Williamwood, bundle 133.

37. Hanover, Hann. 92, Nr. 88.

38. Ibid., Hann. 92, Nr. 87.

39. Ibid., Hann. 92, Nrs 87 and 88; Ibid., Cal. Br. 24, Nr. 5369.

40. Ibid., Hann. 92, Nr. 87.

41. Ibid.

42. HHStA, Staatskanzlei, Berichte, Kart. 127.

43. Ibid., Weisungen, Kart. 129.

44. Hanover, Hann. 92, Nr. 87.

45. This particular aspect is examined in greater detail by Carl Haase in Blanning and Haase, 'Kurhannover, der Kaiser und die "Regency Crisis" ', *Blätter für deutsche Landesgeschichte*, 113 (1977), pp. 447-8.

46. Earl Stanhope, *Life of the Right Honourable William Pitt*, 4 vols. (London, 1861-2), II, 24.

47. Ludwig Friedrich von Beulwitz to Joseph Ewart, 18 March 1789, Papers of Monro of Williamwood, bundle 133.

48. George III to Frederick William II, Royal Archives, Windsor Castle, RA 6409. The copy is not dated but a note suggests that it was written in reply to RA 6520, a letter from Frederick William II to George, offering congratulations on his recovery. The letter from von

Beulwitz to Ewart cited in the previous note, however, makes it clear that George's letter was written two weeks earlier.

49. Richard Grenville to Joseph Ewart, 14 April 1789, Papers of Monro of Williamwood, bundle 133.

50. This was Philipp Karl von Alvensleben, not to be confused with Johann Friedrich Carl von Alvensleben, the Hanoverian minister attached to George III in London.

51. Leopold von Ranke, *Die deutschen Mächte und der Fürstenbund*, 2 vols. (Leipzig, 1871-2), II, 79.

52. Papers of Monro of Williamwood, bundle 161.

53. The background to the Hertzberg plan and its progress is discussed in T.C.W. Blanning, *The Origins of the French Revolutionary Wars* (1986), pp. 51-5.

54. Aspinall (ed.), *The Later Correspondence of George III*, p. 399.

55. Aretin, *Heiliges Römisches Reich*, I, 216-17.

56. Felix Salomon, *Wilhelm Pitt der jüngere* (Leipzig and Berlin, 1906), vol. I, pt. 2, pp. 342-51.

57. Dietrich Gerhard, *England under der Aufstieg Russlands* (Munich and Berlin, 1933), p. 255, n. 197.

58. Friedrich Luckwaldt, 'Zur Vorgeschichte der Konvention von Reichenbach: englischer Einfluss am Hofe Friedrich Wilhelms II', *Delbrück-Festschrift, Gesammelte Aufsätze, Professor Hans Delbrück zu seinem 60ten Geburtstage dargebracht von Freunden und Schülern* (Berlin, 1908), p. 240.

59. Ernst August Runge, 'Die Politik Hannovers im deutschen Fürstenbund (1785-1790)', *Niedersächsisches Jahrbuch für Landesgeschichte*, 8 (1931), p. 104.

60. Reviczky to Kaunitz, HHStA, Staatskanzlei, Berichte, Kart. 127. On the subject of George III's popularity, see the important article by Linda Colley, 'The apotheosis of George III: Loyalty, royalty and the British nation, 1760-1820', *Past and Present*, 102 (1984).

CHAPTER 8

Pitt, Grenville and the Control of British Foreign Policy in the 1790s

Michael Duffy

At some time after January 1806 Sir James Bland Burges, formerly Under-secretary of State at the Foreign Office between 1789 and 1795, jotted down notes for a character sketch of William Pitt the Younger. Among these he recorded:

> . . . from 1783 to 1789 he had no person in the Cabinet to influence or oppose him, and things went on prosperously. In 1789 Grenville came in; his application was of great service; but he gradually gain'd an ascendancy, and at length a superiority, which produc'd the catastrophe of 1791. — As this superiority continued, as Dundas and Lord Liverpool were brought into the Cabinet, his free agency was more and more restrained, and things went on worse — all this was increas'd by the admission of the Portland Faction in 1794, after which every thing went on worse, and he gradually was ruin'd . . .[1]

Burges had little love for Grenville, who had forced him from office in 1795, and his respect for Pitt was muted by a feeling that the latter had never recognised his true worth, but his interpretation merits examination as a starting point for reconsideration of the management of foreign policy in the 1790s.

The first of Burges's statements has been widely accepted in foreign policy matters. David Bayne Horn went so far as to assert that 'The relations between Pitt and his foreign minister, Carmarthen, in the 'eighties probably show the high-water-mark of direct control of foreign policy by a prime minister', and John Ehrman has provided abundant evidence of the exercise of this control. Pitt influenced the appointment of diplomats to key posts and even for a while in 1789-90 imposed an under-secretary on Carmarthen against his wishes. He largely took over control of commercial negotiations from the Foreign Office. In times of acute crisis over Holland in the summer of 1787 and against Spain over Nootka Sound in 1790 he took over daily control of negotiations, sent his own agents to report on the situation, corresponded privately with the official British envoys, and drafted important despatches himself.[2] The evidence is imposing though there has been some nibbling away at the edges in recent years. T.C.W. Blanning has shown how far the King was able to play a German policy as Elector of Hanover in 1785 beyond the control of either Carmarthen or Pitt. Even John Ehrman admits that Pitt's interest in foreign affairs did not really develop until 1786, and Jeremy Black has doubted how far Pitt was in control in 1787, pointing out the influence of other ministers such as Lord

Chancellor Thurlow and that Pitt was now following the policy of vigorous hostility to France that Carmarthen had been advocating since 1784.[3]

Carmarthen had generally been dismissed as (in Ehrman's words) 'inexperienced and incompetent' — 'he did his duty as best he could, prided himself on his ideas, and resigned in the end because his advice was ignored. His contribution to foreign policy . . . was thrown into sharp relief by the fact that his successor was William Grenville'.[4] But perhaps such a judgement is too harsh in that it underrates both the difficulties of a foreign secretary in the late eighteenth century and Carmarthen's particular way through them.

Of all the members of the Cabinet the foreign secretary was most subject to the scrutiny of his colleagues and of the King. They saw the incoming despatches from Britain's envoys abroad, and their approval was required for all significant departures in foreign relations. After the shock of the American War there was a general national mood to isolate Britain from foreign matters, and it seems to have been deliberate policy on Carmarthen's part to involve the Prime Minister as the best way of swaying King, Cabinet and Parliament towards his aims. It was by encouraging his envoy Malmesbury to write directly to Pitt from Holland that Carmarthen sought, successfully, to arouse Pitt's interest and bring him to a forward line on the Dutch crisis in 1786-7. As he grew in self-confidence the young prime minister showed an increasing desire to intervene in other areas of administration beyond his own Treasury department. Ministers with controversial or problematical areas of authority welcomed such intervention provided it was exercised to support their own views, and though such intervention eventually led Carmarthen to protest at times at Pitt's imposition of control, generally there is no evidence of Pitt pressing the foreign secretary into any policy directly contrary to the latter's aims until he determined to withdraw from confrontation with Russia in April 1791 — whereupon Carmarthen (by then Duke of Leeds) promptly resigned. There were undoubted differences on occasion as to the means, but not on ends. Carmarthen was not a member of Pitt's intimate circle and without the close, almost daily contact with the prime minister possessed by his successor, Grenville, the foreign secretary had to find other ways to secure Pitt to his aims. Undoubtedly Carmarthen did not have the strength of personality to impose his will on the Cabinet, but perhaps bringing Pitt into play on his side was a legitimate tactic and not a surrender of policy to Pitt. Although the Prime Minister's intervention often imposed a slower pace, Carmarthen eventually got the ultimatum he wanted both in 1787 and 1790.[5]

Leeds also got the ultimatum he wanted in 1791 only to see Pitt withdraw it again within a month. How far was this 'catastrophe of 1791' the result of

Grenville acquiring a 'superiority' over Pitt as Leeds's friend, his under-secretary, Burges, alleged? Evidence for such a charge is in fact scanty and it seems vastly exaggerated. Leeds himself, in his memoranda on the crisis, did not see Grenville as primarily responsible.[6] Burges finds some support from E.D. Adams, whose account of Grenville's influence between 1787 and 1798 has much influenced historians, though many of his judgements must now be modified and even he hesitates to go so far as Burges.[7]

Grenville was deeply involved in a number of ways. He was Pitt's confidant. He was a long-time correspondent with one of the opponents of the policy, Lord Auckland, British envoy to Holland; and as home secretary he was primarily responsible for supervising military operations if war broke out.[8] He was consequently fully informed, but there is no evidence that he made any opposition in the course of the long build-up to the Cabinet ultimatum to Russia on 21-22 March 1791. Indeed, as his biographer Peter Jupp points out, he ceased corresponding with the hositle Auckland in mid-February. At the 21-22 March Cabinets he objected to the means rather than the ends of the policy, but when the decision went against him he pressed for its speedy implementation. A much more vociferous opponent was the Duke of Richmond, but when he repeated his objections at a private meeting with Pitt, Grenville, Lord Chancellor Thurlow and the foreign secretary on the afternoon of the 30th, Grenville 'said little on the subject'.[9]

Dr Jupp rightly notes that most of the evidence produced by Adams for the decisive adverse influence of Grenville comes from the period after the latter became foreign secretary. That was a time when Grenville saw a virtual withdrawal from Europe as the only way out of Britain's embarrassment and hence could readily become the scapegoat of the proponents of a forward European policy. It might also be added that virtually all Adams's evidence probably stemmed from the same informant — Burges.[10] In fairness Adams was more tentative than Burges and suggested that 'The correct view seems to be that Pitt was weakened in his opinion by the attacks of Grenville, and that the ill-will of Parliament furnished the last and convincing argument'.[11]

During the subsequent retreat both Pitt and Grenville stressed the crucial factor as the domestic situation: Parliament seemed unlikely to provide the necessary vote of credit.[12] Adams misinterprets Leeds's account. This does not show Pitt as weakening when Grenville at last indicated a wish to withdraw at the evening Cabinet on 30 March, but it does show him as shaken after further information on the Parliamentary situation next morning. At that stage there was still only a minority of the Cabinet against his policy, and there seems no reason why he should not have imposed his will on it (as he did against Grenville in 1795 and 1797) had he been sure of

Parliamentary support. Leeds would have nothing to do with retraction, so that it was Pitt who drafted the decisive despatch and Grenville who read it to the Cabinet on 16 April. Adams's assertion that Leeds indicated his knowledge of the true author of his reverse by suggesting that Grenville sign the despatch, ignores the need for despatches to be signed by a secretary-of-state, and that Grenville was the only alternative when Leeds refused to sign.[13] Three days later Leeds resigned and Grenville was transferred to the Foreign Office to settle the crisis. Undoubtedly Grenville turned against the confrontation policy before Pitt, but the main reason for the 'catastrophe' was surely Pitt's failure to do what a foreign secretary ultimately required from his prime minster and leader of the Commons, and that was to produce a reliable parliamentary majority. When even Leeds's stratagem of drawing in Pitt to get his policies through failed, then it was time for him to go.

Grenville seems to have taken the Foreign Office rather unwillingly and on three occasions in 1794 indicated a willingness to leave it again. This does not suggest any determined ascendancy over Pitt. Nevertheless he took a firm grip on the organisation and regulation of his department. His biographer Jupp surprisingly depreciates the extent of his impact by describing him as a foreign secretary 'who led by example rather than by wholesale changes in method and personnel, such changes as were made proved to be as much the result of the efforts of other as his own'. However, Jupp's attribution of reform to Burges overlooks how little took place during Burges's under-secretaryship under Leeds compared with the amount between 1793 and 1795 under Grenville. It also ignores the further period of reforming activity, after Burges's removal, between 1799 and 1801. In contrast is C.R. Middleton's view that 'of those who had the seals between 1782 and 1810 Grenville was clearly the most able . . . He also had the greatest impact on the office'.[14]

Jupp stresses Grenville's 'clear preference for tradition rather than innovation', but his clearest preference was for organisation and efficiency. Hence the tenets of 'economic reform' were applied vigorously. Gratuities were refused, overcharging suppliers called to account, and Grenville backed the regulation of the offices of the Secretaries of State in 1795 which saw personnel removed from a fee'd to a salaried system. In late 1793 he moved the Foreign Office to larger premises in Downing Street where business was reorganised into northern and southern departments, each supervised by a separate under-secretary. Further review resulted in 1799 in detailed regulation of duties and attendance of the clerks. Grenville's reorganisation and regulations of the official correspondence will be shown later, and indeed the flow of regulations from Grenville's pen ranged widely, stretching from entry into the diplomatic service (c.1792-3) to the conduct of government messengers in 1799.[15]

The quality of the diplomatic service was perhaps the major problem Grenville never satisfactorily solved. He hoped to upgrade its status by bringing young men of rank in at the bottom and pushing them up rapidly through the ranks as they acquired experience. Results in the short term, however, were disappointing, and Grenville ultimately resorted to appointing men short of diplomatic experience but whom he trusted to important stations over the heads of what he clearly considered a diplomatic corps of limited talent. Taken with the high turnover of under-secretaries (six saw service during his tenure), this amounted to substantial changes in personnel and betokens a demanding taskmaster determined to run his department to his own satisfaction.[16]

In contrast to Carmarthen, Grenville possessed three particular assets which meant that he did not have to resort to his predecessor's devious methods to secure his ends. The first was his intimacy with his cousin, Pitt, and with the other principal 'man of business' in the Cabinet from 1791, Henry Dundas. Burges described Pitt and Grenville in 1791 as 'two friends . . . so inseparably connected that there is but one sentiment between them', and the diplomat Lord Auckland in the same year considered that 'whatever is written to the one may be considered as written to the other'. If in the course of time tensions developed between the strategic perceptions of Grenville and Dundas, they retained a healthy respect for each other's business abilities and continued to operate with Pitt as an inner cabinet through to 1800.[17]

Grenville's second asset was the strength of his personality — many called it obstinacy — which made him prepared to take on his colleagues if necessary by himself on issues where his mind was made up, and the third was his 'application', already noted by Burges, which won the respect of Pitt, Dundas, his cabinet colleagues and the King.

Above all this 'application' was demonstrated by the way he sought, recorded and presented information. 'Well-informed' was one of the most frequently used adjectives of his colleagues to describe Grenville.[18] He eagerly sought relevant information of all sorts in private letters from his envoys abroad. The extent of the collection of his private papers is in itself testimony to his care in storing information. Among his reforms of the Foreign Office the précis of foreign correspondence, formerly in the hands of a junior clerk, was upgraded to a separate senior post in 1793 and added to the official establishment in 1795. In 1799 the care and management of the official correspondence was newly regulated, and virtually Grenville's last act in 1801 was to order the recovery of all previous foreign correspondence from the State Paper Office to be housed in a new Librarian's Department of the Foreign Office.[19] It all meant that not only did Grenville have access to private information beyond the official despatches seen by his colleagues but he also had the ability to retrieve information from former despatches and to present it to his colleagues in the form of summaries with its own editorial comments. During wartime when the number of official despatches and private letters increased vastly, Grenville's capacity to control such a vast source of information gave him powers to overawe his colleagues. Even Dundas, after questioning Grenville's certainty of a Dutch revolt in 1799, conceded that

> Perhaps any shade of difference [that] may be between us on this view of the question, may be accounted for by the superior knowledge you have upon it. You are in the daily habit of receiving the intelligence, and of combining it, and drawing your conclusions from it. I am therefore very much disposed to think that your ideas are more just than mine; and you may rest assured that I am decided to act upon your ideas (in which Mr Pitt perfectly concurs) rather than upon any doubts of my own.[20]

Within weeks of Grenville taking office, Burges declared that 'our foreign politics . . . are solely and exclusively those of Lord Grenville's . . . Pitt gives way to him in a manner very extraordinary'. Was Burges over-reacting to a different relationship than he had been used to between Pitt and Leeds? Pitt's intervention did not now need to be so ostentatious since the two cousins, living closely together and constantly exchanging views, were in close agreement. Discussions over dinner and meetings in advance of Cabinet with Dundas, as well as frequent exchange of letters, produced a generally harmonious relationship.[21] The most frequent interruptions until 1800 were less policy disputes than the endless patronage requests from Grenville's demanding and over-sensitive eldest brother, the Marquess of Buckingham, which on one occasion led to Grenville seeking to communicate an urgent foreign matter to Pitt via Dundas for fear that his own urgings would be misinterpreted.[22]

It is probably unwise to look for the clear superiority of any one of the ruling triumvirate over the others. Contemporary opinion differed. In 1794 Burges reported without disagreement the view of Liverpool's son that 'Mr Pitt has hitherto been absolute, and other members [of the Cabinet] have had no more to do than to give their opinions and submit to his, unless when Grenville chose to make a stand'. Yet a year later the Russian ambassador was describing Grenville as the strongest man in the Cabinet, while in late 1797 another Cabinet member, Windham, thought that 'Dundas ruled despotically'.[23] The relationship was however much more one of a working partnership, and the extent of disagreement within it has been considerably exaggerated by historians influenced by Adams's seminal study.

Adams identified the manifestos published in late 1793 as occasioning the first difference of opinion between Pitt and Grenville on the conduct of the war with France (and their first difference after Grenville became foreign secretary). The allied armies were across the French border. Toulon had declared for Louis XVII and welcomed in the British fleet. The Vendée was in open rebellion. Hence it was thought time to address the French people on Britain's aims in France. Grenville drafted a general manifesto in which, asserted Adams, he acted as restraining influence on Pitt who sought to commit Britain more deeply to the monarchical cause. Following this lead, J. Holland Rose considered Grenville's attitude as more flexible than Pitt's, while Jupp, comparing the apparently cautious phraseology of Grenville's general manifesto with the separate manifesto to the inhabitants of Toulon (which is assumed to have been written by Pitt and which Adams described as 'much more emphatic in favour of the restoration of monarchy than the former'), has criticised the government for talking with two voices, adding that not for the first or last time Grenville 'played the role of cautious diplomat to Pitt's opportunistic strategist'.[24]

The concept of a battle of the manifestos, however, is insecurely based. Grenville's criticism, cited by Adams, were not of the Toulon manifesto, but of the instructions for the British Commissioners at Toulon, being drawn up by one of them, Sir Gilbert Elliot, in conjunction with Pitt and Lord Chancellor Loughborough. Indeed there is no clear evidence that the Toulon manifesto was in fact Pitt's brainchild and it may simply have been a variant on Grenville's manifesto produced several weeks earlier, for there was no great difference of opinion between the two. Pitt liked 'very much' the general plan of Grenville's paper. He urged 'a more pointed recommendation of monarchical government with proper limitations . . . specifying monarchy as the only system in the re-establishment of which we are disposed to concur', and Grenville's final declaration only promised British support to those who would declare for monarchy. Adams overlooks this by citing its apparently cautious beginning, but the tenor of both manifestos was the same and differences in tone can be accounted for by the fact that Grenville was addressing himself to the unconverted French nation as a whole and seeking therefore to lead them logically towards his concluding endorsement of monarchy, whereas the apparently more enthusiastic and forthright advocacy of Louis XVII in the Toulon manifesto was addressed to committed royalists.[25]

Another persistent misinterpretation of their relationship in the early years of the war is of a continual clash between Grenville as an Austrophil and Pitt as a Prussophil.[26] Again the extent of their differences before 1795 has been greatly exaggerated and too much has been read back from that crisis. Ideally they each wanted the support of both German powers. Grenville came to despair of Prussian support earlier than Pitt and hesitated to go so far as Pitt in seeking to reactivate the Prussians, but only in early 1795 did he see a clear choice as having to be made between Prussia and

Austria. Till then he was ready to make some effort to attract continued Prussian participation, even at Austria's expense. Pitt never saw a choice as having to be made and certainly never had any intention of jettisoning Austria for any supposed partiality for a Prussian alliance. There were indeed occasions when he was prepared to go further than Grenville in concessions to strengthen the Austrian connection.[27]

Adams, followed by Sherwig, portrays a clash emerging over the Prussian request for a subsidy in late 1793, with Grenville totally against and Pitt for testing the ground. Allegedly unable to agree, they submitted the matter to a Cabinet on 9 October to decide, which it did in Grenville's favour. However, Pitt proposed that their most experienced diplomat, Lord Malmesbury, be sent to Berlin and persuaded a further Cabinet in mid-November to accept his views.[28] Re-examination of the documents must modify this interpretation. There was no total disagreement which necessitated their calling for Cabinet arbitration. The letter misdated to 4 February 1794 in H.M.C. *Dropmore* on which Adams based his account was also misdated to 4 October by Adams himself. It is clearly a reply to a letter by Grenville of 8 October enclosing his draft reply to the Prussians for Cabinet consideration. Pitt responded that 'The Prussian draft is, I think, extremely improved and in most parts perfectly right'. Pitt went on to talk of Malmesbury going to the Prussians, and Adams, Sherwig and Jupp have consequently seen this as Pitt's initiative, but part of the original Grenville letter (omitted in Holland Rose's printed version) shows that he made the original suggestion. There was thus much more agreement between the two than is commonly supposed. If the Cabinet approved Grenville's draft, it also accepted Pitt's inclination to soften it. Thereafter military reverses in Europe converted Grenville to a greater willingness to investigate the utility of a subsidy, though more pessimistic about its chances than Pitt.[29]

Adams continues his interpretation of a clash of policies into 1794 by showing Grenville in June as seeking to stop the subsidy when the Prussian army remained immobile. He asserted that Grenville 'yielded with good grace' to promptings for its continuation from Pitt and the Duke of Portland (leader of their new Cabinet coalition partners) only because the time was right for him to launch his own policy of an Austrian alliance. Yet Grenville was not acting out of Prussophobia. He always took a strong line with allies who did not fulfil their obligations and in the subsequent financial negotiations with Vienna incorporated tough terms to prevent a repetition of the Prussian evasion — terms so tough that the Austrians rejected them. Nor was the approach to Vienna peculiarly the responsibility of Grenville. Lord Auckland's mention of Grenville's 'great plan', eagerly seized on by Adams, related to a reshuffle of envoys, not to the Austrian overture. The latter had become necessary because of Austria's defeat and withdrawal from the Netherlands. Pitt and Grenville clearly concerted it together, the Cabinet thought it necessary, and Portland and their new colleagues warmly endorsed it.[30]

Burges saw the inclusion of the Portland Whigs in the Cabinet in June 1794 as completing Pitt's ruin, but it is difficult to see how. They were zealous supporters of the war and readily backed both the continuance of the Prussian subsidy and the overture to Austria. Once in Cabinet they seldom acted as a united pressure group and proved ineffectual opponents of Pitt's later attempts to make peace. When conflict really did first erupt between Pitt and Grenville in early 1795 they split between the two.

The first major difference of opinion between Pitt and Grenville occurred in the spring of 1795 and has been interpreted by Adams and Sherwig as the climax of Pitt's Prussophilia versus Grenville's Austrophilia. The difference however was more subtle and has to be seen in the context of the massive £6-million loan which Pitt and Grenville offered to Vienna to carry the main burden of the continental war in December 1794. The fall of Holland led Grenville on 6 February to attempt again to draw Russia into active intervention. Pitt wished to go further and bring Prussia back into the war for the specific purpose of recovering Holland. Grenville, however, had grasped that a confrontation had developed between Russia and Austria on one side and Prussia on the other over the final partition of Poland. Besides doubting Prussian good faith, he was convinced that any approach to Berlin would wreck Britain's relations with the other two to whom they were looking for the main effort. Pitt was unwilling to accept that a choice would have to be made. He was not devoted to Prussia and looking to switch allies. Far from allowing the Austrian negotiation to 'dangle' as Sherwig suggests, he at no stage showed any antipathy to the project and sanctioned Grenville pressing it repeatedly (the dangling was on the Austrian side). Rather Pitt looked to supplement Austrian efforts in the one area of vital British interest where they were unable to act. Prussia had an army available and Pitt had devised a new formula involving part-payment by results which might obviate Prussian treachery. He opened the idea inconclusively at a Cabinet dinner on 18 February and pressed it when two days later news was received of a breakdown in Prussia's peace negotiations and of Austrian objections to the loan terms and inability to help Holland.[31]

The account of the struggle that followed needs updating from documents which have come to light since Adams wrote his still-influential version. These show a more complex picture involving other players and provide much insight into decision-making structures.

In the first place Grenville's protest at Pitt's independent approach to the Prussian envoy Jacobi, tentatively dated to 12 October 1794 by J. Holland

Rose, is almost certainly the start of this crisis on 23 February 1795.[32] Seeking to break away from Grenville's control of information, Pitt and Dundas saw Jacobi only for the foreign secretary to find out apparently through a secret office intercept of the Prussian's mail. Grenville protested the need for an agreed policy and sought a discussion prior to any further Cabinet meeting. Their difference was not resolved and Grenville indicated that he must resign if Pitt's proposal was accepted. The threat was double misery for Pitt since it came at a time when Irish matters threatened crisis with their Portland Whig allies, and he fought hard to reconcile his cousin. It was Pitt who took the initiative in drafting instructions on the lines of his proposal and summoning the next Cabinet to consider them, but he asked Grenville to see him an hour before the meeting in an effort to persuade him.[33]

Pitt's draft minute of that Cabinet meeting on 1 March is the second important addition to the picture, for it indicates the closeness of his victory and explains his actions over the following week. Loughborough, Cornwallis, Dundas, Portland and another Portland Whig, Windham, backed Pitt, while Chatham, Hawkesbury, and two other Portland Whigs, Mansfield and Spencer, sided with Grenville.[34]

Far from that ascendancy suggested by Burges, Grenville at once offered to discuss with Pitt the mode and timing of his departure if the ultimate decision 'takes the shape, which I will fairly say with your decided opinion on the subject I think it ought . . .' But Pitt could not simply push the decision through by a diktat. The closeness of the 1 March decision precluded that and the premier worked hard to hold his cabinet together and secure unanimity. He sought to stall Grenville by hinting that a further Cabinet might reach a different decision and he played on his cousin's loyalty by pressing the need to avoid an 'éclat' at a delicate time and that he should defer resignation till near the end of the Parliamentary session.[35] Above all Pitt turned to the King.

George III's part in this crisis has been surprisingly neglected. The resignation of a minister was bound to involve him as Grenville indicated on 2 March when asking Pitt how best to inform the King. But the King had stronger reasons for involvement. At a time of great uncertainty over Prussian intentions he had a valuable source of information beyond those of the British government through his Hanoverian Regency. Apparently unaware of the Cabinet debates, he raised the matter himself on 2 March by sending Pitt the gist of Prussia's reply to a Hanoverian enquiry as to what Berlin would do against the French threat to Westphalia. Pitt seized upon the chance to trump the well-informed Grenville and eagerly begged the exact details from the King, indicating that there was a difference of opinion and stating his own preference for making a further financial offer to Prussia.

George, as Elector, declared his favour for the proposal to save threatened Hanover, but added that as King he doubted Parliament would agree. He suggested limiting the proposal to Prussia initially to the offer of essential military stores with a guarantee of full payment of the subsidy by the Dutch after Holland had been recovered. Pitt quickly communicated this to Grenville as 'a line which may in some degree unite opinions'. In the week that followed Pitt worked hard to bring the King into play on his side in the Cabinet contest and on 8 March succeeded in getting royal approval in advance of a minute he would submit to the Cabinet. Taken in isolation, that minute has been used to show Pitt acting as a strong premier, but in the light of the 1 March minute it shows a premier desperately seeking to strengthen a weak position.[36]

In fact as Pitt sought to strengthen his position it was undermined by news from the continent on 5 and 8 March that Prussia would accept French peace terms. The Cabinet on 9 March, which should have finally endorsed Pitt's Prussian overture, pressed ahead instead with proposals for a Triple Alliance between Britain, Austria and Russia.

Britain was not however a major military power and foreign policy oscillated with the varying news received from those continental military powers on whom it depended to implement its objects. On 12 March came news that Austria could not defend Hanover, which possibly decisively decided George III in favour of the Prussian overture so that he was ready to press it when opportunity offered. On 28 March came 'very unpleasant letters from Vienna' which seemed to destroy hopes of the Austrian loan and others indicating the chance of Prussian co-operation. The misplacement in Aspinall's *Later Correspondence of George III* of an exchange of letters between George and Pitt on 29 March has implied that Pitt saw the chance and took the initiative first when in fact it was the opposite.[37] The King told Pitt that he felt 'a little staggered on the subject' and desired his premier to 'with attention read over these papers'. When the Prussian possibility was confirmed by Lord Malmesbury, who arrived from Germany on 5 April, George again pressed his premier that 'there is not a minute to be lost in coming to a decision . . .' Pitt admittedly needed little prompting, but the news and the King's zealous endorsement must have played their part in bringing all the Cabinet except Grenville to accept the Prussian proposal on 8 April.[38]

Grenville fought the decision to the very end, but when it went against him he contented himself with having his dissent officially recorded on the minute. Contrary to Adams and Sherwig, he gave no indication of resigning on this occasion and instead accepted the King's proposal that Dundas should provide the necessary secretary of state's signature to the instructions if he was unwilling. Aspinall suggested that his mode of recording dissent instead of resigning was a precedent, though Pitt had produced the formula in his draft 1 March minute. Whether Grenville would have carried on or whether he would have resigned at the end of the Parliamentary session is uncertain since news arrived on 16 April that Prussia had made peace and put an end to Pitt's project.[39]

To Adams the coalition with the Portland Whigs marks the beginning of a growing apart of Pitt and Grenville while the vindication of the latter's stance on Pitt's Prussian proposals gave him 'a distinct following' in the Cabinet. Jupp too sees Grenville as assuming a more independent role from 1795, asserting that his ties with Pitt and Dundas were weakening while those with the Portland group strengthened. The evidence however is insubstantial. In so far as there had been a weakening of the relationship between Grenville and Pitt it had been as far back as 1792 when Grenville purchased Dropmore and married. Thereafter he was less frequently in the close company of his bachelor cousin, but absences were overcome by a constant flow of correspondence. Their letters during their difference on the Prussian overture reveal their continued regard for each other. Nor is there much sign of any strengthening relationship with the Portland group, at least until 1797 when their dislike of peace coincided, and even then not at a personal level: Jupp's suggestion of a personal tie with Windham falls down on investigation.[40] Right through to 1801 Grenville always considered himself closer to Pitt and Dundas than to the Portland Whigs. In late summer 1795 he co-operated closely with Pitt in persuading Portland of the need to approach Vienna on the possibility of joint negotiations for peace. He also contributed with his cousin in the preparation of Auckland's pamphlet examining the bases on which peace might be made.[41]

All this makes unlikely Jupp's tentative suggestion that Pitt probably sensed a drift apart and possibly tried to check it by installing his own protégé, George Canning, as under-secretary at the Foreign Office. Rather Canning's appointment shows the continued close relationships of the cousins. Grenville had for over a year wished to replace his two under-secretaries, but he shared with his cousin a fault remarkable in two such strong personalities in that they were both poor sackers. He sought to buy his subordinates out in 1794. When they refused his offers he did nothing till summer 1795 when he again offered Burges an embassy. When that was again rejected he turned to the First Lord of the Treasury to provide bigger bait. Pitt obliged with a baronetcy, a £1200 p.a. pension and the office of Knight Marshall for the joint lives of Burges and his son. Grenville was thus enabled to fulfil his wish, as Pitt explained to Burges, to have a person of his own as under-secretary and George Hammond was appointed. Pitt also provided the office of Muster-Master General to persuade the other under-secretary, Aust, to resign. In return Grenville appointed Canning.

Pitt had been looking for a business post for his protégé since May. He tried for a vacant under-secretaryship in Portland's office but found it already promised. Grenville's were the next vacancies that occurred, and having got Hammond, he readily and without any signs of coercion or acrimony gave the other to Canning who seemed a promising man of business. It was a matter of mutual favours and there is no need to suspect underhand motives.[42]

The close co-operation of Pitt and Grenville continued through 1796 and was indeed vital in forcing the King to accept, against his strongly declared wishes, first, a peace enquiry to France and, second, a new overture for Prussian intervention which involved cessions to Berlin of the territory of petty German rulers which the Elector of Hanover was bound to disapprove.[43] Only by a strongly united front could these unpalatable measures be forced on the King and they marked the real decline of royal influence on foreign policy. Not in Pitt's ministry hitherto nor in all his long reign had George III suffered two such consecutive foreign policy defeats. The two cousins were still united when the first peace negotiations actually took place in late 1796.

Both Adams and Holland Rose portray Grenville as seeking to sabotage Pitt's intentions in the 1796 negotiations by the restraints he imposed on the British envoy, Malmesbury, against any hasty conclusion of peace and by his subsequent tough demands. They overlook the real need for delay while Britain's ally, Austria, was consulted. Adams (wrongly) blames the instructions of 7 November for the failure of the negotiations, overlooking that they were drafted by Pitt in the absence of Grenville due to the death of his sister. Rose (rightly) blames the 11 December instructions but fails to point out that British expectations had been legitimately raised by Austrian victories, by the successful loyalty-loan and by the short-lived prospect of Russian intervention. Each claims that the tougher line resulted from Grenville's superiority over Pitt, in disregard of statements by Windham and the Russian envoy, Vorontsov, of the exact opposite relationship at this point. This was not a case of a bellicose Grenville winning out over a pacific Pitt but again of the two working together.[44]

Far different was the situation six months later when the first really fundamental breach between the two cousins exploded and led Wilberforce to record in his diary that they were near to breaking their friendship.[45] Between December 1796 and May 1797 an attempted French invasion of Ireland, financial panic and suspension of cash payments, Austria's defeat by Bonaparte, and mutiny in the fleet seriously undermined the national will to fight on. So long as Vienna held out Grenville was willing to offer joint peace negotiations out of loyalty to his ally and to enhance their bargaining position. When the Austrians made a separate peace, however, he was unwilling to approach the French separately lest it was interpreted as a sign of Britain's weakness and encouraged French ambitions. He saw Britain's salvation as achievable only through firmness which might bring the French to moderation. Pitt, on the other hand, increasingly felt that peace must be had. Negotiation might contain the demoralisation at home and might also reveal whether a peace 'consistent with the safety and honour of the country' was obtainable.

The result was a basic split on matters of fundamental principle. The dispute over the Prussian overture had been about means of continuing the war rather than ends. Now the dispute was about the ends themselves, for, to Grenville, to go running to France was a path likely to lead to further and further concession, to peace without safety or honour: '. . . one by one every government in Europe', he wrote, 'has been shaken and many overthrown, by weakness and by the very system of palliatives and temporizing measures on which we are now acting.' He was for toughing it out against the 'dejection, cowardice and disaffection at home' that so concerned Pitt, and his remarks on the difference of opinion with his cousin are revealing, both on this crisis and their relationship hitherto: 'Nothing has surprized me more in all this history than finding these opinions adverse to the sentiments of those with whom I have so long been used to act and think. It makes me doubt, but it cannot alter my conviction . . .'[46]

In consequence a violent two-month struggle occurred before Canning announced jubilantly at the end of June that 'He [Pitt] *has* asserted himself. An *explosion* was very near. It turned on the point of a moment, on the chance of half an hour's good or ill temper. But it is over for the moment. However he has asserted himself, and is really master now'. For the first time Canning was forced to take sides between his patron, and his departmental chief, and he urged on and abetted Pitt with all the means in his power. His diary provides an illuminating and surprisingly unused insight into the power struggle to control Britain's foreign policy on this occasion.[47]

Pitt was in fact slow to assert himself. Canning spoke to him as early as 10 May on the need for a direct approach to Paris. Pitt agreed with him but indicated that 'some are counteracting it all'. Grenville was digging in his heels. It was not until 31 May that Pitt forced the issue by putting the proposal to the Cabinet. He was clearly uneasy as the dispute with his cousin came into the open. Canning noted that it was decided upon 'after violent disputes', and Windham recorded Pitt avoiding a vote on the 31st, instead showing 'an affection in speaking of it as a thing rather agreed', and he only pressed a final decision next day.

The real battle however would be if the French returned a favourable reply. Canning doubted Pitt's resolution and sought to steel him against Grenville's wrath. On 7 June he rode with him and 'Exhorted him to be stout in Cabinet — to carry points that he thought essential. Reviewed the points which he had thought right in Foreign Politicks during the last three months, and had given up to others'. On the 11th on another ride he 'resumed and went over our former conversation particularly about persons, and the necessity of his being firm to his own opinions'.

The French reply dictated that Britain should negotiate a definitive and separate peace at Lille, remote from continental transactions and separate from its remaining ally Portugal. This precipitated the confrontation Canning feared. Pitt was for pressing on; Grenville for a high-toned reply. The Cabinet on 14 June saw 'violent disputes' after which Canning walked with Pitt and talked over Grenville's draft reply. Pitt was determined to alter it and not give way, and later in the day he sent for Canning to show him his alterations. Next morning the Cabinet met again with 'more violence'. Ministers narrowly supported Pitt by 5-4, with all the Portland Whigs siding with Grenville in the minority, till an undecided Liverpool finally came out on Pitt's side too and provided the premier with a more decisive margin.[48]

Although discussion was to resume in the evening, Pitt had at last brought matters to a decisive vote. He drew up his own note to present to the evening meeting and summoned Canning again for his observations. Grenville spent a tortured afternoon vainly trying to reconcile his own and Pitt's notes and eventually summoned his brother Tom for a family discussion on his future. Yet again he was torn by conscience and loyalty. Should he implement a measure in his own department which he abhorred or should he resign, which at a time of national crisis might give a disastrous impression of weakness and division 'among those by whom alone the country can be saved'?

Grenville conceded that it was clear which way the decision on the negotiation would go, but he nevertheless fought it all the way — unlike Windham who deliberately avoided the evening meeting. The Cabinet in consequence went on past midnight. 'Séance orageuse', recorded Windham from what he heard later. 'Great violence. Ld.G. nearly going out', wrote Canning. But Pitt stood firm and Grenville's hand was called. Rather than jeopardise the ministry, Grenville suffered himself again to have his dissent recorded on the Cabinet minute of 16 June which finally settled the matter. He contented himself with explaining his conduct in a long letter to the King.[49]

In so doing, Grenville was not apparently attempting to incite the King, but nevertheless Pitt's victory was uncertain until George III's approval was secured. The two cousins united had forced the reluctant King into peace negotiations in the previous year. Now they were divided, he might play a more independent line. Pitt's own letter to his sovereign handled the difficulty adroitly. Having gone thus far, he explained, they could not cut the overture short before coming to matters of substance because that would preclude any chance of peace and also lose the best means of rallying the country in case of failure. Insidiously he concluded by playing on the King's well-known predilection for consistency of purpose: 'he knows that Your Majesty will feel that, the line of negotiation having once been taken, ought not to be hastily departed from'.[50]

While Pitt made it difficult for George to say no, the King's reply was scarcely less skilful. He accepted the Cabinet minute but evaded complete submission. Besides Grenville's recorded dissent, he presumed that of Windham and Liverpool who were absent from the 16 June Cabinet, so that by implication ministers were far from united. His own view was that the tone of Pitt's note was too low and he expressed to Pitt his happiness that Grenville had not resigned, as his talents would be very material to the negotiation. To Grenville he gave the green light to continue his firm line. It was 'absolutely essential' for him to remain in his post 'for he will be able to stave off many further humiliations that might be attempted'.[51]

Perhaps this encouraged Grenville's continued resistance when the next French reply came. Pitt was satisfied by it, Grenville was not, but his proposed answer was rejected by Pitt at a Cabinet on 24 June. 'Great violence', recorded Canning, adding that Grenville indeed stormed out of the meeting: 'Ld.G left the Cabinet, taking leave'. Yet again Pitt stood his ground. A not inconsiderable obstacle to his independent line was that, at a time when so much depended on an exact conveyance of meanings, Grenville was easily the best linguist in the Cabinet. Pitt therefore had to draw up his alternative note in English and had Canning get the French expert George Ellis to translate it. He also decided that he must now bring Grenville's continued opposition to an issue, and before the Cabinet on 25 June he made it plain that Grenville must agree or go out. Yet again Canning busied himself against his chief before the meeting, calling on Pitt's intended negotiator, Lord Malmesbury, and on Pitt himself, though there was little need in the event, for Grenville again gave way — provided, he told Pitt, that 'I can have some certainty of a stand being made somewhere'.[52]

It was at this point that Canning proclaimed Pitt to be 'really master now'. However, that mastery was tenuous, for the ruling triumvirate was in total disarray. Dundas had supported Pitt thus far but he was clear that when they came to terms Britain should retain its colonial conquests and he was disillusioned enough with Pitt's soft line for there to be talk of his resigning and taking a peerage at the peace. From the same note in Canning's diary it seems as if Grenville too would move office at the peace, but until then, backed as he was by the King, Pitt could hardly move him and he therefor remained in official control of the negotiation, drawing up and signing all official instructions.[53]

Here then was Pitt's continued problem. It was one thing to gain the decision in Cabinet but much more work was needed to see it implemented. Grenville would negotiate for peace, but he was looking for high terms appropriate for 'a great and dignified country'. To counteract the danger from Grenville's continued supervision of the negotiations Pitt had three weapons. One was his own strength of will which, when put to the test, had proven stronger than his cousin's. He clearly felt he now had Grenville's measure, telling Malmesbury that 'collatoral difficulties may, I think, always be overcome by a mixture of firmness and temper'.[54] Second was his relationship with the actual envoy, Malmesbury, whom he briefed privately before his departure on his personal commitment to peace and who was encouraged to correspond directly with the prime minster throughout the negotiation. In this way Pitt had access to information independent of Grenville.[55]

Thirdly and even more decisively Pitt was able to combat Grenville's greatest personal strength — his control of the collection and dissemination of information — by use of Canning. Grenville himself opened the opportunity for this by removing himself as frequently as possible from the distasteful business to the refuge of his beloved Dropmore, leaving Canning in executive superintendence of communications in London. Canning rather than Grenville thus had control of the sources of information and manipulated them on Pitt's behalf. When on 31st July Henry Wesley and on 8 August Leveson-Gower returned from Lille with details of a secret approach to Malmesbury by part of the French delegation, Canning had them produce edited versions to send to Grenville at Dropmore, while he summoned Pitt to hear their full accounts (less still was communicated to the Cabinet). When on 19 August Grenville's dispatches and private letter to Malmesbury took a line 'apparently hostile and intended to break off negotiation', Canning summoned Pitt who read them over and then wrote privately to Malmesbury himself. When Malmesbury complained to Canning that Grenville's despatches tied him too firmly, Canning again saw Pitt who engaged to have new softer despatches written and that if Grenville would not agree, then he would have a Cabinet to oblige him to do so. Equally, Canning undertook to convey Pitt's views in 'Most Private' letters in the reverse direction — to Malmesbury. On this occasion therefore Pitt availed himself of the facility now available to him to infiltrate Grenville's communication-chain.[56]

Grenville was never totally contained. He removed a fourth weapon utilised by Pitt when on 19 July he secured a Cabinet undertaking to keep the negotiations secret — according to Canning so as to stop Pitt leaking information to stimulate public support for his policy. He also continued to lobby hard those with influence on Pitt: two letters in one day on 16 August to Dundas pressed the need for firmness. Pitt nevertheless felt confident enough to press resolutely on. There is scant evidence to support Adams's view that Pitt's hold was weakening by September and that Grenville had formed a party in Cabinet strongly anti-peace and whose strength was daily increasing. Pitt still called the tune both in the negotiations at Lille and in the consequent secret overtures. There was only one Cabinet on foreign policy (on 11 September) between 17 August and 21 September by when it was known that Malmesbury had been dismissed from Lille, so that it is hard to detect the influence of an increasingly belligerent Cabinet group. The negotiations ultimately failed through events in France rather than growing opposition in Britain.[57]

Adams concluded his survey of Grenville's influence on 'Pitt's foreign policy' at the collapse of the 1797 negotiations, asserting that 'Grenville quietly resumed his former predominance in the determination of foreign policy, while the old conditions of friendly intercourse and confidence with his chief were renewed', so that 'Grenville's war policy became Pitt's policy'.[58] The extent of his predominance between autumn 1797 and spring 1799 can however be exaggerated. His plan for a new concert of Europe was in response to an initiative of the Duke of Brunswick, backed by the Hanoverian Regency and warmly endorsed by the King.[59] It needed Pitt's urgings to encourage him to persist in combating Admiralty objections to sending a fleet back into the Mediterranean so as to induce Austria to come forward again in spring 1798.[60] When he sought to implement the concert plan with full British financial backing in August 1798 he was held back by Dundas and Pitt for fear of alienating the British public which had just been worked up to the taxes needed to sustain a defensive war.[61]

However, as the strains of prolonged war began to affect the health first of Pitt, who almost annually from autumn 1797 suffered some sort of breakdown, and then of Dundas, so Grenville's powers of endurance stood out. When Europe started to gear itself for war again in late 1798, so the foreign secretary's self-confidence soared. He tightened his hold on the diplomatic service by inserting in key posts his own men from outside its ranks — brother Tom in Berlin, Lord Minto in Vienna, William Wickham in Switzerland. He renewed his regulation of the Foreign Office and he began to extend his influence into strategic military planning.[62]

This torrential energy, and the deluge of information with which he swamped opposition, enabled him to secure an ascendancy in the triumvirate recognised by others in the Cabinet. Windham, looking for help for the French Royalists, wrote to Grenville in July 1799 with an 'earnest request, that he set his shoulder to the wheel, without which nothing likely to be done'. For a while he was indeed unstoppable.[63] Pitt no longer had his own Foreign Office source to check on his cousin after Canning transferred to the India Board in March 1799. Grenville played a hard policy line with Britain's potential partners. Prussia had no right to a full confidence of Britain's intentions until it entered the war, nor Austria until it fulfilled past financial obligations. It was a hard line that disturbed Pitt, who repeatedly urged his cousin to be more open for the sake of obtaining a harmonious co-operation. 'I hardly like to adhere to an opinion so opposite to yours', he wrote to Grenville in urging assurances to Vienna over the future of the Netherlands in order to ensure Austria's continued co-operation in the Swiss offensive. But he did not force the issue until too late. In September he pressed on the reluctant Grenville a plan to offer Piedmont to Vienna and had brought him to the point of giving way when news arrived of the Austrian withdrawal from Switzerland, leaving Pitt only able to express his frustration. Nevertheless within a month he returned to the attack and took the matter to the Cabinet. Once again he looked for his alternative advisers and summoned Canning to talk about '*my* Vienna Project' (author's italics). On 26th the Cabinet agreed but again the premier was thwarted by news from Vienna that the offer was going beyond what the Austrians wanted and was therefore needlessly risking offence to their Russian ally.[64]

By autumn 1799 therefore there were signs that Grenville's continuing predominance would depend on developments on the Continent. Pitt would not be battered into submission as in the summer. In November he told Canning it was his policy 'in which Grenville quite concurs' to persist in trying against hope for continued Austro-Russian co-operation. The relationship was moving into equilibrium again. The cousins anticipated and concerted their response to Bonaparte's peace proposals following his coup d'état, and though Grenville drafted the tart reply, both Pitt and Canning advised on the format.[65]

Although Dundas was becoming increasingly restless at Grenville's disregard of British maritime interests in his excessive concentration on the continental war, Pitt and Grenville continued to operate in harmony until the summer of 1800 when that war was clearly lost.[66] By then Grenville was becoming concerned that the 'wet' in Pitt would re-emerge, as in 1797, and this time he made wider efforts to control that tendency. In July a naval clash with a Danish frigate threatened the emergence of a Baltic armed neutrality. Grenville typically believed only firmness could see them through, but he was sufficiently uncertain of Pitt as to have his senior under-secretary, Hammond, write to his friend Canning to hope that Pitt would not be shaken by any difficulties raised by the Admiralty and urging Canning: 'do implore him to be inflexible'. In the event Pitt withstood the

Admiralty but nevertheless pulled up Grenville for sending instructions which he considered in part too summary and peremptory, whereas Cabinet discussion had thought it wiser to avoid too harsh a tone. In consequence the foreign secretary added a supplementary instruction intended to be less grating to Danish feelings.[67]

In the same month came news of Austria's defeat at Marengo, and that was followed by proposals for an armistice and possible joint peace negotiations. Grenville's concern was to sustain their Austrian ally, but again he was alarmed at how far Pitt might go down the road to concession. Not only did he draw up for Pitt a detailed specification of his intended firm negotiating position but this time he ensured that his own brother Tom, rather than Malmesbury, should be the British envoy at any peace negotiation.[68]

It was the failure of the armistice discussions that at last roused Pitt to a policy independent of his cousin. Concluding that the main obstacle to peace would be France's now clear intention to hold on to Egypt, he backed Dundas's plan to send an expedition to neutralise the French bargaining position there. Grenville remained obstinately loyal to his allies on the continent, demanding the troops be sent to the Austrians in Italy or to Portugal against threatened Spanish invasion. With the triumvirate divided, the issue was thrown on the Cabinet for resolution, but ministers were divided there too. The Admiralty objected to the Egyptian plan; others wanted the troops brought home; others still backed Grenville. Even Dundas virtually gave up when it looked as though his scheme would not be accepted, and it was left to Pitt to win out against his cousin not, as in 1797, by 'firmness and temper' but this time by sharp dealing. Liverpool later recalled:

> that Lord Grenville complained that Pitt had authorized him to give assurances to Vienna and other courts of military co-operation, which he afterwards suffered to be overruled in the Cabinet; that Pitt, finding Lord Liverpool was for the Egyptian plan, called out (contrary to custom) for Liverpool's opinion — 'I wish to hear Lord Liverpool's sentiments'; that on voting those who gave an opinion were nearly equal, but Pitt, summing up, counted those of three members who had not given any opinion and so the matter was decided.[69]

In failing health Pitt was now reduced to devious means to get his way. He saw the Egyptian expedition as preparing the ground for peace, but he could expect further violent argument with his cousin when he tried to open negotiations, and Piers Mackesy has suggested that the prospect may have made the ailing premier more willing to resign when crisis erupted with the King over Catholic Emancipation in February 1801. There may have been no Machiavellian intention involved, but it is an ironic fact that Pitt almost certainly had more influence with a lot less bother over the eventual peace negotiations in 1801, when he was out of office and his advice was relied upon by the new minsters, than he would have had if he and his cousin had remained at their posts.[70]

Looking back on his own experience in 1803, Pitt stressed that power must rest with the 'First Minister', though this was

> no ways incompatible with the most cordial concert and mutual exchange of advice and intercourse amongst the different branches of executive departments; but still, if it should come unfortunately to such radical difference of opinion that no spirit of conciliation or concession can reconcile, the sentiments of the [First] Minister must be allowed and understood to prevail . . .[71]

Although this was written to combat a proposal for a joint administration, it nevertheless reflects Pitt's view of his style of government and provides the other side to the face of the coin suggested by Burges at the start of this chapter. Pitt sought involvement in all major aspects of his administration, constantly demanding information and making suggestions of his own in consequence. That involvement however was usually that of a dabbler. With so many calls on his time he lacked the staying power to keep a tight grip on foreign policy. This was where Grenville was essential to him, as was Dundas in his field. He needed someone to provide the necessary information for decision-making,[72] to suggest decisions for consideration[73] and then to ensure their implementation. In such a role Grenville excelled, and Pitt was prepared to allow Grenville the general initiative on foreign policy provided always that he was informed and consulted. Grenville thus had first say and, through his control of information, might influence Pitt to accept his chosen line of action, but ultimately foreign policy was the result of decisions taken in partnership. Pitt was always ready to offer his own view,[74] and where they disagreed the issue was talked out, often with Dundas involved too. In order to prevail if his well-informed cousin proved excessively obstinate, Pitt had to provide the means to convince the rest of the Cabinet, by finding alternative sources of information to break Grenville's hold on that key to decision-making. In major clashes he also secured alternative means of implementation by way of precaution — though once decisions had been taken he could usually rely on Grenville's loyalty to defer to them.[75]

In the light of conflicts within the triumvirate in 1800, Piers Mackesy has wondered why Pitt persisted with this discordant partnership.[76] However, it had a good track record of collective decision-making and Pitt clung to the hope of its continuation. On the whole it was an effective mode of give and take in which only occasional acrimony intervened. In contrast to Burges's view, there are more obvious examples of Pitt prevailing over Grenville in the 1790s than vice-versa, but there is much more evidence of a harmonious co-operation and identity of ideas. Grenville's expression of surprise when they differed in 1797 makes this point, and so too does their relationship with the Cabinet and the King. The triumvirate had little regard for their colleagues and so far as possible made important decisions privately in advance and then, where Cabinet approval was required, pushed them through Cabinet in concert.[77] Only if they disagreed was the Cabinet called upon for arbitration and that was rare. Neither Grenville nor Pitt tried to build up more lasting parties within the Cabinet to support their own foreign policy views — they preferred to deal directly with each other. Agreement within the triumvirate also steadily reduced the King's means of influencing foreign and war policy in the course of the 1790s, and in the final crisis of the ministry in 1801 there are signs of revolt by some Cabinet members and by the King, resentful at having been squeezed out of the policy-making process.[78]

NOTES

1. 'Concise Diary of Events', Bodleian Library, Burges Mss. The most questionable assertion here relates to Liverpool who backed Grenville on 1 March 1795 against Pitt, but otherwise supported Pitt against Grenville in 1797 and 1800. His role in foreign affairs was extremely subordinate and when he opposed Jay's Treaty in 1794 he was easily overcome. J. Ehrman, *The Younger Pitt*, II (London 1983), 246, 513-4.

2. Horn, 'The machinery for the conduct of British foreign policy in the eighteenth century', *Journal of the Society of Archivists*, III (1965-9), 236. On appointments, Ehrman, I, 310, though as Jeremy Black points out, this was not new: Black, 'The Marquis of Carmarthen and relations with France 1784-1787, *Francia*, 12 (1985), 285; on commercial negotiations Ehrman, I, 330, 428, 430, 478, 510; on personal agents, *ibid.*, 532, 534, 566-7; on drafting despatches, *ibid.*, 531, 534, 543, n.1, 550 n.4, 561.

3. T.C.W. Blanning, ' "That horrid Electorate" or "Ma Patrie Germanique"'?: George III, Hanover and the Fürstenbund of 1785', *Historical Journal*, 20 (1977), 311-44; Ehrman, I, 469; Black, *Francia*, 12, 283-303.

4. Ehrman, I, 131, 184-5, 475-6.

5. Ibid., 525-7, 554, 560-1; 3rd Earl of Malmesbury (ed.), *Diaries and Correspondence of James Harris, First Earl of Malmesbury* (London 1844), II, 258; O. Browning (ed.), *The Political Memoranda of Francis, Fifth Duke of Leeds* (Camden Soc., 2nd Series, Vol. 35), 148; Black, *Francia*, 12, 300-1.

6. Browning, *Leeds Memoranda*, 151-73 provides the only inside account. Lack of evidence presumably leads Ehrman to say so little on the issue of Grenville's influence in his authorative account, *Pitt*, II, 3-41.

7. E.D. Adams, *The influence of Grenville on Pitt's Foreign Policy, 1787-1798* (Washington D.C., 1904) is based on his reading of the first three published volumes of Grenville's papers (Historical Manuscripts Commission, *Report on the Manuscripts of J.B. Fortescue, Esq., preserved at Dropmore* — hereafter H.M.C. *Dropmore* — London, 10 vols., 1892-1927).

8. Ehrman, I, 570-1 shows Grenville in this role and involved in foreign relations during

the Nootka crisis of 1790. There were reports in early March 1791 that Grenville was likely to replace Leeds as foreign secretary *(Leeds Memoranda,* 148).

9. Jupp, *Lord Grenville 1759-1834* (Oxford 1985), 123; *Leeds Memoranda,* 151, 153, 155.

10. Adams, 11-13, particularly 13 n.3; Jupp, 124; Malmesbury *(Diaries,* II, 441) had it in Berlin almost certainly from the British envoy Ewart, who had it from Burges (J. Hutton (ed.), *Selections from the Letters and Correspondence of Sir James Bland Burges,* London 1885, 172). Ewart died in the following January apparently inveighing bitterly against Grenville, but although he was in London during the crisis he seems to have made no accusation against Grenville before Burges wrote to him on 6 May. Burges provided no evidence for this earliest statement of his accusation.

11. Adams, 13 n.3.

12. Ehrman, II, 24-5, citing Ewart's account of a conversation with Pitt on 14 April; H.M.C. *Dropmore,* II, 50-1. M.S. Anderson, *Britain's Discovery of Russia 1553-1815* (London 1958), 159-181 considers parliamentary and public opinion. Perhaps the best indication of Grenville's belief in its decisiveness is the care with which he nursed along public opinion during the crisis leading to the outbreak of war with France in 1793: see in particular S. Vorontsov to A. Vorontsov, 21 January 1793, in P.I. Bartenev (ed.), *Archives Woronzow* (Moscow 1870-95), IX, 285.

13. *Leeds Memoranda,* 164-6, 153-5; Adams, 13 n.4.

14. Jupp, 127, 134-5; Middleton, 'The early years of the old foreign office 1782-1810', *Procs. of the Consortium on Revolutionary Europe 1750-1830* (1980), 97. For Grenville's readiness to retire in 1794, see H.M.C. *Dropmore,* II, 513, 595-6, and Grenville to Pitt, 13 October, Cambridge University Library, Add Mss 6958/8/1513.

15. Jupp, 131-5; C.R. Middleton, *The Administration of British Foreign Policy 1782-1846* (Durham N.C., 1977), 17, 155, 161-2; Hutton, *Burges,* 253; Burges to Cooper, 27 July 1792, 'Transcripts of Sir James Burges political papers 1793', Crawford to Burges, 25 July 1795, 'Sir James Burges, letters mainly about public affairs 1795-6', Bodleian Lib., Burges Mss; *The Times,* 4 April 1793; 'Arrangement of Business in the Foreign Department', 1 April 1799, British Library Add Mss 59,229; 'Order respecting Messengers' certificates', 3 June 1799, Public Record Office FO 366/671.

16. H.M.C. *Dropmore,* II, 168-9, 255. Grenville's interposition of his own envoys began with his sending his brother Tom to Vienna in 1794 and his friend Wickham to Switzerland in 1795; it reached a peak in 1799 and concluded with sending his brother-in-law Carysfort to Berlin in 1800. He removed both under-secretaries he inherited from Leeds at the close of his first period of reform in 1795.

17. *Ibid.,* 414; Hutton, *Burges,* 174; G. Hogge (ed.), *The Journals and Correspondence of William Lord Auckland* (London 1860-2), II, 414. In 1794 Grenville worked hard to retain Dundas as war minister during coalition negotiations with the Portland Whigs with a handsome defence of his 'infinite merit': to T. Grenville, 6 July, B.L. Add Mss 42058 f165.

18. Hutton, *Burges,* 170; E. Bickley (ed.), *The Diaries of Sylvester Douglas, Lord Glenbervie* (London, 1928), I, 296; Malmesbury, *Diaries,* III, 590; H. Brougham, *Historical Sketches of Statesmen who flourished at the time of George III* (London, 1839), I, 255; Lord Holland (ed.), *Memoirs of the Whig Party during my time* (London, 1852-4), I, 187.

19. *Burges,* 173; Grenville's papers are now British Library Add Mss 57804-57837 and 58855-59494, with further files waiting to be catalogued; Middleton, *Admin. British Foreign Policy,* 170-3; 'Regulations respecting the official correspondence', 7 April 1799, FO 366/671.

20. H.M.C. *Dropmore,* V, 215; VI, 368; Jupp, 215; some memoranda are in BL Add Mss 59306. As a rough guide to the growth of business there is an increase of just over three-

quarters in the number of files (and considerably more despatches per file) in the Foreign Office general correspondence 1793-1801 compared with the previous nine years 1784-92.

21. Hutton, *Burges,* 172; H.M.C. *Dropmore,* IV, 337, 354-5, 458; VI, 170; J. Holland Rose, *Pitt and Napoleon, Essays and Letters* (London 1912), 270.

22. Grenville to Dundas 9 Jan. 1794, Ann Arbor, Michigan, Melville Papers.

23. Burges to Anne Burges, 9 July 1794. Burges Mss, 'Correspondence with Anne, Lady Burges'; A.C. Morris (ed.), *The Diary and Letters of Gouverneur Morris* (London 1889), II, 95; *Malmesbury Diaries,* III, 590.

24. Adams, 22-5; *Cambridge History of British Foreign Policy* (Cambridge 1922), I, 243; Jupp, 153-4. A more balanced view is provided by Ehrman, *Pitt,* II, 310 n.3, 311.

25. H.M.C. *Dropmore,* II, 432 (where however Pitt's letter is misdated to 5 October when it should be 21 September); FO7/34, Grenville to Eden 27 Sept; Elliot's journal for late September (National Library of Scotland, Minto Papers, Ms 11159) shows the authorship of the Toulon instructions. The two manifestos are printed in *The Parliamentary History of England,* XXX, cols. 1057-60, 1060-1.

26. Adams, 28-9; J.M. Sherwig, *Guineas and Gunpowder: British Foreign Aid in the Wars with France 1719-1815* (Harvard 1969), 59-65; Jupp, 164-8.

27. M. Duffy, British War Policy: the Austrian Alliance, 1793-1801 (Oxford D.Phil. Thesis, 1971), 40-2, 54-7, 80, 83-4 for Grenville, 56 n.1 for Pitt.

28. Adams, 25-6; Sherwig, 28-31.

29. Adams, 26 n.3 concerning H.M.C. *Dropmore* II, 503; Grenville's letter to Pitt of 8 October is largely printed in Rose, *Pitt and Napoleon,* 259-60, while a copy of the full original is in Camb. U.L. Add Mss 6958/7 no. 1331; Jupp, 166-8; Duke of Buckingham (ed.), *Memoirs of the Court and Cabinets of George the Third* (London 1853), II, 247.

30. Adams 27-8, especially 27 n.8 (followed by Sherwig 59-60 n.20) which takes Auckland's comment completely out of context in G. Hogge (ed.), *Journal and Correspondence of Auckland,* III, 241. Duffy, thesis, 105-9, 121-5.

31. Grenville to Eden, 18 Dec. 1794, FO 7/39, to Whitworth 9 Feb. 1795, FO 65/29; H.M.C. *Dropmore,* III, 29; Sherwig, 63; Mrs H. Baring (ed.), *The Windham Diary* (London 1866), 334. Malmesbury to Grenville, Private, 3 Feb. FO 64/36; Eden to Grenville, 21 Jan. FO 7/40.

32. Rose, *Pitt and Napoleon,* 260, omits the final paragraph of the letter dated 'Monday 4 o'clock', in PRO 30/8/140/1 f.75 relating to the Committee in Council's consideration of the report on the Secretary of State's Office to be confirmed on 'Friday'. The Order in Council regulating the Foreign Office was issued on Friday, 27 Feb. 1795. Middleton, *Admin. F.O.,* 155 n.24 also backs 23 Feb. for the letter though without reasons.

33. H.M.C. *Dropmore,* III, 25-26, Pitt to Grenville, 'Feb 20-28', is located by Ehrman as 26 February (*Pitt,* II, 549 n.2).

34. A copy of Pitt's draft minute is in Camb. U.L. Add Mss 6958/9 no.1661. Jupp, 180-1, mistakenly describes only Grenville as dissenting.

35. H.M.C. *Dropmore,* III, 30-31 (both letters of 2 March — see Camb. U.L. Add Mss 6858/9 no. 1664).

36. A. Aspinall (ed.), *The Later Correspondence of George III,* II, (Cambridge 1968), 309, 312; Camb. U.L. Add Mss 6958/9 no.1667 (note by Pitt); Pitt to Grenville, '2-7 March' (3 March) H.M.C. Dropmore III, 31; J. Steven Watson, *The Reign of George III, 1760-1815* (Oxford 1960), 301.

37. Aspinall, *L.C. George III,* II, 323-4, has dated Pitt's letter as 'Sunday 28 March 1.30 p.m.' before the King's of 29 March 10.28 a.m. Sunday was, however, the *29th* March.

38. Spencer to Grenville, 21, 23 Feb. FO 64/37; Grenville to Whitworth, 9 March FO

65/29; Eden to Grenville, 11 Feb. FO 7/40; H.M.C. *Dropmore,* III, 50; Aspinall, *L.C. George III,* II, 323-4, 327, 330-1.

39. *Ibid.,* 330-1, 332; Aspinall, 'The Cabinet Council', *Procs. of the British Academy,* xxxviii (1952), 217; Adams, 34, 50; Sherwig, 67. The proposals were finalised at a Cabinet on 10 April *(Windham Diary,* 335). Comparison of Grenville's minute of objections (H.M.C. *Dropmore,* III, 26-30) with Pitt's minutes of 1 March, 8 April, and Dundas's instructions of 10 April (WO 1/408) shows his objections relate to the April proposal.

40. Adams, 30-1, 35-6; Jupp, 187. Jupp cites a reference in Windham, *Diary,* 359, in 1797, but usage of names in the *Diary* suggests that it refers to Grenville's brother, Tom, rather than to the foreign secretary. In September Windham complained that the latter was 'so reserved and *caché,* that it was impossible for him to be a great Minister. *He knew nobody and was known by nobody'* (Malmesbury *Diaries,* III, 590).

41. Pitt to Portland, 20 Sept., Rose, *Pitt and Napoleon,* 254-5; Grenville to Portland, 20 Sept., Nottingham Univ. Lib., Portland Mss, P.W.F. 4467a; Auckland to Elliot, 2, 17 Nov. 1795. Nat. Lib. Scot., Minto Mss M69.

42. Jupp, 187-8; Grenville to Burges, 19 Aug., Burges to Anne Burges, 1 Sept. 1794, 21 Aug., 1, 22, 30 Sept. 1795, 'Sir James Burges, Correspondence with Anne Lady Burges', Grenville to Burges, 22 Aug. 1795, 'Original Letters to Sir J. Burges. B-Y', Bod. Lib., Burges Mss; Middleton, *Admin F.O.,* 263; D. Marshall, *The Rise of George Canning* (London 1938), 100-12.

43. For George III's strong lobbying against peace in early 1796, see Rose, *Pitt and Napoleon,* 288-9; Earl Stanhope, *Life of the Rt. Hon. William Pitt* (London 1861), II, appendix, xxxi-xxxii; Aspinall, *L.C. George III,* II, 455. His resistance to the new Prussian proposal is in H.M.C. *Dropmore,* III, 174, 227, 230. Adams, 37-44 here provides a well-balanced account of Pitt-Grenville relations. Grenville initiated the latter proposal since the Polish Partition was now settled and he believed he had positive Russian backing and a territorial lure to ensure Prussian reliability.

44. Adams, 45-50; Rose in *Camb. Hist. Brit. For. Pol.,* I, 269-72. The author has discussed their interpretation more fully in his thesis, 255-71, 501-2, and has since been supported by Ehrman, *Pitt,* II, 645-9 and Jupp, 200-201.

45. R.I. and S. Wilberforce, *The Life of William Wilberforce* (2nd ed. London 1839), II, 223.

46. Grenville to Dundas, 16 Aug. 1797, Scottish Record Office, Melville Papers, G.D. 51/1/528 (1) (2); *Court and Cabinets of G.III,* II, 377; Pitt to Carlisle, 4 June 1797, PRO 30/8/102.

47. Canning to Leigh (30 June) 1797, Leeds Central Library, George Canning Papers, Bundle 14. The Canning diary is contained in Bundle 29d.

48. Canning diary entries for 10 May, 7, 11, 14 June; Wilberforce *(Life,* II, 220) believed that he had brought Pitt to make the effort by his exhortations on 27 May. Windham, *Diary,* 365, 367-8 gives insight into the Cabinet row.

49. Grenville to Pitt, 'Thursday 6 o'clock', PRO 30/8/140 is certainly of 15 June and was probably preceded by the note dated '[July-August]' in Rose, *Pitt and Napoleon,* 262. Grenville to T. Grenville, 15 June, B.L. Add Mss 41,852. Windham *Diary,* 15 June, 368; Canning Diary, 14 June; H.M.C. *Dropmore,* III, 329, 331.

50. Pitt to George III, 16 June 1797, Rose, *Pitt and Napoleon,* 242.

51. H.M.C. *Dropmore,* III, 330-1. Pitt clearly and surprisingly passed his double-edged letter from the King on to Grenville, presumably because it contained the royal authorisation to despatch the note to France.

52. Canning diary, entries and observations, 24, 25 June; Windham, *Diary,* 25 June, 368; Grenville to Pitt, 26 June, PRO 30/58/(2).

53. Canning diary, 10 July; Countess of Minto (ed.), *Life and Letters of Sir Gilbert Elliot, First Earl of Minto*, II, 408. On 18 July Dundas produced a long memorandum urging separate negotiations with Holland and Spain so as to avoid returning British conquests (SRO GD 51/1/526).

54. Malmesbury, *Diaries*, III, 554. Adams (65-6) misses the point of this statement by including it in a section portraying Pitt's hold as weakening.

55. Malmesbury also sent private letters to Canning which he intended should be passed on to Pitt. *Diaries*, III, 369, 400 n.1, 464-7 *et passim*.

56. Canning to Leigh, 24 July, 5 Sept., Canning Papers, bundle 14; Canning diary, 31 July, 8, 19 Aug., 1 Sept. 1797; D. Marshall, *Rise of George Canning*, 170-4; H.M.C. *Dropmore*, III, 337-43.

57. Canning diary, 19 July; SRO GD 51/1/528 (1) (2); Adams 65-6.

58. Adams 70, 73.

59. Jupp, 211-2 stresses George III's initiative on 4 November 1797 though this was a response to Brunswick's overture already made to him via de Luc. See Steinberg to de Luc 3 Oct., Royal Archives, Windsor, 8632-3.

60. H.M.C. *Dropmore*, IV, 166.

61. See Dundas's letter of 19 Aug. and its misplaced enclosure H.M.C. *Dropmore*, IV, 284, 433-5; Windham, *Diary*, 400-1.

62. For the ill-health of Pitt and Dundas, see R. Reilly, *Pitt the Younger* (London, 1978), 276, 284, 298-9; P. Mackesy, *War Without Victory: The Downfall of Pitt 1799-1802* (Oxford, 1984), 15-17, 173-6. Grenville's soaring military confidence can be seen by contrasting his letter to Pitt on 17 June 1793 (Camb. U.L. Add Mss 6958/7) with that to Tom Grenville on 17 May 1799 (H.M.C. *Dropmore*, V, 55).

63. Windham Mss diary entry, 30 July 1799, B.L. Add Mss 37,923. The extent of Grenville's dominance in 1799 is shown by P. Mackesy, *The Strategy of Overthrow 1798-1799* (London 1974), 158-80 *et passim*.

64. H.M.C. *Dropmore*, V, 152, 224, 234-5, 380, 396, 404; Rose, *Pitt and Napoleon*, 264-5; Windham, *Diary*, 416; Pitt to Canning, 22 Oct. 1799, Leeds C.L., Canning Papers, Bundle 14.

65. Pitt to Canning, 23 Nov., *Ibid;* to Canning, 3 Dec 1799, *Ibid.*, Bundle 30; to Grenville, 3 Jan. 1800, H.M.C. *Dropmore*, VI, 96.

66. For Dundas's fight to win back control of strategy from Grenville, see Mackesy, *War without Victory*, 7-16, 69-94, 119-62.

67. Hammond to Canning, 29 July 1800, Canning Papers, Bundle 76; Ole Feldbaeck, *Denmark and the Armed Neutrality 1800-1801* (Copenhagen 1980), 52.

68. G. Pellew, *The Life and Correspondence of the Rt. Hon. Henry Addington, First Viscount Sidmouth* (London 1847), I, 256-60; Grenville to Canning, 6 Sept. 1800, Canning Papers, Bundle 63.

69. *Glenbervie Diaries*, I, 159-60; Mackesy, *War without Victory*, 142-58.

70. Stanhope, *Pitt*, III, 351-2, Malmesbury, *Diaries*, IV, 59.

71. Pellew, *Sidmouth*, II, 116.

72. H.M.C. *Dropmore*, VI, 13, 357, 368.

73. *Ibid.*, II, 447; IV, 283; V, 172-3.

74. Such intervention ranged down to suggested minor alterations to despatches, see *Ibid.*, II, 88, 322.

75. Dundas retained the Prussian correspondence for some months after 11 April 1795 (WO1/408), Canning was the medium in 1797. Grenville readily accepted that if Pitt's mind was made up, then he should prevail, see Rose, *Pitt and Napoleon*, 260-1, 264-5.

76. Mackesy, *War without Victory*, 39, 176-7.

77. H.M.C. *Dropmore*, IV, 228-9; V, 422, 486-7; VI, 170, 232. For attempts to bypass the need for Cabinet meetings, see *ibid.*, VI, 35, 232.

78. R. Willis, 'William Pitt's Resignation in 1801', *Bulletin of the Institute of Historical Research*, 44 (1971), 239-257.

Selective Bibliography

This brief list is intended only as an introduction to the very extensive literature available. For reasons of space the list is restricted to work in English and concentrates on material published since 1960. Unless otherwise cited, place of publications is London.

Adams, E.D., *The Influence of Grenville on Pitt's Foreign Policy, 1787-98* (Washington D.C., 1904).

Anderson, M.S., 'Great Britain, Russia and the Russo-Turkish War of 1768-74', *English Historical Review* (1954).

Anderson, M.S., *Britain's Discovery of Russia 1553-1815* (1958).

Baugh, D.A., 'Great Britain's "Blue-Water" Policy, 1689-1815', *International History Review* (1988).

Baxter, S.B., *William III* (1966).

Baxter, S.B., 'The Myth of the Grand Alliance', in Baxter and P.R. Sellin (eds.), *Anglo-Dutch Cross Currents in the Seventeenth and Eighteenth Centuries* (Los Angeles, 1976).

Birke, A.M. and Kluxen K. (eds.), *England and Hanover* (Munich, 1986).

Black, J.M., 'George II Reconsidered', *Mitteilungen des Österreichischen Staatsarchivs* (1982).

Black, J.M., 'An "ignoramus" in European affairs', *British Journal for Eighteenth-Century Studies* (1983).

Black, J.M., 'The Development of Anglo-Sardinian Relations in the First Half of the Eighteenth Century', *Studi Piemontesi* (1983).

Black, J.M., 'Parliament and the Political and Diplomatic Crisis of 1717-18', *Parliamentary History Yearbook* (1984).

Black, J.M., 'Sir Robert Ainslie: His Majesty's Agent-provocateur? British Foreign Policy and the International Crisis of 1787', *European History Quarterly* (1984).

Black, J.M., *British Foreign Policy in the Age of Walpole* (Edinburgh, 1985).

Black, J.M. and Schweizer, K. (eds.), *Essays in European History in honour of Ragnhild Hatton* (Lennoxville, 1985).

Black, J.M., 'The Marquis of Carmarthen and Relations with France, 1784-1787', *Francia* (1985).

Black, J.M., *Natural and Necessary Enemies: Anglo-French Relations in the Eighteenth Century* (1986).

Black, J.M., 'British Foreign Policy and the War of the Austrian Succession', *Canadian Journal of History* (1986).

Black, J.M., 'The Anglo-French Alliance 1716-1731', *Francia* (1986).

Black, J.M., 'Fresh Light on the Fall of Townshend', *Historical Journal* (1986).

Black, J.M. (ed.), *The Origins of War in Early Modern Europe* (Edinburgh, 1987).

Black, J.M., *The English Press in the Eighteenth Century* (1987).

Black, J.M., 'British Foreign Policy in the Eighteenth Century: A Survey', *Journal of British Studies* (1987).

Black, J.M., *The Collapse of the Anglo-French Alliance 1727-1731* (Gloucester, 1987).

Black, J.M., 'Anglo-Russian Relations after the Seven Years' War', *Scottish Slavonic Review* (1987).

Black, J.M. and Woodfine P.L. (eds.), *The British Navy and the Use of Naval Power in the Eighteenth Century* (Leicester, 1988).

Black, J.M., 'Anglo-French Relations in the Age of the French Revolution 1787-1793', *Francia* (1988).

Blanning, T.C.W., ' "That horrid Electorate" or "Ma patrie germanique"?: George III, Hanover and the Fürstenbund of 1785', *Historical Journal* (1977).

Blanning, T.C.W., *The Origins of the French Revolutionary Wars* (1986).

Boxer, C., 'Some second thoughts on the third Anglo-Dutch War', *Transactions of the Royal Historical Society* (1969).

Bromley, J.S. and Hatton R. (eds.), *William III and Louis XIV* (Liverpool, 1967).

Bromley, J.S., *Corsairs and Navies 1660-1760* (1988).

Brown, G.S., 'The Anglo-French Naval Crisis, 1778: a study of conflict in the North Cabinet', *William and Mary Quarterly* (1956).

Browning, A., *Thomas Osborne, Earl of Danby* (Glasgow, 1951).

Browning, R., 'The Duke of Newcastle and the Imperial Election Plan, 1749-1754', *Journal of British Studies* (1967-8).

Browning, R., *The Duke of Newcastle* (New Haven, 1975).

Butterfield, H., 'British Foreign Policy 1762-65', *Historical Journal* (1963).

Chance, J.F., *George I and the Northern War* (1909).

Chance, J.F., *The Alliance of Hanover* (1923).

Clapham, J.H., *The Causes of the War of 1792* (Cambridge, 1899).

Clark, G.N., *The Dutch Alliance and the War against French Trade 1688-1697* (Manchester, 1923).

Clayton, T.R., 'The Duke of Newcastle, the Earl of Halifax, and the American Origins of the Seven Years' War', *Historical Journal* (1981).

Cobban, A., *Ambassadors and Secret Agents: The Diplomacy of the First Earl of Malmesbury at the Hague* (1954).

Conn, S., *Gibraltar in British Diplomacy in the Eighteenth Century* (New Haven, 1942).

Coombs, D., *The Conduct of the Dutch. British Opinion and the Dutch Alliance during the War of the Spanish Succession* (The Hague, 1958).

Dalrymple, Sir J., *Memoirs of Great Britain and Ireland* (1773).

Dippel, H., 'Prussia's English Policy after the Seven Years' War', *Central European History* (1971).

Doran, P.F., *Andrew Mitchell and Anglo-Prussian Relations during the Seven Years' War* (New York, 1986).

Duffy, M., ' "A particular service": the British government and the Dunkirk expedition of 1793', *English Historical Review* (1976).

Duffy, M., 'British Policy in the War against Revolutionary France', in C. Jones (ed.), *Britain and Revolutionary France: Conflict, Subversion and Propaganda* (Exeter, 1983).

Duffy, M., *The Englishman and the Foreigner* (Cambridge, 1986).

Duffy, M., *Soldiers, Sugar and Seapower. The British Expeditions to the West Indies and the War against Revolutionary France* (Oxford, 1987).

Duffy, M., 'British Diplomacy and the French Wars 1789-1815', in H.T. Dickinson (ed.), *Britain and the French Revolution, 1789-1815* (1989).

Dull, J.R., *A Diplomatic History of the American Revolution* (New Haven, 1985).

Dunthorne, H., *The Maritime Powers 1721-1740. A Study of Anglo-Dutch Relations in the Age of Walpole* (New York, 1986).

Ehrman, J., *The British Government and Commercial Negotiations with Europe, 1788-93* (Cambridge, 1962).

Ehrman, J., *The Younger Pitt: the Years of Acclaim* (1969).

Ehrman, J., *The Younger Pitt: the Reluctant Transition* (1983).

Eldon, C.W., *England's Subsidy Policy towards the Continent during the Seven Years' War* (Philadelphia, 1938).

Elliot, D.C., 'The Grenville Mission to Berlin', *Huntington Library Quarterly* (1954-5).

Ellis, K.L., 'British Communications and Diplomacy in the Eighteenth Century', *Bulletin of the Institute of Historical Research* (1958).

Ellis, K.L., 'The Administrative Connections between Britain and Hanover' *Journal of the Society of Archivists* (1969).

Evans, H.V., 'The Nootka Sound controversy in Anglo-French diplomacy', *Journal of Modern History* (1974).

Feiling, K., *British Foreign Policy 1660-1672* (1930).

Feldbaek, O., 'The Anglo-Danish Convoy Conflict', *Scandinavian Journal of History* (1977).

Fisher, H.E.S., *The Portugal Trade: a study of Anglo-Portugese Commerce 1700-1770* (1971).

Fryer, W.R., *Republic or Restoration in France 1794-1797* (Manchester, 1965).

Geyl, P., *Orange and Stuart* (1969).

Gibbs, G.C., 'Parliament and Foreign Policy in the Age of Stanhope and Walpole', *English Historical Review* (1962).

Gibbs, G.C., 'Newspapers, Parliament and Foreign Policy in the Age of Stanhope and Walpole', *Mélanges offerts à G. Jacquemyns* (Brussels, 1968).

Gibbs, G.C., 'The Revolution in Foreign Policy', in G. Holmes (ed.), *Britain after the Glorious Revolution* (1969).

Gibbs, G.C., 'Laying Treaties before Parliament in the Eighteenth Century', in R. Hatton and M.S. Anderson (eds.), *Studies in Diplomatic History* (1970).

Gill, C., *Merchants and Mariners of the eighteenth century* (1961).

Glover, R., 'Arms and the British Diplomat in the French Revolutionary Era', *Journal of Modern History* (1957).

Goebel, J., *The Struggle for the Falkland Islands* (New York, 1927).

Graham, G.S., *Empire of the North Atlantic: the Maritime Struggle for North America* (1958).

Haley, K.H.D., *William of Orange and the English Opposition, 1672-4* (Oxford, 1953).

Haley, K.H.D., *An English Diplomat in the Low Countries: Sir William Temple and John De Witt, 1665-1672* (Oxford, 1986).

Harlow, V.T., *The Founding of the Second British Empire 1763-1793* (2 vols., 1952-64).

Harvey, A.D., 'European attitudes to Britain during the French Revolutionary and Napoleonic Era', *History* (1978).

Hattendorf, J.B., *England in the War of the Spanish Succession. A Study of the English View and Conduct of Grand Strategy, 1701-1712* (New York, 1987).

Hatton, R., *Diplomatic Relations between Great Britain and the Dutch Republic 1714-1721* (1950).

Hatton, R., *George I* (1978).

Hatton, R., *The Anglo-Hanoverian Connection 1714-1760* (1982).

Helleiner, K., *The Imperial Loans* (Oxford, 1965).

Hertz, G.B., 'England and the Ostend Company', *English Historical Review* (1907).

Horn, D.B., *Sir Charles Hanbury-Williams and European Diplomacy 1747-58* (1930).

Horn, D.B., *British Diplomatic Representatives 1689-1789* (1932).

Horn, D.B., *British Public Opinion and the First Partition of Poland* (1945).

Horn, D.B., 'The diplomatic experience of Secretaries of State, 1660-1852', *History* (1956).

Horn, D.B., *The British Diplomatic Service 1689-1789* (Oxford, 1961).

Horn, D.B., *Great Britain and Europe in the Eighteenth Century* (Oxford, 1967).

Horn, D.B., 'The Duke of Newcastle and the Origins of the Diplomatic Revolution', in J.H. Elliott and H.G. Koenigsberger (eds.), *The Diversity of History* (1970).

Hotblack, K., 'The Peace of Paris, 1763', *Transactions of the Royal Historical Society* (1908).

Hutt, M., *Chouannerie and Counter-Revolution: Puissaye, the Princes and the British Government in the 1790s* (Cambridge, 1983).

Hutt, M., 'The 1790s and the Myth of "Perfidious Albion" ', *Franco-British Studies* (1986).

Hutton, R., 'The Making of the Secret Treaty of Dover, 1668-1670', *Historical Journal* (1986).

Jarrett, D., *The Begetters of Revolution: England's involvement with France* (1973).

Jones, G.H., *The Mainstream of Jacobitism* (Cambridge, Mass., 1954).

Jones, G.H., *Charles Middleton* (Chicago, 1967).

Jones, J.R., *The Revolution of 1688 in England* (1972).

Jones, J.R., *Country and Court: England 1658-1714* (1978).

Jones, J.R., *Britain and the World 1649-1815* (1980).

Kennedy, P.M., *The Rise and Fall of British Naval Mastery* (1976).

Kent, H.S.K., *War and Trade in Northern Seas: Anglo-Scandinavian Economic Relations in the mid-eighteenth century* (Cambridge, 1973).

Kenyon, J.P., *Robert Spencer, Earl of Sunderland* (1958).

Konopozynski, W., 'England and the First Partition of Poland', *Journal of Central European Affairs* (1948-9).

Langford, P., *Modern British Foreign Policy: The Eighteenth Century, 1688-1815* (1976).

Lodge, R., *Great Britain and Prussia in the Eighteenth Century* (Oxford, 1923).

Lodge, R., *Studies in Eighteenth Century Diplomacy, 1740-1748* (1930).

Lojek, J., 'The International Crisis of 1791', *East-Central Europe* (1970).

McKay, D. and Scott, H.M., *The Rise of the Great Powers, 1648-1815* (1983).

McKay, D., *Allies of Convenience. Diplomatic Relations between Great Britain and Austria 1714-1719* (New York, 1986).

Mackesy, P., *Statesmen at War. The Strategy of Overthrow 1798-99* (1974).

Mackesy, P., *War without Victory. The Downfall of Pitt, 1799-1802* (Oxford, 1984).

McLachlan, J., *Trade and Peace with Old Spain, 1667-1750* (Cambridge, 1940).

Madariaga, I. de, *Britain, Russia and the Armed Neutrality of 1780* (1962).

Marshall, P.J., 'British Expansion in India in the eighteenth century: Historical Revision', *History* (1975).

Mediger, W., 'Great Britain, Hanover and the Rise of Prussia', in R. Hatton and M.S. Anderson (eds.), *Studies in Diplomatic History* (1970).

Metcalf, M.F., *Russia, England and Swedish Party Politics 1762-1766* (Stockholm, 1977).

Meyer, J. and Bromley, J., 'The Second Hundred Years' War (1689-1815)', in D. Johnson, F. Bedarida and F. Crouzet (eds.), *Britain and France: Ten Centuries* (1980).

Middleton, C.R., *The Administration of British Foreign Policy 1782-1846* (Durham, North Carolina, 1977).

Middleton, R., *The Bells of Victory: the Pitt-Newcastle Ministry and the Conduct of the Seven Years' War 1757-1762* (Cambridge, 1985).

Miller, D.A., *Sir Joseph Yorke and Anglo-Dutch Relations 1774-1780* (The Hague, 1970).

Miller, J., *James II* (Hove, 1978).

Mitchell, H., *The Underground War against Revolutionary France: the Missions of William Wickham 1794-1800* (Oxford, 1965).

Murray, J.J., *George I, the Baltic and the Whig Split of 1717* (1969).

Oakley, S.P., *William III and the Northern Crowns during the Nine Years' War 1689-1697* (New York, 1987).

Pares, R., *War and Trade in the West Indies 1739-1763* (Oxford, 1936).

Pares, R., 'American versus Continental Warfare 1739-1763', *English Historical Review* (1956).

Pares, R., *Colonial Blockade and Neutral Rights 1739-1763* (Oxford, 1938).

Ramsey, J.F., *Anglo-French Relations 1763-1770* (Berkeley, 1939).

Rashed, Z.E., *The Peace of Paris 1763* (Liverpool, 1951).

Reading, D., *The Anglo-Russian Commercial Treaty of 1734* (New Haven, 1938).

Reddaway, W.F., 'Great Britain and Poland, 1762-72', *Cambridge Historical Journal* (1932-4).

Rice, G.W., 'Great Britain, the Manila Ransom and the First Falkland Islands Dispute with Spain, 1766', *International History Review* (1980).

Richmond, H., *Statesmen and Sea Power* (Oxford, 1946).

Ritcheson, C.R., 'The Earl of Shelburne and Peace with America, 1782-1783', *International History Review* (1983).

Roberts, M., 'Great Britain and the Swedish Revolution, 1772-1773', *Historical Journal* (1964).

Roberts, M., *Splendid Isolation 1763-1780* (Reading, 1970).

Roberts, M., *Macartney in Russia* (1974).

Roberts, M., *British Diplomacy and Swedish Politics, 1758-1773* (1980).

Rose, J.H., *William Pitt and the National Revival* (1911).

Rose, J.H., *William Pitt and the Great War with France* (1911).

Schroeder, P., 'The collapse of the Second Coalition', *Journal of Modern History* (1987).

Schweizer, K.W., 'The Non-Renewal of the Anglo-Prussian Subsidy Treaty, 1761-1762', *Canadian Journal of History* (1978).

Schweizer, K.W., 'William Pitt, Lord Bute and the Peace Negotiations with France, 1761', *Albion* (1981).

Schweizer, K.W. and Leonard, C.S., 'Britain, Prussia, Russia and the Galitsyn Letter: a Reassessment', *Historical Journal* (1983).

Schweizer, K.W. (ed.), *Lord Bute. Essays in Re-interpretation* (Leicester, 1988).

Scott, H.M., 'Great Britain, Poland and the Russian Alliance, 1763-1767', *Historical Journal* (1976).

Scott, H.M., 'British Foreign Policy in the Age of the American Revolution', *International History Review* (1984).

Sherwig, J.M., *Guineas and Gunpowder, British Foreign Aid in the Wars with France, 1793-1815* (Cambridge, Mass., 1969).

Sherwig, J.M., 'Lord Grenville's plan for a concert of Europe', *Journal of Modern History* (1962).

Spencer, F. (ed.), *The Fourth Earl of Sandwich: Diplomatic Correspondence 1763-1765* (Manchester, 1961).

Sutherland, L.S., 'The East India Company and the Peace of Paris', *English Historical Review* (1947).

Tarling, P.N., *Anglo-Dutch Rivalry in the Malay World 1780-1824* (St. Lucia, Queensland, 1962).

Thomson, M.A., *The Secretaries of State, 1681-1782* (Oxford, 1932).

Tracy, N., 'Parry of a Threat to India, 1768-1774', *Mariner's Mirror* (1973).

Tracy, N., 'The Gunboat Diplomacy of the Government of George Grenville, 1764-65', *Historical Journal* (1974).

Tracy, N., 'The Administration of the Duke of Grafton and the French Invasion of Corsica', *Eighteenth-century Studies* (1974-5).

Tracy, N., 'The Falklands Islands crisis of 1770: use of naval force', *English Historical Review* (1975).

Van Alstyne, R.W., 'Great Britain, the War for Independence and the "Gathering Storm" in Europe 1775-1778', *Huntington Library Quarterly* (1964).

Van Alstyne, R.W., *Empire and Independence: the International History of the American Revolution* (New York, 1965).

Ward, A.W., *Great Britain and Hanover: Some Aspects of the Personal Union* (Oxford, 1899).

Ward, A.W. and Gooch, G.P., *Cambridge History of British Foreign Policy 1787-1919. I: 1783-1815* (1922).

Williams, B., *Stanhope* (1932).

Williams, B., *Carteret and Newcastle* (Cambridge, 1943).